OXFORD READINGS IN POLITICS
AND GOVERNMENT

MARXIST THEORY

OXFORD READINGS IN POLITICS
AND GOVERNMENT

General Editors: Vernon Bogdanor and Geoffrey Marshall

The readings in this series are chosen from a variety of journals and other sources to cover major areas or issues in the study of politics, government, and political theory. Each volume contains an introductory essay by the editor and a select guide to further reading.

MARXIST THEORY

EDITED BY
ALEX CALLINICOS

OXFORD UNIVERSITY PRESS

1989

Oxford University Press, Walton Street, Oxford OX2 6DP
Oxford New York Toronto
Delhi Bombay Calcutta Madras Karachi
Petaling Jaya Singapore Hong Kong Tokyo
Nairobi Dar es Salaam Cape Town
Melbourne Auckland
and associated companies in
Berlin Ibadan

Oxford is a trade mark of Oxford University Press

Published in the United States
by Oxford University Press (USA)

Introduction and compilation © A. T. Callinicos 1989

British Library Cataloguing in Publication Data
Callinicos, Alex, 1950–
Marxist theory.—(Oxford readings in politics and government)
1. Marxism. Theories
I. Title
335.4'01
ISBN 0–19–827294–4
ISBN 0–19–827295–2 Pbk

Library of Congress Cataloging-in-Publication Data
Marxist theory / edited by Alex Callinicos.
p. cm.—(Oxford readings in politics and government)
1. Marx, Karl, 1818–1883. 2. Marx, Karl, 1818–1883—Influence.
I. Callinicos, Alex. II. Series.
HX39.5.M378 1989   335.4—dc19   88–28720
ISBN 0–19–827294–4
ISBN 0–19–827295–2 (pbk.)

Set by Hope Services, Abingdon
Printed in Great Britain
at the University Printing House, Oxford
by David Stanford
Printer to the University

CONTENTS

PREFACE AND ACKNOWLEDGEMENTS

I would like to thank the following for helping, in different ways, to make the appearance of this collection possible: Vernon Bogdanor and Geoffrey Marshall, the editors of the series in which it appears; Henry Hardy, Leofranc Holford-Strevens and David Edmonds at Oxford University Press; Robin Blackburn, Jerry Cohen, Andrew Levine, and Erik Olin Wright.

I am also grateful to the following for granting permission for republication of the articles collected here: *New Left Review* for chapters 1 and 7; Elsevier Scientific Publishing Company for chapters 2, 3 and 4; New York University Press for chapter 5; and the Canadian Association for Publishing in Philosophy for chapter 6.

Some of the items cited as 'forthcoming' in the footnotes to the following chapters have now been published, and I have added the appropriate information in square brackets.

INTRODUCTION:
ANALYTICAL MARXISM

ALEX CALLINICOS

I

Before the late 1970s one would have been hard put to name much original theoretical work by English-speaking Marxists. This is not to say that there were no important empirical applications of Marxism in the English-speaking world—on the contrary, the work of such historians as Christopher Hill, Rodney Hilton, Eric Hobsbawm, and Edward Thompson was quite outstanding, as was Tony Cliff's path-breaking study of the USSR. And, of course—as Thompson insisted—creative empirical enquiry often expands the boundaries of the theory it embodies. Nevertheless, with few exceptions (perhaps the most important of which was the encounter between Marxism and pragmatism in the United States during the 1930s), very little of much interest was written in English on such topics as the basic explanatory principles of historical materialism and their relationship to philosophical doctrines and debates. High theory was a continental monopoly, its pursuit slowly spreading from central Europe (Kautsky, Adler, Bauer, Lukács, Bloch, Korsch, Horkheimer, Adorno, Marcuse, Habermas) to Italy (Labriola, Gramsci, della Volpe, Colletti), and then to France (Sartre, Merleau Ponty, Althusser), but halting at the Channel.

By the early 1980s things were very different. Perry Anderson could write: 'the geographical pattern of Marxist theory has been profoundly altered in the past decade. Today the *predominant* centres of intellectual production seem to lie in the English-speaking world, rather than in Germanic or Latin Europe, as was the case in the inter-war and post-war periods respectively.'[1] One of the most striking elements of this change was the emergence of a group of theorists who sought to use the kind of philosophical approach embodied in the analytical tradition in order to elucidate and resolve problems within Marxism. Analytical Marxism's most famous work is G. A. Cohen's *Karl Marx's Theory of History*, first published in 1978. Cohen's reconstruction of historical materialism was governed, he tells us, by 'two constraints: on the one hand, what Marx wrote, and, on the other, those standards of clarity and rigour which distinguish twentieth-century analytical philosophy'.[2] This way of proceeding provided something of a model for other analytical Marxists, though they can by no means be said to constitute a school united by shared doctrine. On the contrary, their history has involved a number of major disagreements, some of which are reflected in the articles collected here. Nevertheless, despite these differences analytical Marxism—whose main practitioners also include Jon Elster, John Roemer, Philippe van Parijs, Adam Przeworski, Andrew Levine, Erik Olin Wright, and Robert Brenner—is distinguished by the use of 'state of the art methods of analytical philosophy and "positivist" social science'.[3]

2

This analytical turn is remarkable, since Marxists have traditionally insisted on the fundamental methodological divide which separates them from all forms of bourgeois thought. Thus one of the main themes of the Frankfurt school's early writings was a critique of analytical philosophy (represented chiefly by the Vienna circle) as a prime instance of the alienated instrumental reason produced by twentieth-century bourgeois society. Hilferding and Bukharin

---

[1] P. Anderson, *In the Tracks of Historical Materialism* (London, 1983), p. 24.

[2] G. A. Cohen, *Karl Marx's Theory of History: A Defence* (hereinafter *KMTH*) (Oxford, 1978), p. ix.

[3] J. Roemer, editor's introduction to *Analytical Marxism* (Cambridge, 1986), pp. 1–2.

sought to show that neoclassical economics merely registers the surface appearances of monopoly capitalism—yet the 'rational-choice' Marxism which Elster and Roemer in particular have sought to construct rests on axioms which are essentially generalizations of neoclassical postulates. Cohen and his co-thinkers have casually crossed the supposedly impassable border between Marxism and the academic mainstream in philosophy and social theory.

There are no doubt many reasons for the rise of 'Anglo-Marxism', and any proper explanation would have much to say about socio-political developments (the impact of the student movement of the 1960s on English-speaking universities, the continental 'crisis of Marxism' in the 1970s, and so on).[4] One strictly intellectual development that formed, in my view, a necessary condition for the emergence of the analytical strain some of whose contributions fill the pages which follow was the expulsion of Hegelian modes of thinking from Marxist theory. It is only a slight exaggeration to say that analytical Marxism is post-Hegelian Marxism. One might even say that it is post-Althusserian Marxism. Although Althusser's assumptions and idiom are almost wholly alien to the work of Cohen, Elster, Roemer, et al., his intervention helped to clear the space within which analytical Marxism took shape.

Before Althusser the distinction drawn by Marx in his afterword to the second German edition of the first volume of *Capital* and by Engels in 'Ludwig Feuerbach and the End of German Classical Philosophy' between Hegel's method and system was largely a commonplace of Marxist theory. The thought was that while Hegel's philosophical system had to be rejected since its absolute idealism required the reduction of all reality to manifestations of Spirit, he had forged a dialectical method which, in its focus on the contradictions inherent in things, was indispensable to revolutionary socialist thought. The main disagreement among Marxist philosophers after Marx was over the nature of this dialectical method. Most accepted what came to be regarded as the orthodoxy shaped by Engels, according to which certain dialectical

---

[4] See, for example, Anderson, *Tracks*, and my review of this book, 'Perry Anderson and "Western Marxism"', *International Socialism*, 2. 23 (1984).

principles which had been extracted from Hegel's *Logic* constituted the most general laws of nature governing the physical as well as the social world. Adherents to dialectical materialism thus conceived included the main figures of the Second and Third Internationals, Lenin and Trotsky as well as Kautsky and Plekhanov. A smaller, though philosophically much more sophisticated, group rejected the idea of a dialectic of nature, arguing that the distinctively Marxist method was concerned with elucidating the relationship between conscious human subjects and objective social structures. Lukács's *History and Class Consciousness* is the most cogent statement of this view, but it was shared by the other great Hegelian Marxists of the 1920s, principally Gramsci and Korsch, and later by Sartre in his Marxist phase. Even Adorno, the major Marxist philosopher before Althusser most critical of Hegel, never escaped from an intellectual framework shaped by Lukács.

Althusser's main achievement was to break out of the Hegelian strait-jacket. In particular, he challenged the distinction drawn since Engels between Hegel's idealist system and his supposedly materialist method. Althusser showed that the very structure of the Hegelian dialectic contained implicit within it its author's conception of reality as the progressive unfolding of the Absolute's self-consciousness. Any version of Marxism which possessed Hegelian conceptual structures would therefore be liable to certain idealist 'deviations': in the case of 'orthodox' dialectical materialism a tendency to conceive history as a teleological process moving towards an inevitable goal, in the case of Hegelian Marxism a liability to reduce social structures to forms of consciousness. The core of historical materialism consisted in those of Marx's mature writings, notably *Capital*, least shaped by Hegelian forms of thought.[5] These arguments formed what one might call Althusser's negative contribution, and despite the fury they aroused on their first appearance in the mid-1960s, they met with no convincing rebuttal.

[5] Althusser's clearest statement of his case is 'Marx's Relation to Hegel', in *Montesquieu, Rousseau, Marx* (London, 1982). The idea that Hegel's method can be separated from his system is demolished in M. Rosen, *The Hegelian Dialectic and its Criticism* (Cambridge, 1982).

Althusser was, however, less successful in his positive attempt to reconstruct Marxism on consistently non-Hegelian lines. He remained convinced that there was a distinctively Marxist method (or 'problematic', as he called it), which he sought to elucidate, using philosophical assumptions and arguments drawn from what came in the 1960s to be known as structuralism, the extension to disciplines such as anthropology (Lévi-Strauss) and psychoanalysis (Lacan) of Saussure's structural linguistics. What Althusser himself described as his 'flirt' with structuralism was generally accounted a failure. Nevertheless, he can be said in three respects to have laid the basis of analytical Marxism. First, he established the incompatibility of historical materialism with the Hegelian modes of thinking previously adhered to by Marxist philosophers, and therefore the need to re-examine the basic principles of Marxism. Secondly, the attempts by Althusser and Balibar in *Reading Capital* to rethink historical materialism along non-Hegelian lines inaugurated 'the systematic interrogation and clarification of basic concepts and their reconstruction into a more coherent theoretical structure' which Wright holds to be characteristic of analytical Marxism.[6] Thirdly, the failure of the Althusserian project acted as a kind of negative proof, encouraging what Levine calls the 'tentative conclusion reached by the careful study of Marx undertaken in the past decades by investigators with analytical training . . . that, despite what is so often proclaimed, there is, finally, nothing distinctive about Marxian *methodology*—at least in so far as it yields defensible, substantive positions'.[7]

By no means all the essays included in this collection can be identified with analytical Marxism *stricto sensu*, and certainly not with the narrower 'rational-choice' approach pioneered by Elster and Roemer. Nevertheless, they are linked at least by family resemblance, in that all are written in the analytical idiom, and are concerned with problems which arise, at least in their most acute form, once a Hegelian conceptual

[6] E. O. Wright, *Classes* (London, 1985), p. 2. See also Cohen's remarks on Althusser in *KMTH*, p. x.

[7] A. E. Levine, review of J. Elster, *Making Sense of Marx*, in *Journal of Philosophy*, 83. 12 (1986), p. 728 n. 25.

framework has been abandoned. I shall try to illustrate the latter aspect by considering in the remainder of this Introduction three issues: history, ethics, and method.

3

Marx's most distinctive claim is that the character of social production explains both the nature of every society and the transformations it undergoes. He contrasts two aspects of social production, namely the forces and relations of production. The productive forces comprise (minimally) the material elements of production—labour-power and the means of production (tools, land, etc.) which it uses to produce goods and services. The development of the productive forces is cumulative, and reflected in the growth of labour productivity. Production relations consist (again, minimally) in the relations of effective control over these productive forces exercised by different groups, and in the forms of exploitation that arise when a minority exerts sufficient control over the forces to compel the direct producers to work, not simply for themselves and their dependants, but for this minority, thus performing what Marx calls surplus-labour. Exploitive productive relations give rise to classes, and, given the antagonistic interests between exploiters and exploited, to class struggle. Marx argues, most systematically in the 1859 preface to *A Contribution to the Critique of Political Economy*, that each set of production relations (slavery, feudalism, capitalism, etc.), passes through two phases, the first where it is a stimulus to the development of the productive forces, the second where it becomes a fetter on their development. The latter phase ushers in a period of social revolution, in which the class struggle intensifies until the old production relations are overthrown and replaced by a new set permitting the further development of the productive forces. Communist relations of production, which will replace capitalism, are distinctive, in that they will always be a form of development of, and never a fetter on, the productive forces.

As even this brief sketch should make clear, this theory of history raises a series of difficult questions to which both

Marxists and their critics have devoted much attention. One set of issues arises from the problem of how to draw the line between productive forces and relations. Another concerns the nature of the relationship between the forces and relations on the one hand, and politics, culture, law, etc. on the other (the question of base and superstructure). The third deals with the relationship between the forces and relations themselves. I shall concentrate on this latter issue, since it is here that Cohen has made his most distinctive contribution. Some Marxists—principal among them Kautsky and Plekhanov—have defended the primacy of the productive forces over the production relations to the extent of claiming that once the relations have become fetters on the forces a social revolution introducing a new progressive set of relations becomes inevitable. Many Western Marxists have, however, resisted this technological determinism, some of Althusser's followers going as far, under the influence of the Chinese Cultural Revolution of the late 1960s, as to reverse the relationship, so that the relations of production have primacy over the productive forces.

The position Cohen defends in these debates is in no sense distinctive. He describes it as 'an old-fashioned historical materialism . . . in which history is, fundamentally, the growth of human productive power, and forms of society rise and fall accordingly as they enable or impede that growth'.[8] More specifically, he advances two claims: (1) the Development Thesis—the productive forces tend to develop throughout history; and (2) the Primacy Thesis—the nature of the production relations of a society is explained by the level of development of its productive forces. These views place Cohen clearly on the Kautsky-Plekhanov side of the debate. Nevertheless, the arguments which Cohen uses for these conclusions are almost wholly novel. The Development Thesis is justified by appeal to what Levine and Wright call in Chapter 1 below certain 'transhistorical' facts about human beings, namely that being 'somewhat rational' and intelligent enough to improve their situation, and confronted by circumstances of material scarcity, they will be disposed to increase their productive powers. The consequent tendency for the

[8] *KMTH*, p. x.

productive forces to grow provides history with its impulse for development. The Primacy Thesis specifies what will occur when, as a result, the forces and relations of production come into conflict. The forces' primacy is not, Cohen claims, a causal one: if that were so the thesis would founder on Marx's demonstration in the first volume of *Capital* that capitalist production relations antedated the emergence of a distinctively capitalist labour-process in the sense of artificially powered mass production. Rather, the productive forces functionally explain production relations, where a functional explanation accounts for a phenomenon in terms of its tendency to bring about certain effects. In this case, production relations are explained by their tendency to promote the development of the productive forces. Techno-logical transformations brought about by capitalist relations, far from contradicting the Primacy Thesis, are a consequence of this tendency. Similarly Cohen argues that the economic base functionally explains the politico-ideological super-structure, in that non-economic institutions tend to stabilize the prevailing relations of production.[9]

So elegant and ingenious are Cohen's arguments for a highly orthodox version of historical materialism that it is little wonder that they have dominated subsequent discussion. Three main lines have been followed by his critics. The first casts doubt on the Development Thesis, and more specifically on the idea that there is an autonomous tendency for the productive forces to develop which arises from some general human interest in technological progress. Thus Levine and Wright argue in Chapter 1 that no such interest exists, and that the growth of the productive forces depends on historically specific classes having both interests in, and capacities to secure these forces' advance, a condition which is by no means necessarily met. Historical cases of 'blocked development'—for example, the stagnation of the Chinese economy after 1300—lend support to this argument, and to the stronger claim that class relations in precapitalist societies systematically impede improvements in labour productivity.[10]

---

[9] *KMTH*, chs. 6, 8, 9, 10.

[10] See J. Cohen, review of *KMTH*, in *Journal of Philosophy* 79. 5 (1982), and R. Brenner, 'The Social Basis of Economic Development', in Roemer

Objections to Cohen's version of historical materialism have focused, secondly, on the Primacy Thesis. It is, more particularly, his use of functional explanations to explicate the relationship between the forces and relations of production that has invited the strongest criticism. Thus Elster argued that functional explanations are valid under only very restrictive conditions not usually met by those theories which rely on them. Elster linked this argument (for example, in Chapter 2) to the claim that much of Marxist social theory is vitiated by a reliance on often very crude versions of functionalism which, for example, appeal to supposedly beneficial consequences for capitalism in order to explain a variety of phenomena, perhaps most notably the state. Cohen's response in Chapter 3 turns, first, on the claim that historical materialism is only tenable if functional explanations are valid, and, secondly, on a defence of his analysis of such explanations. The latter issue itself depends on whether, as Elster originally argued, a valid functional explanation must specify the mechanism responsible for a phenomenon having the consequences which (functionally) explain it. Cohen contends that while some such mechanism must exist, it is not necessary for the explanation to mention it—an argument which Elster has now, perhaps surprisingly, come to accept.[11]

Elster's attacks on functionalist social theory are related to a broader attempt to reconstruct Marxism along methodological-individualist lines. Functionalism, he argues, ultimately derives from a teleological conception of history in which the basic explanatory principle is some underlying long-term tendency—a conception which Marx and his heirs have often been guilty of holding. The only alternative, Elster contends, lies in a rigorous insistence on accounting for social phenomena in terms of individual human agents, their properties, beliefs, and desires. The main models for such an approach are

(ed.), *Analytical Marxism*. See now, in reply to this line of criticism, G. A. Cohen and W. Kymlicka, 'Human Nature and Social Change in the Marxist Conception of History', in *Journal of Philosophy*, April 1988, and in G. A. Cohen, *History, Labour and Freedom* (Oxford, 1988).

[11] See J. Elster, 'Further Thoughts on Marxism, Functionalism and Game Theory', in Roemer (ed.), op. cit.

provided by rational-choice theory—neoclassical economics, game theory, and the like. This rational-choice Marxism— expounded by Elster in Chapter 2 and perhaps most systematically developed by Roemer in his work on exploita- tion and class—naturally invites the question whether the choice between functionalism and methodological individualism is indeed exhaustive. The most prominent contemporary social theorist to have sought to challenge this stark polarity is Anthony Giddens. Giddens argues that the best way of understanding the relationship between social structures and human agents is in terms of interaction, so that structures both enable and constrain agents, but agents alter structures.[12] While not a Marxist, Giddens has sought to integrate what he regards as historical materialism's valid insights into a broader social theory, an attempt which I discuss in Chapter 4.

Giddens's basic argument is one that goes back to Max Weber, and which has been made recently by other sociolo- gists (for example, Michael Mann and Frank Parkin). It is that class exploitation is merely one form of social domination. The others—sexual and racial oppression, for example, and the conflicts between nation-states—are irreducible to, and inexplicable in terms of, the contradiction between the forces and relations of production. This argument specifies the third main objection to Cohen's orthodox historical materialism, namely that its focus upon production is too narrow to capture the range and diversity of human behaviour. Interestingly, this criticism is entertained by Cohen himself in Chapter 5. Here he casts doubt upon Marx's conception of human nature, and more particularly upon the idea that human beings 'flourish only in the cultivation and exercise of their manifold powers'. This view of people as essentially productive is one-sided, Cohen argues, because it ignores other basic needs—for example, for an identity shared with others within a common culture, a need which finds one expression in nationalism. Other objections have been raised

---

[12] See especially A. Giddens, *Central Problems in Social Theory* (London, 1979). Other explorations of a similar approach include R. Bhaskar, *The Possibility of Naturalism* (Brighton, 1979), and A. Callinicos, *Making History* (Cambridge, 1987).

to Marx's philosophical anthropology: for example, Elster
argues that the idea that under communism human beings
will be able to realize all their potential in a rounded and
harmonious fashion is Utopian.[13]

<h1 style="text-align:center">4</h1>

Marx's conception of human nature is also an important issue
in another main area of debate, that concerning the place of
ethics in his thought. Here again, the attention given the issue
is a consequence of the break with Hegel. Hegel believed that
he had succeeded in transcending the opposition between 'is'
and 'ought', between factual and evaluative discourse, an
opposition he regarded as distinctive to Kant's essentially
subjective philosophy. Hegel was able to make this move
because the dialectic involves an objective teleology such that
reality is striving towards the realization of a goal—the self-
consciousness of Absolute Spirit—that is immanent within it.
The result is a conception of thought in which what Richard
Hare calls the descriptive and the prescriptive are inextricably
mingled. Marx, in this respect at least, remained a good pupil
of Hegel: *Capital* is notoriously a work in which objective
analysis and passionate condemnation figure alongside one
another. Critics have, however, often pointed to the apparent
contradiction between Marx's willingness to make ethical
judgements and the readiness which he and his followers
showed to dismiss morality as the embodiment of capitalist
class-interests.

There have long been Marxists ready to reinstate the distinction between fact and value—most importantly, perhaps, the
Austro-Marxists, themselves heavily influenced by neo-Kantian
philosophy. Hilferding, for example, described Marxism as
'logically an objective, value-free science', and argued that 'it
is one thing to acknowledge a necessity, and quite another to
work for that necessity'.[14] Generally, however, the treatment
of morality as a distinct discourse independent of class
interests has been associated, at least since the time of Eduard
Bernstein at the end of the last century, with attempts to

[13] J. Elster, *Making Sense of Marx* (Cambridge, 1985), pp. 82–92.
[14] R. Hilferding, *Finance Capital* (London, 1981), pp. 23–4.

revise Marxism by denying a central thesis of historical materialism, namely that it is class interest not moral conviction which moves people to change society.[15]

Nevertheless, once Hegelian teleology has been abandoned, it becomes difficult to avoid the question of the place of ethical thought in Marxism. The 1970s indeed saw a resurgence of interest in the issue, in various forms. One was the debate provoked by Edward Thompson's *The Poverty of Theory*, a principal theme of which was the indispensable role played by a socialist morality in an acceptable version of Marxism. Another was the controversy over whether or not Marx had a theory of justice, which generated an enormous literature, principally by North American philosophers (for a partial bibliography see Chapter 7 by Norman Geras). One stimulus to this debate was undoubtedly John Rawls's *A Theory of Justice*, which succeeded in rehabilitating political philosophy as substantive theory rather than merely the explication of concepts. But it is doubtful whether developments in mainstream philosophy would have such an impact had not many Marxists come to doubt the plausibility of a conception of history involving, in John Dewey's words, 'the belief that human ends are interwoven into the very texture and structure of existence'.[16]

How serious one thinks the problems posed here for Marxism by the break with Hegel depends partly on one's precise conception of morality. Bernard Williams distinguishes between the ethical, by which he understands a broad range of considerations responding in different ways to Socrates' question 'how should one live?', and the 'peculiar institution' of morality, 'a particular development of the ethical', introduced above all by Kant, which consists in a set of general obligations absolutely binding on agents who are conceived as pure subjects abstracted from their particular situations and social circumstances.[17] Williams is one of a number of

[15] For a critique of recent such attempts see E. Wood, *The Retreat from Class* (London, 1986).

[16] J. Dewey, 'Means and Ends', in L. Trotsky *et al.*, *Their Morals and Ours* (New York, 1973), p. 73.

[17] B. Williams, *Ethics and the Limits of Philosophy* (London, 1985), esp. chs. 1, 10.

contemporary philosophers to whom Aristotle's ethical theory, which focuses on the virtues, those dispositions the actual members of concrete societies have tending towards, and indeed partially constitutive of human well-being, seems the most attractive alternative to either Kantian morality or utilitarianism. Their arguments are relevant in two respects. First, it is what Williams calls morality which attracts the bulk of Marxist criticism, and which indeed can be plausibly related to the kind of abstract individualism promoted by capitalist society. Secondly, as Richard Miller argues in Chapter 6, there are striking parallels between Marx's and Aristotle's thought, particularly in their philosophical anthropologies. One possible resolution of the debate about Marx and morality might be to attribute to him a quasi-Aristotelian conception of the ethical.[18]

There remains, however, the difficulty that Marx on some occasions eschews ethical judgements, and on others apparently makes them. Much of the discussion on whether Marx thought that capitalist exploitation was unjust has grappled with this problem, and it forms the focus of Geras's magisterial survey of the debate in Chapter 7. His conclusion is the same as Cohen's, who writes: 'at least sometimes, *Marx mistakenly thought that Marx did not believe that capitalism was unjust*, because he was confused about justice.'[19] Whether or not this solution finds acceptance (it is doubtful whether it would with Miller, for example), Geras's essay is outstanding for the care with which both sides to the argument are summarized and the different issues explored.

5

It is nevertheless difficult to read, say, the discussions provoked by Roemer's work on exploitation, without a feeling that one has come a long way from the preoccupations of

[18] Though this is a course which Miller himself rejects: see 'Marx and Morality', in J. Roland Pennock and John W. Chapman (eds.), *Marxism* (*Nomos XXVI*, New York, 1983).

[19] G. A. Cohen, review of Allen W. Wood, *Karl Marx*, in *Mind*, 92 (1983), 444.

classical Marxism (Marx, Engels, Lenin, Trotsky, Luxemburg, Gramsci) with the political economy of capitalism, the analysis of class struggle, and the strategy and tactics of socialism. For one thing, analytical Marxism is just as much an essentially academic discourse as Western Marxism, without the direct engagement in political practice characteristic of the Marxisms of the Second and Third Internationals. For another, analytical Marxists tend to deny much of the substance of Marx's thought—above all, the labour theory of value and the theory of economic crises which he developed with its help. Thus Elster concludes his monumental study of Marx by declaring: 'It is not possible today, morally or intellectually, to be a Marxist in the traditional sense.' He nevertheless regards himself as a Marxist in the sense that 'most of the views that I hold to be true and important, I can trace back to Marx.'[20] Now this kind of position is by no means distinctive to the writers I have been discussing. Some theorists who were influenced by Althusser but who moved on to quite differnt views adopted a rather similar stance—Paul Hirst and Ernesto Laclau, for example. What perhaps distinguishes the analytical Marxists, however, is not that they reject various of Marx's theories, but that they deny that there is anything of value which distinguishes his method from that of mainstream social science.[21] As a result, Roemer concedes that 'it is not at all clear how analytical Marxists will differ from non-Marxist philosophers like Ronald Dworkin, John Rawls, and Amartya Sen.'[22]

The denial that there is any distinctively Marxist method may, however, have been too hasty. It all depends on what you mean by method. Analytical Marxists are in part reacting

[20] Elster, *Making Sense*, p. 531.

[21] Elster does indeed argue that 'there is a specifically Marxist method for studying social phenomena' (*Making Sense*, p. 3), but his candidate for this role—an emphasis on 'the unintended consequences of human action'—is in no sense distinctively Marxist, since it was an important theme of Smith's and Hegel's writings, and was taken up by the defenders of neoclassical economics from Carl Menger to Karl Popper.

[22] J. Roemer, ' "Rational-Choice" Marxism: Some Issues of Method and Substance', in Roemer (ed.), *Analytical Marxism*, p. 199.

against the kind of reduction of Marxism to method whose most extreme version was expressed by Lukács:

Let us assume for the sake of argument that recent research had disproved once and for all every one of Marx's individual theses. Even if this were proved, every serious 'orthodox' Marxist would still be able to accept all such modern findings without reservation and hence dismiss all of Marx's theses *in toto*—without having to renounce his orthodoxy for a single moment. Orthodox Marxism, therefore, does not imply the uncritical acceptance of the results of Marx's investigations. It is not the 'belief' in this or that thesis, nor the exegesis of a 'sacred' book. On the contrary, orthodoxy refers exclusively to *method*.[23]

One doesn't have to be a follower of Karl Popper to find the idea of a theory which would survive the empirical refutation of every one of its specific propositions absurd. Lukács seems to have thought of method as a kind of form or conceptual framework which is then given empirical content by particular, dispensable theories. There are general reasons for resisting such a separation of form and content, quite aside from the uses to which Lukács puts it here.[24] But there are other, more acceptable ways of distinguishing between the more and less fundamental features of a theory. Imre Lakatos, for example, argued that philosophers of science would do well to think in terms not of discrete hypotheses, but of scientific research programmes each consisting of a series of theories unified by a shared heuristic. This heuristic involves a 'hard core'— certain theories treated as immune to empirical refutation and common to all versions of the programme. Surrounding the hard core is a 'protective belt' of auxiliary hypotheses which are liable to modification in the light of their success or failure, in conjunction with the heuristic, in predicting 'novel facts'.[25] This approach to the philosophy of science is not without difficulties, but it does have the merit of treating method not as a formal framework, but as those propositions which give a body of scientific thought its distinctive identity. It might also help to answer the question, raised by Cohen in Chapter 5, of

[23] G. Lukács, *History and Class Consciousness* (London, 1971), p. 1.
[24] D. Davidson, 'On the Very Idea of a Conceptual Scheme', in id., *Inquiries into Truth and Interpretation* (Oxford, 1984).
[25] I. Lakatos, *Philosophical Papers*, i (Cambridge, 1978).

how historical materialism can be judged to have been
corroborated or refuted by empirical evidence.

There have been several attempts to use Lakatos's methodology of scientific research programmes to elucidate the
character of Marxism.[26] Their value will depend on whether
or not they assist in determining the extent to which Marxism
as a scientific research programme has been borne out by the
history of capitalism over the past century. The difficulty,
however, for analytical Marxists is that any such view of
Marxism as a relatively unified body of theory possessing a
hard core (the central propositions of historical materialism,
perhaps, plus the principal theses of Marx's analysis of
capitalism) will simply highlight the question implicit in
the direction their work has taken: given the rejection,
particularly by rational-choice theorists such as Elster and
Roemer, of most of Marx's principal theories, and their use of
the methods of mainstream social science, in what sense does
calling them Marxists refer to more than facts about their
individual political and intellectual biographies? The impact
especially of Cohen's work has been salutary in sharply
raising the standards of intellectual rigour required in Marxist
theoretical debate, and in drawing attention to certain
important issues discussed in the pages that follow. But even
he had by the mid-1980s settled for political objectives
little different from those espoused by contemporary social-
democratic thought—'a workers' co-operative mixed economy
with fiscal devices to ensure rough equality'.[27] Whether
analytical Marxism represents a development of, or an exit
from, the revolutionary socialist tradition therefore remains to
be seen.

[26] A. Callinicos, *Is There a Future for Marxism?* (London, 1982), chs. 7, 8,
and A. Gilbert, 'The Storming of Heaven: Politics and Marx's *Capital*', in
Pennock and Chapman (eds.), *Marxism*.

[27] G. A. Cohen, 'Peter Mew on Justice and Capitalism', *Inquiry* 29
(1986), 320. Compare, for example, G. Hodgson, *The Democratic Economy*
(Harmondsworth, 1984).

RATIONALITY AND CLASS STRUGGLE

ANDREW LEVINE AND ERIK OLIN WRIGHT

It is commonplace for writers on Marx, whether Marxists of various tendencies or critics of varying degrees of sympathy for Marxism, to hold that among Marx's major theoretical achievements was the inauguration of a new 'theory' of history, designated 'historical materialism'. While aspects of this theory were intimated throughout Marx's writings, only rarely did it get explicit and sustained discussion, most notably in the celebrated *Preface* (1859) to *The Critique of Political Economy*. None the less, for all its acknowledged importance, historical materialism has fared poorly in the Marxist literature. The schematic assertions of the 1859 *Preface*, while hardly transparent, seem disarmingly simple, lending themselves to easy adoption in the 'orthodox' Marxisms of the Second and Third Internationals. In consequence, what is hardly more than a sketch of a theory has been effectively frozen into dogma, immune from the often facile but sometimes trenchant criticisms levelled against it, and impervious to theoretical elaboration or even clarification. It is only with the disintegration of orthodoxy that the pressing need for an *account* of historical materialism, and a sustained defence or criticism of it, has come to be recognized. Despite the virtual absence of direct discussion, it is clear that the cutting edge of twentieth century Western Marxism, as it has developed in more or less overt opposition to the official Marxisms of the Communist Parties, has tended to oppose the historical materialism of the *Preface*: though, to be sure, Western Marxists have seldom, if ever, acknowledged doing so; and

From *New Left Review*, 123 (1980), pp. 47–68. Used with permission.

sometimes even outdo those they write against in professing allegiance to 'historical materialism'. The reasons for opposing the classical formulation of historical materialism are nonetheless readily apparent.

QUESTIONING THE PRIMACY OF PRODUCTIVE FORCES

There is, first of all, a rigidly determinist cast to the historical materialism of the *Preface* that accords poorly with the general tendency of Western Marxist thought. There are also political grounds for opposition. Indisputably, the *Preface* accords causal primacy (of a sort it does not clearly explain) to what Marx calls 'productive forces' (*Produktivkräfte*) over 'relations of production' (*Produktionsverhältnisse*); thus suggesting precisely the kind of 'evolutionary' or 'economist' political posture Western Marxists have opposed with virtual unanimity. If it is indeed the case, as Marx contends in the *Preface*, that 'no social formation ever perishes before all the productive forces for which there is room in it have developed', and if 'new, higher relations of production never appear before the material conditions of their existence have matured in the womb of the old society itself', then it would seem that socialist transformation depends less on revolutionizing production relations directly, as Western Marxists tend to maintain, than on the development of productive forces.[1]

---

[1] A more straightforward reading of Marx's injunctions would suggest the folly of attempting to build socialism anywhere but in the most advanced capitalist centres, a position universally adhered to by the Marxists of the Second International, including the Bolsheviks, who in overthrowing bourgeois rule in Europe's most backward capitalist country, sought to spark world revolution by attacking imperialism at its 'weakest link'. Bolshevik success in maintaining political power in the USSR and the failure of the Revolution elsewhere in Europe, complicated efforts to develop a politics (and a political theory) based on this position. Read sympathetically, Stalin's notion of 'socialism in one country', though plainly contrary to what all Marxists before the October Revolution believed, is an attempt to develop such a politics. So too is the Trotskyist theory of Permanent Revolution. This is not the place to compare these positions, nor to assess their success in translating the classical Marxian account of the primacy of productive forces into a politics appropriate for the world situation that developed after the October Revolution. The point is just

This conclusion has indeed been drawn by the Communist Parties, as by many others; and has inspired a political programme in the Soviet Union and elsewhere from which virtually all Western Marxists outside the Communist Parties, and many within, in varying degrees dissent. The litany of Soviet sins, committed for the sake of developing productive forces, is all too well known: the brutal collectivization of agricultural production, the hierarchical structure and 'productivist' ideology that governs the factories, the selective and technocratic structure of education, the severe centralization of political power, the indefinite prolongation of police terror and the progressive (and apparently intractable) growth of bureaucratic despotism. Needless to say, commitment to the theoretical positions of the 1859 *Preface* does not entail the political programmes adopted by the leaders of the Soviet Union; and it is likely that even under the conditions the Soviet Union and other Communist states face, and without slackening the development of productive forces, a more 'human face' is an historic possibility. In any case, the best Marxist thought in the West has sought to distance itself from the Soviet experience; and so, sometimes inadvertently, sometimes deliberately, from the theoretical positions that Soviet politics seems to presuppose.

The Cultural Revolution in China (or, at least, Western perceptions of it), in proclaiming 'politics in command', in apparently aiming at the revolutionary transformation of relations of production, while neglecting or even disparaging the development of productive forces, provided, at last, a model of an official Marxism at odds with the 1859 *Preface*. It is not surprising, then, that the tendency in Western Marxist thought most solidly (implicitly) with the Cultural Revolution, and also most intent upon developing Marx's contributions to a theory of history—the tendency developed by Louis Althusser, Etienne Balibar and their co-thinkers— should break expressly with the evolutionary account of historical materialism dominant in the Second and Third Internationals. Even if they did not quite repudiate the 1859

that, for both Trotsky and Stalin, what is crucially important in socialist transformation, and what must therefore have primacy in any socialist politics, is the society's productive forces and their development.

Preface, they so qualified their acceptance of it, that they might as well have struck the text from the Marxist canon.[2] Like so many other major Western Marxists, Althusser and Balibar look with ill-disguised embarrassment on the simple declarations of the 1859 *Preface*, and thus on historical materialism as traditionally understood. To be sure, Althusserians remain adamant defenders of what they call 'historical materialism'. But their 'historical materialism' has little to do with what the term has traditionally meant to generations of Marxists. They retain the term at the cost of altering its meaning. 'Historical materialism', for Althusser and Balibar, has come to be synonymous with 'Marxist social science' (or, as they would prefer, with the Marxist 'science of history'). Thus it is distinguished, in their view, from rival accounts of history and society by its methodological positions (its view of causality and explanation, its concept of 'contradiction', its logic of concept formation and theory construction) and not at all by its substantive theoretical claims about the primacy of productive forces. And what the Althusserians do more or less explicitly, other Western Marxist tendencies do too, though often even less self-consciously and perspicaciously. Thus historical materialism, in the sense of the 1859 *Preface*, has effectively been abandoned in the most lively and penetrating Marxist currents.

However, the resurgence of interest in Marxist theory in the English-speaking world, particularly among philosophers trained in the analytic tradition, has kindled a new and generally sympathetic interest in the positions of the 1859 *Preface*. This emerging tendency, at odds both with earlier orthodoxies and also with the main currents of Western Marxism, has been given major theoretical expression in a new book by G. A. Cohen, *Karl Marx's Theory of History: A Defence*.[3]

---

[2] Cf., for example, Etienne Balibar, 'The Basic Concepts of Historical Materialism', in L. Althusser and E. Balibar, *Reading Capital* (NLB, London, 1970), esp. pp. 202–8.

[3] G. A. Cohen, *Karl Marx's Theory of History: A Defence* (Oxford University Press, 1978). Other recent work, elaborating similar positions, include: John McMurtry, *The Structure of Marx's World View* (Princeton, 1978); and William Shaw, *Marx's Theory of History* (Stanford, 1978).

Without in the least slackening the critical political stance characteristic of the best of Western Marxism, Cohen boldly and remarkably takes exception to the widespread abandonment of the theses of the 1859 *Preface*. In arguing the case for the primacy of productive forces, Cohen mounts what is likely the most substantial defence of historical materialism (in the traditional sense) ever launched; while throwing down a challenge to the best Marxist thought of the past decades. Cohen sets out unabashedly to reconstruct and defend the 'technological determinism'[4] Western Marxists have, virtually without exception, inveighed against; and thus to rehabilitate—not as dogma, but as defensible theory—the positions of the 1859 *Preface*.

Western Marxism's stance on the kind of position Cohen defends was originally a reaction (in large measure) to the dogmatism of the official Marxisms of the Second and Third Internationals. Gradually, this stance has itself become, if not quite a new dogma, at least an automatic response. Views that accord primacy to productive forces over production relations (and, in turn, over the legal and political 'superstructure') are everywhere faulted as crude and 'vulgar'; as leading to a 'mechanistic' politics that denies the effective historical role of individual and class agency, and even the theoretical and practical importance of class struggle. Cohen shows, beyond any question, that this kind of response to the traditional view is woefully facile and inadequate. The traditional view, whatever our final assessment of it, is eminently serious and, as Cohen would have it, defensible. Moreover, it is very likely Marx's own position, as Cohen convincingly argues. However, we are not convinced that the position Cohen defends, at least as it presently stands, is at all adequate. The consensus against technological determinism, even if not nearly so obvious as it formerly appeared, is still, we think, basically sound.

Cohen's central contention, designated the Primacy Thesis, holds that social relations of production are explained by the level of development of productive forces. We will examine the

[4] Not 'economic determinism', as is often supposed. On Cohen's account, the productive forces that are accorded primacy are not, strictly speaking, part of the economy!

case for the Primacy Thesis as such, and also for a number of more fundamental claims Cohen advances with a view to defending it. Our thesis, in short is that Cohen's account neglects what is crucial for any adequate account of revolutionary social transformations: the question of class capacities. Thus the theory of history Cohen defends is, at best, partial and one-sided; and in consequence, defective both theoretically and politically. But even if we do not finally agree with Cohen, the challenge his work poses is extremely welcome. Too often, discussions of historical materialism, as of much else of pertinence to Marxist thought, when not entirely insensitive to the requirements of rational reconstruction and defence, lapse into that dreadful obscurantism that, for all its positive achievements, plagues Western Marxism. Cohen has given us a standard of clarity to which subsequent discussions of Marx's theory of history, as well as of other aspects of Marxist theory, must aspire. It is not the least virtue of this book that its theses and arguments are sufficiently clear and rigorous that they can be constructively criticized.

THE CASE FOR THE PRIMACY THESIS

The Primacy Thesis, again, maintains that: 'the nature of a set of production relations is explained by the level of development of the productive forces embraced by it (to a far greater extent than vice versa.)'[5] (p. 134) The burden of *Karl Marx's Theory of History* is to defend this position. It is the Primacy Thesis, on Cohen's account, that distinguishes Marx's theory of history.

Productive forces are said to explain relations of production *functionally*.[6] A given set of relations of production is determined

---

[4] In chs. 1 and 2 Cohen provides a very lucid and useful gloss on these key notions of historical materialism. Very roughly, 'productive forces' (*Produktivkräfte*) designates the technical organization of the labour process; while 'relations of production' (*Produktionsverhältnisse*) designates forms of real social ownership and control.

[6] In brief, functional explanations explain the existence or form of phenomena by virtue of their effects. A classic example is Malinowski's explanation of the existence of magic rituals among Trobriand Islanders as functional for the reduction of fear and anxiety elicited by dangerous forms

by the functional requirements necessary for the expansion of productive forces. Specially, 'the production relations are of a kind R at time t because relations of kind R are suitable to the use and development of the productive forces at t, given the level of development of the latter at t.' (p. 160) And again: 'when relations endure stably, they do so because they promote the development of the forces. . . . The property of a set of productive forces which explains the nature of the economic structure embracing them is their disposition to develop within a structure of that nature.' (p. 161)

Cohen's task is to give an account of the structure of interconnections between forces and relations of production which make functional explanations of this sort defensible. In this section, we outline the salient features of Cohen's argument (omitting virtually all of the fine and intricate detail). This reconstruction (and simplification) of Cohen's position then forms the basis for the critical remarks that follow in the next section.

The overall argument can be decomposed into five relatively independent theses: A given level of development of productive forces is compatible with only a limited range of relations of production (Thesis 1). Since the forces of production tend to develop over time (Thesis 2), these forces eventually reach a level at which they are no longer compatible with existing relations of production (Thesis 3). When this occurs, the relations are said to 'fetter' the productive forces. Because rational human, beings will not in the long run tolerate the fettering of productive forces, they will transform these relations of production (Thesis 4), and substitute new relations that are optimal for the further development of productive forces (Thesis 5). We shall consider each of these theses in turn.

1. *The Compatibility Thesis: A given level of development of productive forces is compatible with only a limited range of relations of production.* This thesis is plainly essential for the Primacy

of fishing. On functional explanation in social science, see Arthur Atinchcombe, *Constructing Social Theories* (New York, 1968), and also Cohen's own, very important discussion in chs. 9 and 10 of *Karl Marx's Theory of History*.

Thesis. If a given level of development of productive forces were compatible with any relations of production whatsoever, then the forces could hardly *explain* the relations. Cohen, however, offers no general defence of this claim. Instead, he supports it by citing examples. Thus: 'Slavery . . . could not be the general condition of producers in a society of computer technology, if only because the degree of culture needed in labourers who can work that technology would lead them to revolt, successfully, against slave status.' (p. 158).

As his examples make clear, 'compatibility' has a precise sense: forces and relations of production are compatible whenever the relations allow for the further development (or, as Cohen adds in Chapter 11, the effective deployment) of productive forces; and where these productive forces help to strengthen and reproduce existing relations of production. Compatibility thus designates a system of reciprocal effects, as the following diagram illustrates:

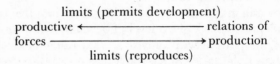

$$\text{limits (permits development)}$$
$$\text{productive} \longleftarrow \text{relations of}$$
$$\text{forces} \longrightarrow \text{production}$$
$$\text{limits (reproduces)}$$

Productive forces impose limits on the range of possible relations of production (since only certain relations will be reproduced by these forces), and relations of production impose limits on productive forces (since only certain productive forces can be properly utilized and developed within those relations).

Cohen uses the Compatibility Thesis to develop a general typology of correspondences between forms of production relations (economic structures) and levels of development of productive forces. This typology is summarized in the following table (cf. p. 198):

Form of Economic Structure		*Level of Productive Development*
1. Pre-class society		No surplus
2. Pre-capitalist class society	Corresponding to	Some surplus, but less than
3. Capitalist society		Moderately high surplus, but less than
4. Post-class society		Massive surplus

This table of correspondences is admittedly roughly drawn: it fails to distinguish at all among the various forms of pre-capitalist class societies, and it provides no criteria for distinguishing the different levels of productive development. None the less, it does indicate the general contours of Cohen's position.

The rationale for these correspondences is plain enough. Class relations are impossible without some surplus, since a class (for Marx) is, by definition, determined by its relation to other classes in the social process of appropriating an economic surplus. Pre-class society (primitive communism) is therefore incompatible with any level of development of productive forces capable of generating a small surplus. And a small surplus, in turn, is incompatible with capitalist class relations. Capitalism requires a moderately high surplus (and thus a moderately developed level of the forces of production), in order to allow for 'repeated introduction of new productive forces and thus for regular capitalist investments.' (p. 198) When a moderately high level of surplus is reached, pre-capitalist relations of production increasingly fetter the further development of productive forces, and therefore come to be superseded by distinctly capitalist social relations. Likewise a moderately high level of development of productive forces is incompatible with what Cohen calls post-class society, a society of collective control of the surplus by the direct producers. Since the development of productive forces from moderate to high levels requires great deprivation and toil, the direct producers would never freely impose such sacrifices on themselves. Only a production system dominated by market imperatives, forcing a logic of accumulation on both direct producers and owners of means of production can accomplish this development.

The Compatibility Thesis thus maintains, albeit roughly, a systematic relation of correspondence between forces and relations of production. But it does not itself establish the primacy of productive forces. As Cohen writes: '. . . some Marxists who accept the primacy of the forces are content to equate it with the constraints they impose on the production relations. But that is unsatisfactory. For the constraint is symmetrical. If high technology rules out slavery, then slavery rules out high technology. Something must be added to mutual constraint to establish the primacy of the forces.' (p. 158) That 'something' is the Development Thesis.

2 *The Development Thesis: The productive forces tend to develop throughout history.* This tendency, Cohen argues, is based on specific characteristics of human nature, the human condition and human capacities. Human beings are at least somewhat rational, and 'rational beings who know how to satisfy compelling wants . . . will be disposed to seize and employ the means to satisfaction of those wants.' (p. 152) Under conditions of (relative) scarcity, where few if any wants are satisfied immediately and without effort, the development of productive forces becomes a 'compelling want' on the part of rational agents. Then, inasmuch as human beings 'possess intelligence of a kind and degree which enables them to improve their situation' (p. 152), they will in fact seize the means for satisfaction of their wants by continuously and progressively developing productive forces (assuming, of course, that no countervailing tendencies of sufficient strength intervene). Thus human beings are moved by a permanent impulse to try to improve their abilities to transform nature to satisfy their wants. In consequence, Cohen concludes, there is a tendency for productive forces to develop over time. Further, these improvements will generally be cumulative. Inasmuch as human beings are rational, having once improved their situation by developing the productive forces they find at hand, they will not revert to less developed forces, except under extraordinary circumstances beyond their control.

The Development Thesis introduces the asymmetry lacking in the Compatibility Thesis. These two theses together imply a further thesis, not formulated as such by Cohen, but a plank of his argument nonetheless. We call this third claim: the Contradiction Thesis.

3. *The Contradiction Thesis: Given the reciprocal constraints that exist between forces and relations of production (the Compatibility Thesis), and the tendency of the productive forces to develop (the Development Thesis), with sufficient time, the productive forces will develop to a point where they are no longer compatible with (i.e. contradict) the relations of*

production under which they had previously developed. Thus while, at any given time, forces and relations of production are mutually determining (each imposing limits on the other), their relation becomes asymmetrical over time in virtue of those rational adaptive practices that progressively augment the level of development of productive forces. To return to our diagram:

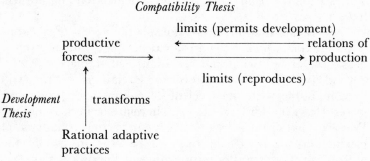

Compatibility Thesis

The Contradiction Thesis, then, asserts the inevitability of 'contradictions' (intensifying incompatibilities) between forces and relations of production. The relations come to 'fetter' the development of the forces. This contradiction might in principle be resolved by an adaptation downward of the productive forces, by a regression sufficient to restore compatibility. But this kind of resolution is ruled out by the Development Thesis. Thus the contradictions that inevitably occur can be resolved only through a transformation of the relations of production. Or, in other words:

4. *The Transformation Thesis: When forces and relations of production are incompatible (as they will always eventually become, so long as class society persists), the relations will change in such a way that compatibility between forces and relations of production will be restored.* Where contradictions between forces and relations of production emerge, as they inevitably will in class society, the resolution will always be in favour of the forces, not the relations; it is the relations of production that give. As Marx wrote, 'in order that they may be deprived of the results attained (by the development of productive forces) and forfeit the fruits of civilization, they are obliged from the moment

when their mode of intercourse no longer corresponds to the productive forces acquired, to change all their traditional social forms.'[7]

'Why', Cohen asks, 'should the fact that the relations restrict the forces foretell their doom, if not because it is irrational to persist with them given the price in lost opportunity to further inroads against scarcity?' (p. 159) Thus Thesis 4 follows from Theses 2 and 3 (which follows, in turn, from Theses 1 and 2).

The Transformation Thesis 'fortells the doom' of relations of production which fetter productive forces, but by itself it does not foretell what new relations will replace the old, beyond specifying that, whatever these relations are, they will be compatible with the level of development of productive forces. However, for forces to explain relations in the sense the Primacy Thesis requires (to explain actual relations of production), it is crucial that we be able to specify the outcome of those transformations that, if Thesis 4 is right, we know to be necessary. This is the point of the Optimality Thesis.

5. *The Optimality Thesis: When a given set of relations of production become fetters on the further development of productive forces and are thus transformed, they will be replaced by relations of production which are functionally optimal for the further development of the productive forces.* In Cohen's words, 'the relations which obtain at a given time are the relations most suitable for the forces to develop at that time, given the level they have reached by that time'. (p. 171) The rationale for this claim apparently derives, again, from the Development Thesis, now in conjunction with the Transformation Thesis. If fettering relations of production are abandoned because they conflict with a rational desire for development, it would be irrational to replace them with anything short of those relations of production that, in the circumstances, are optimal for the further development of productive forces. Thus Thesis 5 follows, on Cohen's account, from Theses 2 and 4.

Moreover, Thesis 5 is necessary for the full defence of the

[7] Marx to Annenkov, 23 Dec. 1846, cited in Cohen, p. 159.

Primacy Thesis. If for a particular level of development of productive forces, more than one set of relations of production would in fact stimulate further development, and if the productive forces did not, so to speak, 'select' the optimal relations from among the set of possible relations, the character of actual relations of production would not be explained (functionally) by the productive forces. In other words, without the Optimality Thesis, the force of the Primacy Thesis would be severely and perhaps fatally, mitigated. It is, we think, because this claim is so crucial for the Primacy Thesis that Cohen insists on it vehemently, even in the face of obvious counter-examples. Pre-capitalist class relations, for the most part, can hardly be said to have encouraged the development of productive forces. Nonetheless, Cohen argues, they were optimal for their time. 'Even a set of relations which is not the means whereby the forces within it develop', Cohen insists, 'may be optimal for the development of the forces during the period when it obtains.' (p. 171)

Since the Optimality Thesis depends on the Transformation Thesis, if the latter is fatally flawed, then so too is the former. We will argue in what follows that this is indeed the case; and we will thus not discuss the Optimality Thesis directly in our assessment and critique of the Primacy Thesis as a whole.[8]

[8] While we will not criticise the Optimality Thesis in a systematic way, it is worth noting some of its theoretical and political implications. In particular, the Optimality Thesis is an important element in the argument that capitalism is the necessary form of social relations of production for the rapid development of industrial forces of production. Cohen goes to great length to defend this proposition, arguing that only under the compulsion of the market and the domination of use value by exchange value can sufficient sacrifices be imposed on the direct producers to allow for the rapid development of industrial forces of production. Capitalism is thus the optimal structure for such development. This argument, which recapitulates the shared wisdom of Marxists prior to the October Revolution, is plainly directed against those who hold that socialism too can rapidly and systematically develop the productive forces. Cohen insists that a high level of development of productive forces (and thus a massive surplus) is a necessary condition for socialism, rather than a task to be achieved under socialism; and that without a massive surplus already in place, attempts at constructing socialism will fail. 'Premature attempts at revolution', Cohen argues, 'whatever their immediate outcome, will eventuate in a restoration of capitalist society.' (p. 206) The possibility of class relations in which

In any case, with Thesis 5, the case for the Primacy Thesis is now complete. Our reconstruction of Cohen's argument has, of course, left out much of what is most valuable in Cohen's discussion: the subtlety of his argumentation and the many insights and clarifications he provides *en passant*. But the broad outline of his central contention is now sufficiently clear. The productive forces functionally explain the relations of production in that the effects of the relations on the tendentially developing forces determine what the relations of production are, and whether they will continue to exist or be transformed.

In the section that follows, we question the Primacy Thesis as such, and the sort of rationale Cohen provides for its defence. Then in the next section we focus directly on the specific theses Cohen uses to argue for the Primacy Thesis.

RATIONALITY AND CLASS CAPACITY

Although Marx spoke disparagingly of the contractarian tradition in social and political theory, the theory of history advanced in the 1859 *Preface* is itself derived in contractarian fashion. Of course Marx would have resisted this character-ization and perhaps so too would Cohen; but Cohen's reconstruction of the argument for historical materialism, an argument Marx himself never provides directly, is contractarian nonetheless.

In its more familiar uses in political and social philosophy, contractarianism is a methodological programme for dealing with normative questions, for discovering the principles that determine how political and social institutions ought to be organized. The normative principles that ought to

production is not directed towards the accumulation of exchange value, but where systematic imperatives for the development of means of production nonetheless exist—not as 'capital' (accumulated exchange value), but as expanded capacities for the production of use values—is never directly confronted. Cohen's analysis is thus silent on the various arguments concerning post-capitalist class societies as developed by such theorists as Rudolph Bahro in *The Alternative in Eastern Europe* (NLB, 1978), G. Konrad and I. Szeleyni in *Intellectuals on the Road to Class Power* (London and New York, 1979), and others.

govern the state are those these individuals would choose. Contractarianism supposes, then, that individuals have a certain capacity for acting rationally in an instrumental sense; that they are able, to some extent at least, to adapt means to ends in order to realize their goals. And it supposes that their situation in a state of nature leads them, as Rousseau put it in *The Social Contract*, to seek 'to change their mode of existence'.

The same method lends itself to other speculative investigations, even where there is no question of determining normative principles. Thus as Marx pointed out in his methodological *Introduction* to the *Grundrisse*, the classical economists, with their 'isolated hunters and fishermen', were effectively contractarians: building an economic theory out of a logically prior notion of individual (instrumental) rationality in a milieu of (relative) scarcity. And so too, whether consciously or not, and despite all Marx has to say against contractarianism, is Marx himself. The classical formulation of historical materialism, though arguably corroborated by the 'facts' of concrete history, is defended, as Cohen demonstrates, by an extended thought-experiment in which the general contours of human history are derived, as in the classical economists, from a logical prior claim about individual (instrumental) rationality and about individuals' capacities to realize their ends in a milieu of (relative) scarcity. Individuals, in a word, have a stake in the development of productive forces in order to overcome that scarcity; and it is in virtue of this overwhelming interest that the course of human history proceeds.

The radical individualism Marx inveighs against in the classical economists is muted in Cohen's reconstruction, because individuals are located in classes and thus have interests not only in the overall development of productive forces, but also in the maintenance or overthrow of existing forms of class society.[9] Still, in Cohen's view, class interests are reducible to individuals' interests; that is, to the interests of individuals situated differentially in a social structure. Thus even if the appeal is not to 'isolated hunters and fishermen',

[9] As Cohen argues in ch. 2 of *Karl Marx's Theory of History*, the sorting of individuals into social classes is itself a necessary feature of the production process under conditions of (relative) scarcity.

but to serfs and lords or workers and capitalists, it is still, in the final analysis, a reference to individuals.[10]

The issue, then, is whether or not Cohen, following the letter and spirit of the 1859 *Preface*, has in fact derived an adequate, substantive picture of the general contours of human history. We think he has not. Our view, in brief, is that one cannot develop an adequate account of human history just by reference to individuals' or even classes' interests. It is crucial in addition to determine how these interests are translated into social and political practices. Cohen effectively denies that, in the long run, the realization of human interests (in the development of productive forces) can be blocked by social constraints. These interests may be impeded, of course. Indeed, it is their impedance that structures the course of human history, making the transformation of economic structures necessary. But interests in the development of productive forces cannot, on Cohen's view, be finally blocked. Thus at the level of generality at which historical materialism (in the sense of the 1859 *Preface*) is posed, social constraints on the implementation of interests can be overlooked. On this crucial point, we think Cohen is wrong. The transformation of interests into practices is the central problem for any adequate theory of history, as it is for the theory and practice of politics. It is worth noting that this problem is a central motif of the

---

[10] We shall not speculate here whether Marx's own strictures against the individualism of the contractarian programme, against the very notion of a logically prior individual as the starting-point for social or political theory, can be turned against his own (implicit) case for the theses of the 1859 *Preface*; except to note that the introduction of classes and class interests within a still contractarian framework does not in any obvious way avoid the charge of incoherence Marx levels against contractarians in the essay *On the Jewish Question* and elsewhere. And neither shall we dwell on the anomalous use Marx seems to make of the classical and 'vulgar' economists' notion of practical reason as purely instrumental, as pertaining just to the adaptation of means to ends, and not to the character of the ends themselves. That Marx's account of individual and class interests, and his claims about revolutionary motivation, do suppose a view of practical reason as purely instrumental is noteworthy and perhaps damaging; and, in any case, renders his positions vulnerable to some unexpected cricitisms. (See Allen Buchanan, 'Revolutionary Motivation and Rationality', *Philosophy and Public Affairs*, 9.1, Autumn, 1979.) Investigation of these and related issues is, we think, crucial for the critical assessment of Marx's theory of history.

thought of those Marxists who have, in effect, distanced themselves from the positions of the 1859 *Preface*. We agree with them that the theory of history Marx sketches in that text is inadequate to the extent it ignores or effectively minimizes the problem of *class capacities*.

We define class capacities as those organizational, ideological and material resources available to classes in class struggle. Cohen, of course, realizes that there is a distinction to be drawn between class capacities in class struggles and class interests in the outcomes of these struggles. But he treats the problem of capacity as entirely subordinate to the problem of interests. Indeed, he even argues that class interests by themselves somehow generate the capacities requisite for their realization, so long as these interests advance the level of development of productive forces. Thus in discussing the domination of a ruling class, Cohen writes: 'But how does the fact that production would prosper under a certain class ensure its dominion? Part of the answer is that there is a general stake in stable and thriving production, so that the class best placed to deliver it attracts allies from other strata of society. Prospective ruling classes are often able to raise support among the classes subjected to the ruling class they would displace. Contrariwise, classes unsuited to the task of governing society tend to lack the confidence political hegemony requires, and if they do seize power, they tend not to hold it for long.' (p. 292)

On Cohen's view, apparently, class interests determine class capacities. For ascending and progressive ruling classes, class interests somehow breed the capacities for seizing and exercising domination. For historically retrograde classes, in virtue of their interests, the capacity for class rule is correspondingly undone.

Cohen is very likely right that Marx himself saw the growth of class capacities (at least for the ascendant working class under capitalism) as a consequence of the emergence of revolutionary and transformative interests. As capitalism becomes increasingly untenable as an economic system, capitalism's gravediggers, the proletariat, become, Marx thought, increasingly capable of transforming capitalist relations of production. This coordination of interests and capacities is achieved, on Marx's account, by the mutual determination of interests and capacities by the development of productive forces. However, many Marxists have come, with good reason, to question this account. Instead of seeing an inexorable growth in the capacity of the working class to struggle against the intensifying irrationality of capitalism, it has been argued that there are systematic processes at work in capitalist society that disorganize the working class, block its capacities and thwart its ability to destroy capitalist relations of production. These processes range from labour market segmentation and the operation of the effects of racial and ethnic divisions on occupational cleavages within the working class, to the effects of the bourgeois legal system and privatized consumerism in advertising. (We will examine these processes in more detail in our discussion of the Transformation Thesis below.) All of these processes contribute to reproducing the disorganization of the working class rather than the progressive enhancement of its class capacity.

Thus there is no automatic development of working class capacities in consequence of the development of productive forces under capitalism. There are, to be sure, as Marx showed, processes at work that encourage such development. But there are also, as just noted, processes that profoundly, perhaps even overwhelmingly, discourage it. There is no adequate general theory of the balance between these processes; and thus no substitute for what Lenin called 'the soul of Marxism': the concrete investigation of concrete situations.

Moreover, what holds for the emergence of working class capacities under capitalism, Cohen's most likely case, surely pertains in general. There is no necessary relation between the development of an interest in social change on the part of rational agents (situated differentially in a social structure) and an historical capacity for bringing such changes about. A sustained and powerful (rational) interest in the transformation of an economic structure is not a sufficient condition, even in the long run, for the revolutionary transformation of that structure. So far as class capacities, *pace* Cohen, do not derive from the development of productive forces, it is arbitrary, in the end, to ascribe to these productive forces the kind of 'primacy' Cohen alleges.

Collapsing the issue of capacities for action into the problem of determining the rational objectives of action is characteristic of the type of contractarian argument Cohen, and perhaps also Marx, at least in the 1859 *Preface*, employ. By abstracting human beings from their social/historical conditions in order to develop an account of pure rational action, the analysis implicitly takes the position that the structural conditions for the translation of rationality into action are of theoretically secondary interest to the problem of characterizing rational action itself. However, for the concrete investigation of concrete situations, the most powerful determinants of human activity generally lie in the distinctively social determinations contractarians effectively minimize. Human beings may be generally rational in the sense described by Cohen and yet may be generally thwarted from fully acting on the basis of that rationality because of social constraints, relations of domination, organizational incapacities for collective struggle and so on. The abstracted, ahistorical account of rationality may provide an essential element in the philosophical critique of those constraints, but it does not provide a basis for explaining the real determinations and contradictions of those constraints. Cohen has undoubtedly focused on an important component of any adequate explanation; but it is far from clear that in doing so he has advanced our general understanding of the actual course of human history.

To corroborate this conclusion, we will now turn to a critique of Cohen's specific arguments for the primacy of the productive forces.

CRITICISMS OF COHEN'S ARGUMENT

1. The Compatibility Thesis

The Compatibility Thesis involves two interconnected claims: (a) that for a given level of forces of production, there is a limited range of compatible relations of production; and (b) for a given form of relations of production, there is a limited range of compatible forces of production.

The first of these two claims seems hard to fault. It is easy to posit a type of relation of production which would be incompatible with any specified level of the forces of production, and the thesis is supported as long as such examples are forthcoming. The second claim, however, is somewhat less convincingly argued. This is particularly true for Cohen's analysis of capitalism, where it is never entirely clear why there is a ceiling to the development of the forces of production within capitalist relations of production.

Cohen's analysis of 'fettering' in capitalism explictly rejects the conventional falling rate of profit/rising organic composition of capital argument for crisis of accumulation. In that traditional argument, capitalism fetters the development of the forces of production because the crises of accumulation ultimately undermine the capacity of capitalists to invest, since investments occur only in the pursuit of profits and only out of surplus value. The declining rate of profit, therefore, erodes the capacity of capitalism to generate further advances of the forces of production. Cohen, however, explicitly distances himself from such arguments. Indeed, he insists that none of his arguments hinge on the labour theory of value (p. 116), and in this work he remains agnostic on the adequacy of the 'specifically labour-theoretical account of value'. (p. 116) In a later essay he moves one step further and argues for the incoherence of the labour theory of value, thus further removing his general analysis from traditional crisis arguments.[11]

How then does Cohen defend the thesis of the fettering of the forces of production in advanced capitalism? His basic argument is that because capitalism is production for exchange rather than use, capitalist relations of production have a built-in bias for using progress in productive forces to expand output rather than to expand leisure time (where leisure is defined as release from burdensome toil). Cohen writes: 'As long as production remains subject to the capitalist principle, the output-increasing option will tend to be selected and implemented in one way or another. . . . Now the consequence of the increasing output which capitalism

[11] See G. A. Cohen, 'The Labour Theory of Value and the Concept of Exploitation', *Philosophy and Public Affairs*, 8. 4 (Summer, 1979), 338–60.

necessarily favours is increasing consumption. Hence the boundless pursuit of consumption goods is a result of a productive process oriented to exchange-values rather than consumption-values. It is the Rockefellers who ensure that the Smiths need to keep up with the Jones's.' (p. 306)

This generates an incompatibility between the forces and relations of production, not because productive power as such ceases to develop, but because it ceases to be rationally deployed: 'The productive technology of capitalism begets an unparalleled opportunity for lifting the curse of Adam and liberating men from toil, but the production relations of capitalist economic organization prevent the opportunity from being seized. . . . It brings society to the threshold of abundance and locks the door. For the promise of abundance is not an endless flow of goods, but a sufficiency produced with a minimum of unpleasant exertion.' (pp. 306–7)

The Compatibility Thesis is thus equivalent to the claim that the relations of production become irrational with respect to a general notion of improving the human condition. In the past such improvement was achieved by increasing the level of development of the forces of production themselves; in advanced capitalism it is achieved by the rational deployment of the forces of production that already exist. 'Fettering', therefore, is ultimately a fettering of the possibility of rational action. For the Compatibility Thesis to rest on a sound foundation, therefore, it is crucial that Cohen's account of rational action is adequately developed. As we shall see, there are important limitations on this issue.

2. The Development Thesis

At first glance, there seems to be little to criticize in the view that productive forces tend to develop over time, given the rational interests and capacities of human beings in conditions of scarcity. The problem, however, is that the Development Thesis presupposes a transhistorical meaning for 'rationality' and 'scarcity', and thus a transhistorical notion of human beings' interests that likely cannot be sustained. If the content of both rational action and scarcity, and hence of interests, are not given for all time, but are instead endogenous to the social system; if the meaning of these terms is in some important sense determined by the relations of production themselves, then the Development Thesis, however unobjectionable in its own right, would not serve the purpose to which Cohen puts it.

Consider the case of scarcity. How many calories per day are necessary for an adequate or abundant diet? Is physical effort always toil? How much effort or strain is necessary to generate a sufficient aversion to toil to act as a sustained incentive for improvement? Marx argued in effect that these questions have no transhistorical answers. Thus a hut by itself might be seen as adequate shelter, whereas next to a palace it is a hovel. But whether huts are built next to palaces or not is as much a function of the relations of production as the development of the productive forces.

This problem with the definition of scarcity becomes particularly salient in the discussion of the fettering of the forces of production in late capitalism, where as Cohen rightfully notes, scarcity is something imposed by capitalist production relations and ideology, rather than confronted by those relations. But the problem is not unique to capitalism. In feudal society it is not at all obvious that if the consumption of all the parasitic classes (priests, lords, etc.) were redistributed to the peasantry there would have been in any meaningful sense 'scarcity'. Furthermore, if leisure time is a measure of scarcity, then the number of holy days in medieval society— at times nearly as many as work days in the year—would indicate that medieval society was characterized by considerably greater surplus time (if not necessarily surplus product) than is contemporary capitalism.

Yet, there was undoubtedly an impulse for technical change in feudal Europe that needs to be explained. If it is not the result of a universal impulse for human beings to improve their condition by virtue of the kind of animal they are, what was the underlying dynamic of such change? We would argue that the answer to this question requires a shift of the terms of the discussion from universal criteria for scarcity and rationality to class-specific notions of scarcity and rationality.

In feudalism, in these terms, there was systematic scarcity for feudal lords engaged in military competition for command of territories. In order to effectively wage such warfare, they needed revenues, retainers, military equipment, etc. There was thus an incentive for feudal ruling classes to attempt to exact more surplus from peasants and to encourage the development of improved means of waging war. The imperative to improve agrarian means of production thus came not, as Cohen's account suggests, from a rational desire to augment productive capacity in the face of natural scarcity, but as an indirect effect of feudal relations of production.

This argument may not seem inconsistent with Cohen's, since his account of the Primacy Thesis requires that the relations of production be compatible with the development of productive forces, either by permitting development or by actually encouraging it. But recall that the explanatory asymmetry Cohen accords to productive forces over relations of production depends upon an independent argument for the development of the productive forces, one that does not itself hinge on the form of the relations of production. This is why Cohen turns to transhistorical claims about rationality and scarcity. The Development Thesis cannot both follow from the Primary Thesis and, at the same time, be a presupposition of it.

The problem can be restated as follows: the rational peasant (and other subordinate direct producers) in feudal society would probably have preferred a society without feudal lords and military competition; a society where peasants could directly consume all of the surplus product. Indeed, given the very slow rate of development of productive forces under feudalism, most peasants would probably have preferred completely stagnant development of the productive forces without exploitation, to slowly developing productive forces with exploitation. From their point of view, in short, there was nothing 'rational' about the way in which feudalism allowed for the development of the productive forces. But peasants, as a subordinate class, separated from the means of repression, lacked the capacity to translate their rational interests into collective actions. Therefore, the rationality and scarcity of the ruling class was imposed on them by the relations of production. Thus, contrary to what Cohen maintains, relations of production condition the development of productive forces, not because they allow for the translation of universal rationality into historically specific 'moments', but in virtue of the imposition of class specific rationalities and forms of scarcity.

3. *The Contradiction Thesis*

If the critique of the Development Thesis just sketched is correct, it is possible to imagine a class society in which there is no systematic tendency towards a contradiction between forces and relations of production. Or, in other words, it is possible to imagine a society in which no mechanisms exist for translating an *incompatibility* between forces and relations of production into a *contradiction*.

The 'Asiatic Mode of Production', as discussed by Marx and others, is in fact an example of such a possible society. If Marx's account of the Asiatic mode of production is right—that is, if the concept is coherent and actually applies to the analysis of actual or even possible societies—the social form of the relations of production with the attendant form of the state generated a permanent stagnation of the development of the forces of production. There was thus, in Cohen's terms, a clear incompatibility between the further development of the forces of production and the existing relations of production.

But was there a contradiction between the forces and relations of production? A contradiction implies that a stable reproduction of the structure is impossible, that there are endogenously generated imperatives for change. And for there to be such imperatives, there must exist within the society a new potential ruling class that is capable of organizing the development of the productive forces under its rule and the destruction of the old ruling class. If incompatibility does not itself engender such a class, then, incompatibility simply becomes the basis for permanent stagnation.

In the case of classical China there was no class capable of being such a bearer of productive advance. Because of the centralization of state power, the lack of the political and economic independence of the towns, the absorption of merchants into the existing ruling class, etc., there was no social basis for the emergence of a proto-capitalist class in the urban centres. And the peasantry, while it might have had an interest in eliminating the mandarin ruling class, was so fragmented and dispersed into organic peasant communities, that it was unable to act as a revolutionary force. The existing social structure, in other words, contained no potential alternatives to the existing ruling class. And it contained no dynamic which would have generated such a class. It was only with the external assault of Western Capitalism on that social structure that the power of the ruling class was structurally broken.

Incompatibility leads to contradiction only if there exist class actors capable of being bearers of a new society, a new social form that would liberate the development of the forces of production. Whether or not such a new ruling class exists or will be generated depends not upon a dynamic vested in the forces of production, but in the specific historical forms of the social relations of production.[12]

4. *The Transformation Thesis*

Even if we were to assume that the first three theses were correct, there would still be reasons to reject the Transformation Thesis, i.e. the thesis that when a contradiction exists between the forces and relations of production, that it is the relations of production which will change. This thesis is problematic even where there is a potential historical bearer of the new relations of production.

Our criticism of the transformation thesis rests on two interconnected issues: (1) the relationship between class

[12] It appears here that Cohen has taken the transition from feudalism to capitalism in Western Europe as the paradigm of social change and transition for human society in general. In feudalism it was in fact the case that within the old social order the future ruling class—the bourgeoisie— was able to grow. But this does not imply that it was the development of the productive forces as such which even in this case provides the critical explanation of emergence of the bourgeoisie within the fabric of European feudalism. As Anderson and others have argued, it was the peculiar combination of highly parcellized sovereignty, geopolitical location, and the existence of a particular pattern of town-country relations which set the stage for the emergence of this new class. All of these are characteristics of the social structure of European feudalism, not consequences of the productive forces as such.

interests in social change and class capacities for such change; and (2) the relationship between an interest in the *outcome* of change and *interests* in the process of change.

Cohen presents two kinds of arguments for the thesis that class capacities grow simultaneously with an intensifying interest in social transformation. The first is an argument of class alliances: ruling classes whose rule blocks the development of productive forces will lose support and allies; while potential new ruling classes which offer the possibility of the liberation of forces of production will gain allies and support.

The second argument is linked to the analysis of economic crisis:

In our view, Marx was not a breakdown theorist, but he did hold that once capitalism is fully formed, then each crisis it undergoes is worse than its predecessor. . . . Therefore, socialism grows more and more feasible as crises get worse and worse (but not because they get worse and worse). There is no economically legislated final breakdown, but what is de facto the last depression occurs when there is a downturn in the cycle *and* the forces are ready to accept a socialist structure *and* the proletariat is sufficiently class conscious and organized. (pp. 203–4)

Let us examine this argument more closely. The claim that socialism becomes increasingly feasible as productive forces grow seems unproblematic enough, inasmuch as a high level of development of productive forces is, on Cohen's view, a precondition for socialism. The claim that crises become ever more intense, however, is simply asserted. In fact, as already noted, Cohen goes on to define the pivotal contradiction of capitalism in quite different terms: emphasizing its incapacity to deploy productive forces rationally, not its incapacity to develop productive forces at all. Elsewhere Cohen has explicitly attacked the theoretical foundation of Marxian crisis theory: the labour theory of value.[13] Thus there appears to be no basis, on Cohen's account, for the claim that crisis tendencies intensify systematically. Finally, the claim that the proletariat is sufficiently class conscious and organized to support new relations of production is hardly established.

[13] Cf. 'The Labour Theory of Value and the Concept of Exploitation'.

Disillusionment with the bourgeoisie, even if it can be anticipated, is not equivalent to the revolutionary formation of the proletariat. Such disillusionment may be a necessary condition for the proper political organization of a revolutionary proletariat; but it is hardly sufficient.[14]

These arguments for the growth of working class capacities coincident with the development and fettering of the forces of production are doubly inadequate: first, because class capacities are determined by a variety of factors irreducible to the development of the forces of production as such; and, second, because in certain circumstances technological change itself may systematically undermine, rather than augment, the capacities for struggle of the working class.

The capacity of the working class to forge effective organizations for struggle depends upon a wide range of economic, political and ideological factors. At the economic level, for example, labour market segmentation, the development of complex job hierarchies and internal labour markets, etc., undermine the unity of the working class at least in terms of immediate, market-related issues. This economic fragmentation of the working class is further intensified when it coincides with racial, ethnic or national divisions. Thus, while the tendencies towards the homogenization and degradation of labour forecast by Marx may contribute to the growth of working class capacities, these counter-tendencies of differentiation and segmentation undermine those capacities.

The political institutions of capitalist society also contribute systematically to the erosion of working class capacities. Poulantzas has argued in general terms that one of the essential effects of the 'relative autonomy' of the capitalist state is the disorganization of subordinate classes.[15] Przeworski

---

[14] Thus Cohen's rejection of traditional crisis theory is of great consequence for his account. Were it the case that crisis tendencies inexorably lead to permanent stagnation, it could be argued that the maladies of capitalism would eventually constitute a sufficient cause for the formation of the working class as a revolutionary class. Given enough time, with a horizon of deteriorating conditions facing the working class, revolutionary organization might well develop. But on Cohen's account of the particular contradictions of late capitalism, this development is much less likely.

[15] See especially *Political Power and Social Class* (NLB, London), p. 75.

has taken this argument much further in demonstrating precisely how the parliamentary forms of the capitalist state systematically undermine the class character of working class political parties and deflect their programmes from revolutionary towards reformist objectives.[16]

Furthermore, the very proposition that the development of the forces of production tends to increase the capacity of the working class is suspect. While it is true, as Marx argued, that the development of the forces of production in capitalism improves communications among workers, brings workers together into ever larger factories, breaks down certain earlier forms of craft and skill divisions within the working class by degrading labour and so on, it is also true that many aspects of technical change have the effect of weakening the working class rather than strengthening it. The global telecommunications revolution, combined with dramatic improvements in transportation systems has made it much easier for the bourgeoisie to organize capitalist production globally, producing parts for consumer goods in 'world market factories' in the third world. This has meant that it is easier for the bourgeoisie to manipulate national and global divisions within the working class and to isolate technical coordination from direct production. The development of repressive technology has made insurrectionary movements more difficult, particularly in the advanced capitalist world. These and other similar factors do not imply that technological change intrinsically weakens the working class, but they do suggest that there is no simple, monolithic relation between technical change and the growth in the class capacities of the working class.

Cohen has thus failed to demonstrate that class capacities of potentially revolutionary classes grow in step with the development and eventual fettering of the forces of production. This seriously undermines the cogency of the Primacy Thesis. For, if the preconditions for the emergence of the class capacities of the working class depend upon contradictions and dynamics located within the social relations of production and the superstructure, and cannot be derived from the

[16] See Adam Przeworski, 'Social Democracy as an Historical Phenomenon', *New Left Review* (1980), 122.

development of the forces of production as such, then it is not the case that the existing relations of production are functionally explained by their tendency to promote the development of the productive forces. They may be just as fundamentally explained by their tendency to undermine the capacity of rival classes to become effective political forces.

Even if the problem of capacity for transformation is solved, the Transformation Thesis is still in doubt. Let us imagine that through a complex argument of mediations we are able to derive an account of the capacity of workers to transform society from the development (and fettering) of the productive forces. Workers still might not actually engage in such transformation because of the costs of the struggle for socialism.[17] Rational actors do not act simply on the basis of the desirability of outcomes (however that is defined) but on the basis of the acceptability of the costs of the process needed to obtain that outcome. At one point, Cohen acknowledges this problem. In criticizing the view that the vote by workers for bourgeois parties demonstrates that they are captivated by bourgeois ideology, Cohen writes:

This answer no doubt gives a part of the truth, in exaggerated form. But it is important to realize that it is not the whole truth. For it neglects the cost and difficulties of carrying through a socialist transformation. Workers are not so benighted as to be helpless dupes of bourgeois ideology, nor all so uninformed as to be unaware of the size of the socialist project. Marxist tradition expects revolution only in crisis, not because then alone will workers realize what burden capitalism puts upon them, but because when the crisis is bad enough the dangers of embarking on a socialist alternative become comparatively tolerable. (p. 245)

The Transformation Thesis, then, is questionable because (a) even if the working class has a rational interest in transforming capitalism due to the fettering of the productive forces, it will not necessarily recognize capitalism as such as the cause of this fettering; because (b) even if workers in general come to understand that capitalist relations of production are the cause of stagnation, the working class may lack the organizational and political capacity to struggle

---

[17] Cf. Buchanan, 'Revolutionary Motivation and Rationality'.

effectively for a qualitative transformation of capitalism; and because (*c*) even if the working class has the political capacity to achieve a socialist revolution, the costs of such a revolutionary process may be intolerably high even under crisis conditions. This is *not* to say that a socialist transformation is impossible, but simply that the theory of socialist revolution cannot be derived from an account of the fettering of the productive forces.

CONCLUSION

To reject the Primacy Thesis is not to reject the importance of technological development in a theory of social change. Technological development is surely a critical factor for opening up new historical possibilities; and a specification of the level and type of technological development undoubtedly helps in defining the range of possible alternatives to the existing social order. As Cohen and Marx contend, the fettering of the rational development and deployment of a society's productive capacity is crucially important for any explanation of revolutionary change.

What we would deny is the contention that explanatory primacy, in the sense Cohen explains, be accorded to the productive forces. At the very least, historical materialism, as Marx sketches it in the 1859 *Preface* and as Cohen reconstructs it, must be supplemented by a theory of class capacities. Such a theory, if the main lines of Western Marxism throughout the present century are sound, must be based directly on an analysis of the development of social relations of production, the state and ideology.

Socialist political strategies must contend directly with the obstacles in the way of developing appropriately revolutionary class capacities: the institutional form of the capitalist state, divisions within the working class, and between the working class and its (potential) allies, and mechanisms of ideological domination and deflection. Such obstacles are irreducible to the forces of production, and thus the fettering of those forces in no way ensures the eventual erosion of these obstacles to working class capacities.

Cohen's book thus lays down a political as well as a theoretical challenge. A revolutionary theory which sees the building of working class capacities as an inevitable outcome of technological development and which fails to understand the specificity of the role of social structural constraints in the formation of class capacities will, we think, be incapable of informing revolutionary practice constructively. The 'orthodoxy' Cohen has reconstructed and defended is, in our view, ultimately inadequate politically, as well as theoretically, whatever its roots in Marx's writings. Western Marxism, however obscurely, has long recognized these inadequacies, and attempted to correct for them. Whether the best Marxist thought of this century, in any of its very different varieties, has been successful in this endeavour is another matter. What Cohen has done, in effect, is to have made the case for orthodoxy as forcefully and lucidly as it can be made. It remains for those of us who are sympathetic to what we take to be the advances registered in the Marxism of this century to respond with equal force and lucidity.

MARXISM, FUNCTIONALISM, AND GAME THEORY: THE CASE FOR METHODOLOGICAL INDIVIDUALISM

JON ELSTER

How should Marxist social analysis relate to bourgeois social science? The obvious answer is: retain and develop what is valuable, criticize and reject what is worthless. Marxist social science has followed the opposite course, however. By assimilating the principles of functionalist sociology, reinforced by the Hegelian tradition, Marxist social analysis has acquired an apparently powerful theory that in fact encourages lazy and frictionless thinking. By contrast, virtually all Marxists have rejected rational-choice theory in general and game theory in particular. Yet game theory is invaluable to any analysis of the historical process that centres on exploitation, struggle, alliances, and revolution.

This issue is related to the conflict over methodological individualism, rejected by many Marxists who wrongly link it with individualism in the ethical or political sense. By methodological individualism I mean the doctrine that all social phenomena (their structure and their change) are in principle explicable only in terms of individuals—their properties, goals, and beliefs. This doctrine is not incompatible with any of the following true statements. (*a*) Individuals often have goals that involve the welfare of other individuals. (*b*) They often have beliefs about supra-individual entities that are not reducible to beliefs about individuals. 'The capitalists fear the working class' cannot be reduced to the

* From *Theory and Society*, 11 (1982), pp. 453–82. Reprinted by permission of Kluwer Academic Publishers.

feelings of capitalists concerning individual workers. By contrast, 'The capitalists' profit is threatened by the working class' can be reduced to a complex statement about the consequences of the actions taken by individual workers.[1] (c) Many properties of individuals, such as 'powerful', are irreducibly relational, so that accurate description of one individual may require reference to other individuals.[2]

The insistence on methodological individualism leads to a search for microfoundations of Marxist social theory. The need for such foundations is by now widely, but far from universally, appreciated by writers on Marxist economic theory.[3] The Marxist theory of the state or of ideologies is, by contrast, in a lamentable state. In particular, Marxists have not taken up the challenge of showing how ideological hegemony is created and entrenched at the level of the individual. What microeconomics is for Marxist economic theory, social psychology should be for the Marxist theory of ideology.[4] Without a firm knowledge about the mechanisms that operate at the individual level, the grand Marxist claims about macrostructures and long-term change are condemned to remain at the level of speculation.

THE POVERTY OF FUNCTIONALIST MARXISM

Functional analysis[5] in sociology has a long history. The origin of functionalist explanation is probably the Christian

[1] The philosophical point invoked here is that in contexts of belief, desire, etc. it is not in general possible to substitute for each other expressions with the same reference, without change of truth value. We fear an object as described in a certain way, and we may not fear it under a different description.

[2] For an analysis of this idea see my *Logic and Society* (Chichester: Wiley, 1978), pp. 20 ff.

[3] A forceful statement of the need for microfoundations is in John Roemer, *Analytical Foundations of Marxian Economic Theory* (Cambridge University Press, 1981), ch. 1 and *passim*.

[4] I argue in more detail for this claim in ch. 5 of my *Sour Grapes*, forthcoming from Cambridge University Press [1983].

[5] For a fuller statement of my views on functional explanation see ch. 2 of my *Explaining Technical Change*, forthcoming from Cambridge University Press [1983]; see also my exchange with G. A. Cohen in *Political Studies*, 28. 1

theodicies, which reach their summit in Leibniz: all is for the best in the best of all possible worlds; each apparent evil has good consequences in the larger view, and is to be explained by these consequences. The first secular proponent perhaps was Mandeville, whose slogan 'Private Vices, Public Benefits' foreshadows Merton's concept of latent function. To Mandeville we owe the Weak Functional Paradigm: an institution or behavioural pattern often has consequences that are (a) beneficial for some dominant economic or political structure; (b) unintended by the actors; and (c) not recognized by the beneficiaries as owing to that behaviour. This paradigm, which we may also call the invisible-hand paradigm, is ubiquitous in the social sciences. Observe that it provides no explanation of the institution or behaviour that has these consequences. If we use 'function' for consequences that satisfy condition (a) and 'latent function' for consequences that satisfy all three conditions, we can go on to state the Main Functional Paradigm: the latent functions (if any) of an institution or behaviour explain the presence of that institution or behaviour. Finally, there is the Strong Functional Paradigm: all institutions or behavioural patterns have a function that explains their presence.

Leibniz invoked the Strong Paradigm on a cosmic scale; Hegel applied it to society and history, but without the theological underpinning that alone could justify it. Althusser sees merit in Hegel's recognition that history is a 'process without a subject', though for Hegel the process still has a goal. Indeed, this is a characteristic feature of both the main and strong paradigms: *to postulate a purpose without a purposive actor* or, in grammatical terms, a predicate without a subject. (Functionalist thinkers characteristically use the passive voice.) I shall refer to such processes guided by a purpose without an intentional subject as *objective teleology*. They should be distinguished from both *subjective teleology* (intentional acts with an intentional subject) and *teleonomy* (adaptive behaviour fashioned by natural selection). The main difference between subjective teleology and teleonomy is that the former,

(1980), my exchange with Arthur Stinchcombe in *Inquiry*, 23 (1980), and my review of P. van Parijs, *Evolutionary Explanation in the Social Sciences* (Totowa, NJ: Rowman and Littlefield, 1981), forthcoming in *Inquiry* [25 (1982)].

but not the latter, is capable of waiting and of using indirect strategies, of the form 'one step backward, two steps forwards'.[6] To the extent that the Main Functional Paradigm invokes teleonomy, as in the explanation of market behaviour through a natural-selection model of competition between firms, there can be no objection to it. In the many more numerous cases where no analogy with natural selection obtains, latent functions cannot explain their causes.[7] In particular, long-term positive, unintended, and unrecognized consequences of a phenomenon cannot explain it when its short-term consequences are negative.[8]

Turning to examples of functional analysis in non-Marxist social science, consider this statement by Lewis Coser: 'Conflict within and between bureaucratic structures provides

[6] For a fuller statement see ch. 1 of my *Ulysses and the Sirens* (Cambridge University Press, 1979).

[7] Natural selection invokes competition between coexisting individuals. Arthur Stinchcombe (in his contribution to *The Idea of Social Structure: Papers in Honor of Robert K. Merton*, ed. Lewis A. Coser (Harcourt, Brace, Jovanovich, 1975)) points to an analogous model involving selection among successive social states. The model pictures social change as an absorbing Markov process—which for the present purposes may be summarized by saying that institutions undergo continuous change until they arrive in a state in which there is no pressure for further change (the 'absorbing state'). This view could be used as a basis for functional explanation, with the modification that it would explain social states in terms of the absence of destabilizing consequences rather than through the presence of stabilizing ones. I would argue, however, that—unlike the biological case—there are no reasons for thinking that this adaptive process would ever catch up with the changing social environment.

[8] A radically different account of functional explanation is offered by G. A. Cohen, *Karl Marx's Theory of History* (Oxford University Press, 1978). He argues that functional explanations can be sustained by *consequence laws*, of the form 'Whenever x would have favourable consequences for y, then x appears'. If a law of this form is established, we may affirm that x is explained by its favourable consequences for y, even if no mechanism is indicated (although Cohen asserts that some mechanism must indeed exist). To the (partially misguided) objections to this idea stated in my review of his book in *Political Studies* (n. 5 above), I now would like to add the following. First, x and the y-enhancing effect of x might both be effects of some third factor z, and thus related by spurious correlation. Second, the definition of a consequence law is vitiated by the imprecise way in which the time dimension is brought in. The law could in fact be vacuously confirmed by suitably ignoring short-term in favour of long-term consequences.

the means for avoiding the ossification and ritualism which threatens their form of organization.'[9] If instead of 'provides the means for avoiding', Coser had written 'has the consequence of reducing', there could be no methodological quarrel with him. But his phrasing implies objective teleology, a simulation of human intentional adaptation without specification of a simulating mechanism. Alexander J. Field has observed that a similar functional explanation lies behind the Chicago school of 'economic interpretation of the law'.[10] For a somewhat grotesque example, consider a statement by Richard Posner:

The economic case for forbidding marital dissolution out of concern for the children of the marriage is weakened if the parents love the child, for then the costs to the child of dissolution will be weighed by the parents in deciding whether to divorce, and they will divorce only if the gains to them from the divorce exceed the costs to the child, in which event the divorce will be welfare maximizing. If, as suggested earlier, love is a factor of growing importance in the production of children, this might help to *explain* why the law is moving toward easier standards for divorce.[11]

Posner and his school actually tend toward the Strong Functional Paradigm, which most sociologists have abandoned for the more subtle Main Paradigm. Merton, the leading exponent of the Main Paradigm, is also an acute critic of the Strong Paradigm.[12] In Radical and Marxist social science, however, both the crude Strong Paradigm and the less crude (but equally fallacious) Main Paradigm are flourishing. Although my main concern is with Marxism, a few comments on the closely related Radical approach may be in order. As exemplified in the work of Michel Foucault and Pierre Bourdieu, this tends to see every minute detail of social action as part of a vast design for oppression.

[9] 'Social Conflict and the Theory of Social Change', in *Conflict Resolution: Contributions of the Behavioral Sciences*, ed. C. G. Smith (University of Notre Dame Press, 1971), p. 60.
[10] 'What's Wrong with the New Institutional Economics' (mimeograph, Department of Economics, Stanford University, 1979).
[11] *Economic Analysis of the Law* (Little, Brown, 1977), p. 106. Italics added, parentheses deleted.
[12] R. K. Merton, *Social Theory and Social Structure*, rev. edn. (Free Press, 1957), pp. 30 ff.

For an example, we may take Bourdieu's assertion that when intellectuals play around with language and even deliberately violate the rules of grammar, this is a strategy designed to exclude the petty-bourgeois would-be intellectuals, who believe that culture can be assimilated by learning rules and who loose their footing when they see that it is rather a matter of knowing when to break them.[13] This sounds like a conspiratorial view, but actually is closer to functionalism, as can be seen from Bourdieu's incessant use of the phrase *'tout se passe comme si'*.[14] If eveything happens as if intellectuals thought of nothing but retaining their monopoly, then objectively this must be what explains their behaviour. This argument is a theoretical analogue of envy—arising when 'our factual inability to acquire a good is wrongly interpreted as a positive action against our desire'.[15]

Marx recognized the Weak Functional Paradigm, but argued that what Sartre calls 'counterfinality'—the systematic production of consequences that are harmful, unintended, and unrecognized—was equally important. In addition one can certainly trace to him the Main Functional Paradigm, and in at least one passage the Strong Paradigm as well. In the *Theories of Surplus-Value*, Marx reconstructs the rational core of an adversary's argument:

1. The various functions in bourgeois society mutually presuppose each other;
2. The contradictions in material production make necessary a superstructure of ideological strata, whose activity—whether good or bad—is good, because it is necessary;
3. All functions are in the service of the capitalist, and work out to his 'benefit';
4. Even the most sublime spiritual productions should merely be granted recognition, and *apologies* for them made to the bourgeoisie, that they are presented as, and falsely proved to be, direct producers of material wealth.[16]

[13] P. Bourdieu, *La Distinction* (Paris: Editions de Minuit, 1979), p. 285. For a critical discussion of this inverted sociodicy, which proceeds from the assumption that all is for the worst in the worst of all possible worlds, see my review in *London Review of Books*, 5–18 Nov. 1981.

[14] I counted 15 occurrences of this phrase in *La Distinction*.

[15] M. Scheler, *Ressentiment* (Schocken, 1972), p. 52.

[16] *Theories of Surplus-value*, 3 vols. (Moscow: Progress, 1963–71), i. 287.

Although the context is ambiguous and the text far from clear, a plausible reading suggests the Strong Paradigm. All activities benefit the capitalist class, and these benefits explain their presence. This conspiratorial world view, in which all apparently innocent activities, from Sunday picnics to health care for the elderly, are explained through their function for capitalism, is not, however, pervasive in Marx's work. Much more deeply entrenched, from the level of the philosophy of history to the details of the class struggle, is the Main Paradigm.

Marx had a theory of history, embedded in a philosophy of history: an empirical theory of the four modes of production based on class division, and a speculative notion that before and after the division there was, and will be, unity. In the latter idea, clearly, there is also present the Hegelian or Leibnizian[17] notion that the division is necessary to bring about the unity, and can be explained through this latent function. Marx's objective teleology is especially prominent in the 1862–3 notebooks, of which the middle third was published as the *Theories of Surplus-Value*, while the remaining parts are only now becoming available.[18] Consider in particular the argument that

The original unity between the worker and the conditions of production . . . has two main forms. . . . Both are embryonic forms and both are equally unfitted to develop labour as *social* labour and the productive power of social labour. Hence the necessity for the separation, for the rupture, for the antithesis of labour and property . . . The most extreme form of this rupture, and the one in which the productive forces of social labour are also most fully developed, is capital. The original unity can be re-established only on the material foundations which capital creates and by means of the revolutions

[17] 'You know my admiration for Leibniz' (Marx to Engels, 10 May 1870). For the structure of Leibniz's philosophy of history, see ch. 6 of my *Leibniz et la formation de l'esprit capitaliste* (Paris: Aubier-Montaigne, 1975).

[18] The manuscript consists of 23 notebooks, of which bks. 6–15 were published by Kautsky as *Theories of Surplus-Value*. Bks. 1–5 and 16–18 have recently been published in the new *Marx-Engels Gesamt-Ausgabe*, and the remaining will soon be available in the same edition. Just as Marx's *Grundrisse* testify to the influence of Hegel's *Logic*, these manuscripts bear witness to the influence of Hegel's philosophy of history.

which, in the process of this creation, the working class and the whole society undergoes.[19]

Elsewhere Marx states that 'insofar as it is the coercion of capital which forces the great mass of society to this [surplus labour] beyond its immediate needs, capital creates culture and exercises an historical and social function.'[20] He also quotes one of his favourite verses from Goethe:

> Sollte diese Qual uns quälen,
> Da sie unsre Lust vermehrt,
> Hat nicht Myriaden Seelen
> Timur's Herrschaft aufgezehrt?[21]

It is difficult, although perhaps not impossible, to read these passages otherwise than as statements of an objective teleology. Marx, as all Hegelians, was obsessed with *meaning*. If class society and exploitation are necessary for the creation of communism, this lends them a significance that also has explanatory power. In direct continuation, Marx can also argue that various institutions of the capitalist era can be explained by their functions for capitalism, as in this analysis of social mobility:

The circumstance that a man without fortune but possessing energy, solidity, ability and business acumen may become a capitalist in this manner [i.e., by receiving credit]—and the commercial value of each individual is pretty accurately estimated under the capitalist mode of production—is greatly admired by the apologists of the capitalist system. Although this circumstance continually brings an unwelcome number of new soldiers of fortune into the field and into competition with the already existing individual capitalists, it also reinforces the supremacy of capital itself, expands its base and enables it to recruit ever new forces for itself out of the substratum of society. In a similar way, the circumstance that the Catholic Church in the Middle Ages formed its hierarchy out of the best brains in the land, regardless of their estate, birth or fortune, was one of the

---

[19] *Theories of Surplus-Value*, iii. 422–3.

[20] *Marx-Engels Gesamt-Ausgabe*, Further Series, iii, pt. 1 (Berlin: Dietz, 1976), p. 173.

[21] Ibid., 327. The verse is also quoted in Marx's article on 'The British Rule in India' (*New York Daily Tribune*, 25 June 1853) and, in a more ironic vein, in *Neue Oder Zeitung*, 20 Jan. 1855.

principal means of consolidating ecclesiastical rule and suppressing the laity. The more a ruling class is able to assimilate the foremost minds of a ruled class, the more stable and dangerous becomes its rule.[22]

By using the word 'means' in the penultimate sentence, Marx suggests that the beneficial effects of mobility also explain it. In this case the explanatory assertion, although unsubstantiated, might be true, because the Catholic Church was in fact a corporate body, able to promote its interests by deliberate action. This cannot be true of social mobility under capitalism, however, because the capitalist class is not in this sense a corporate body, shaping and channelling everything for its own benefit. That mobility may have favourable consequences for 'capital' is neither here nor there, as capital has no eyes that see or hands that move. Indeed, the German 'capital logic' school represents a flagrant violation of the principle of methodological individualism, when it asserts or suggests that the needs of capital somehow bring about their own fulfilment.[23]

There is, however, one way in which the capitalist class may promote its collective interests: through the state. Here we confront the difficulty of specifying the capitalist character of the state in a capitalist society. Marx did not believe that the concrete states of the nineteenth century were a direct outgrowth and instrument of capitalist class rule. On the contrary, he argued that it was in the interest of the capitalist class to have a noncapitalist government—rule by the

[22] *Capital*, 3 vols. (International Publishers, 1967), iii. 600–1. For the distinction between short-term and long-term functionalism in Marxism see also Roemer, *Analytical Foundations*, p. 9.

[23] For surveys see B. Jessop, 'Recent Theories of the Capitalist State', *Cambridge Journal of Economics*, 1 (1977), 353–74, and the Introduction to J. Holloway and S. Picciotto (eds.), *State and Capital* (London: Edward Arnold, 1978). I should mention here that by 'corporate body' I mean something different from what is later referred to as a 'collective actor'. The former refers to a juristic person, or more broadly to any kind of formal organization with a single decision-making centre. The latter is defined below as any group of individuals who are able, by solidarity or enlightened self-interest, to overcome the free-rider problem. Another way of overcoming it is to create a corporate body with legal or effective power to keep individual members in line, but in the discussion below I mostly limit myself to cooperation emerging by tacit coordination.

aristocracy in England, by the Emperor and his bureaucracy in France. It was useful for the English capitalists to let the aristocracy remain in power, so that the political struggle between rulers and ruled would blur the lines of economic struggle between exploiters and exploited.[24] Similarly, capitalism on the European continent could only survive with a state that apparently stood above the classes. In these analyses Marx asserts that the noncapitalist state was beneficial for capitalism. He never states or implies that this benefit was deliberately brought about by the capitalist class, and yet he strongly suggests that it explains the presence of the noncapitalist state:

The bourgeoisie confesses that its own interests dictate that it should be delivered from the danger of its *own rule*; that in order to restore the tranquillity in the country its bourgeois Parliament must, first of all, be given its quietus; that in order to preserve its social power intact its political power must be broken; that the individual bourgeois can continue to exploit the other classes and enjoy undisturbed property, family, religion and order only on condition that his class be condemned along with the other classes to like political nullity; that in order to save its purse it must forfeit the crown, and the sword that is to safeguard it must at the same time be hung over its own head as the sword of Damocles.[25]

I defy anyone to read this text without understanding it as an *explanation* of the Bonapartist regime. What else is it but a functional explanation? The anti-capitalist state is the indirect strategy whereby the capitalists retain their economic dominance: one step backward, two steps forward. But an explanation in terms of latent functions can never invoke strategic considerations of this kind. 'Long-term functionalism' suffers from all the defects of ordinary functional explanations, notably the problem of a purpose in search of a purposive actor. Moreover, it is *arbitrary*, because the manipulation of the time dimension nearly always lets us find a way in which a given pattern is good for capitalism; *ambiguous*, because the distinction between the short and the long term may be read either as a distinction between transitional effects and steady-

[24] *New York Daily Tribune*, 25 Aug. 1852.
[25] *The Eighteenth Brumaire of Louis Bonaparte*, in Marx and Engels, *Collected Works*, xi (Lawrence and Wishart, 1979), p. 143.

state effects, or as a distinction between two kinds of steady-state effects;[26] and *inconsistent*, because positive long-term effects could never dominate negative short-term effects in the absence of an intentional actor. It is not possible, then, to identify the state in a capitalist society as a capitalist state simply by virtue of its favourable consequences for bourgeois economic dominance.

From Marx I now turn to some recent Marxist writings. Consider first some writings by Marxist historians. In an otherwise important study, John Foster makes the following argument:

> The basic function of feudal social organization was, therefore, to maintain just that balance between population and land which (given technological conditions) would produce the biggest possible feudal surplus. . . . It was enough to ensure that [peasant] marriage and childrearing were strictly tied (by customary practice and religion) to the inheritance of land, and rely on peasant self-interest to do the rest.[27]

But what is the subject of the verbs 'ensure' and 'rely' in the last sentence? This is clearly a case of objective teleology, of an action in search of an actor.

E. P. Thompson writes that in pre-industrial England there were recurring revolts which, although usually unsuccessful in achieving their immediate objectives, had long-term success in making the propertied classes behave more moderately than they would have otherwise. He also seems to conclude that long-term success provides an (intentional or functional) explanation of the revolts. This, at any rate, is how I interpret his rhetorical question of whether the revolts 'would have

---

[26] De Tocqueville, in *Democracy in America*, distinguishes both between the transitional effects of democratization and the steady-state effects of democracy; and between the inefficient use of resources and the efficient creation of resources that are both inherent in democracy as a going concern. For details see ch. 1 of my *Explaining Technical Change*.

[27] *Class Struggle and the Industrial Revolution* (Methuen, 1974), p. 15. Thus Marxist functionalism explains the institutional arrangements of feudalism in terms of their favourable consequences for the surplus product, whereas non-Marxist functionalists such as D. North and R. P. Thomas (*The Rise of the Western World* (Cambridge University Press, 1973)) explain the same arrangements in terms of their favourable consequences for total product.

continued over so many scores, indeed hundreds of years, if they had consistently failed to achieve their objective'.[28] If functional, the explanation fails for reasons by now familiar. If intentional, it fails for reasons related to a crucial difference between individual and collective action. If an individual acts in a way that he knows to be in his interest, we may conclude that he acted for the sake of that interest. But when a group of individuals act in a way that is to their collective benefit, we cannot conclude that they did so to bring about that benefit.[29]

The attempt to read meaning into behaviour that benefits the actors can take one of three distinct forms. First, the functionalist, discussed above. Second, the consequences can be transformed into motives, as in the example from Thompson. This inference, although not always incorrect, is unwarranted in the cases where the benefits emerge only if the actions are performed by *all* the actors concerned, yet the *individual* has no incentive to perform them. For instance, it is beneficial for the capitalist class as a whole if all capitalists search for labour-saving inventions, for then the aggregate demand for labour and hence the wage rate will fall. And it may well be true that historically there has been a trend to labour-saving inventions. Yet the collective benefits cannot explain the trend, for they could never motivate the individual capitalist who, under conditions of perfect competition, is unable to influence the overall wage level. The trend, if there is one, must be explained by some other mechanism, of which the collective benefits are accidental by-products. Third, one may invoke a conspiratorial design and seek one unifying but hidden intention behind the structure to be explained. Thus, if a pattern such as social mobility benefits the capitalist class as a whole, but not the 'already existing individual capitalists', the conspiratorial explanation postulates a secret executive committee of the bourgeoisie. I do not deny that conspiracies occur, or that their existence may be asserted on indirect evidence. I simply argue the need for evidence—preferably direct or, if this is not available, as in the nature of the case it may not be, indirect—pointing to some hidden coordinating

<hr>

[28] 'The Moral Economy of the English Crowd in the Eighteenth Century', *Past and Present*, 50 (1971), 120.

[29] For an analysis of this fallacy see my *Logic and Society*, pp. 118 ff.

hand. Simply to invoke beneficial consequencies supplies no such evidence.

Turning now from Marxist history to Marxist social science proper, we find that functionalism is rampant. Functional explanations pervade the theory of crime and punishment,[30] the analysis of education,[31] the study of racial discrimination,[32] and (most important) the analysis of the capitalist state, a Marxist growth industry during the last decade. Not all Marxist studies fall victim to the functionalist fallacies identified above, but most Marxist authors seem to believe that 'everything that happens in a capitalist society necessarily corresponds to the needs of capital accumulation',[33] so that the 'correspondence between the actions (and structure) of the state and the requirements of capital accumulation [is] taken for granted'.[34] Alternately, the 'assumption is made that the capitalist state is universally functional for reproducing the

[30] Stark examples include W. J. Chambliss, 'The Political Economy of Crime: A Comparative Study of Nigeria and the USA', in *Critical Criminology*, ed. I. Taylor *et al.* (Routledge and Kegan Paul, 1975) and W. J. Chambliss and T. E. Ryther, *Sociology: The Discipline and Its Direction* (McGraw-Hill, 1975), p. 348. The closely related Radical approach is exemplified by M. Foucault, *Surveiller et punir* (Paris: Gallimard, 1975), p. 277 and *passim*.

[31] S. Bowles and H. Gintis, *Schooling in Capitalist America* (Routledge and Kegan Paul, 1976) e.g. pp. 103, 114, and 130 features many such examples. In the same vein is also M. Levitas, *Marxist Perspectives in the Sociology of Education* (Routledge and Kegan Paul, 1974). A Radical version is that of P. Bourdieu and J.-C. Passeron, *La Reproduction* (Paris: Editions de Minuit, 1970), e.g. p. 159.

[32] S. Bowles and H. Gintis, 'The Marxian Theory of Value and Heterogeneous Labour: a Critique and Reformulation', *Cambridge Journal of Economics*, 1 (1977), 173–92; J. Roemer, 'Divide and Conquer: Micro-foundations of a Marxian Theory of Wage Discrimination', *Bell Journal of Economics*, 10 (1979), 695–705. The fallacy involved in both these articles is the belief that because internal cleavages in the working class benefit capitalist class domination, they are to be explained in terms of this benefit. This, however, is to confuse what Simmel (*Soziologie* (Berlin: Dunker und Humblot, 1908), pp. 76 ff.) referred to as, respectively, *tertius gaudens* and *divide et impera*. Third parties may benefit from a struggle even when they have not been instrumental in setting it up.

[33] As Jessop, 'Recent Theories', p. 364, characterizes the 'capital logic' school.

[34] Introduction to Holloway and Picciotto, p. 12, characterizing Yaffe's work.

dominance of the capitalist class'.[35] These neo-Marxist works appear to be guided by the following principles (i) All actions of the state serve the collective interest of the capitalist class. (ii) Any action that would serve the collective interest of the capitalist class is in fact undertaken by the state. (iii) Exceptions to the first principle are explained by 'the relative autonomy of the state'. (iv) Exceptions to the second principle are explained along the lines of Marx in the *Eighteenth Brumaire*: it is in the political interest of the bourgeoisie that the state should not always act in the economic interest of the bourgeoisie. Needless to say, the effect of the last two clauses is to render the first two virtually vacuous. In a seminal article Michał Kalecki[36] raised some of the issues that came to the forefront in recent debates, particularly concerning the limits of state intervention to save capitalism from itself. To the question of why industrial leaders should oppose government spending to achieve full employment, he offers three answers, the two most important of which are these. First,

under a *laisser-faire* system the level of employment depends to a great extent on the so-called state of confidence. . . . This gives to the capitalists a powerful indirect control over Government policy: everything which may shake the state of confidence must be carefully avoided because it would cause an economic crisis. But once the Government learns the trick of increasing employment by its own purchases, this powerful controlling device loses its effectiveness. Hence budget deficits necessary to carry out the Government intervention must be regarded as perilous. The social function of the doctrine of 'sound finance' is to make the level of employment dependent on the 'state of confidence'.

Second, Kalecki argues that capitalists not only oppose this way of overcoming the crisis, but actually need the crisis itself:

[under] a regime of permanent full employment, 'the sack' would cease to play its role as a disciplinary measure. The social position of the boss would be undermined and the self-assurance and class

---

[35] E. O. Wright, *Class, Crisis and the State* (New Left Books, 1978), p. 231.
[36] M. Kalecki, 'Political Aspects of Full Employment', in *Selected Essays on the Dynamics of the Capitalist Economy* (Cambridge University Press, 1971), pp. 139–41.

consciousness of the working class would grow. Strikes for wage increases and improvements in conditions of work would create political tension. It is true that profits would be higher under a regime of full employment than they are on the average under *laisser-faire*; and even the rise in wage rates resulting from the stronger bargaining power of the workers is less likely to reduce profits than to increase prices, and thus affects adversely only the rentier interests. But 'discipline in the factories' and 'political stability' are more appreciated by business leaders than profits. Their class instinct tells them that lasting full employment is unsound from their point of view and that unemployment is an integral part of the normal capitalist system.

In conclusion Kalecki states that 'one of the important functions of fascism, as typified by the Nazi system, was to remove the capitalist objection to full employment.' To the extent that this thesis is only a variation on the inherent dilemma of the capitalist class—*Et propter vitam vivendi perdere causas*[37]—there can be no objection to it. As admirably explained in the work of Amid Bhaduri,[38] the ruling class often faces a change that gives short-term economic profit but has adverse long-term political (and hence economic) effects. But Kalecki never says whether his analysis is intentional or functional, in addition to being causal. He does make the case for a causal relation between unemployment and the interests of capital, but how does the latter explain the former? As any serious historian can imagine, a mass of detailed evidence is required to make an intentional explanation credible—hence the strong temptation to take the functionalist short cut.

Many contemporary Marxists think the state has three main functions: repression, legitimation, and creating the conditions for accumulation. Whereas traditional Marxists stress the first function, their modern counterparts assert the importance of the second. Indeed, legitimation is viewed as 'symbolic violence' that in modern societies is the functional equivalent of repression. The state exerts its legitimating

[37] 'And for the sake of life to sacrifice life's only end' (Juvenal), quoted by Marx in *Neue Oder Zeitung*, 12 June 1855.

[38] A. Bhaduri, 'A Study in Agricultural Backwardness under Semi-Feudalism', *Economic Journal*, 83 (1973), 120–37, and 'On the Formation of Usurious Interest Rates in Backward Agriculture', *Cambridge Journal of Economics*, 1 (1977), 341–52.

function through 'ideological apparatuses' (e.g., education) and the provision of social welfare. The state's function for capital accumulation is mainly to help the capitalist class overcome the particular interests of individual capitalists. In fact, the state is sometimes said to represent 'capital in general', which is (logically) prior to the many individual capitals.[39] This of course is a drastic violation of the tenet of methodological individualism defended here. True, there is often a need for concerted capitalist action, but the need does not create its own fulfilment. The necessary collective action may fail to materialize even if seen as possible and desirable, because of the free-rider problem, and *a fortiori* if the need and possibility go unperceived. Failures of cartelization, of standardization, of wage coordination take place all the time in capitalist societies. Moreover, even when the actions of the state serve the interests of capital against those of individual capitalists, evidence must be given to show that this consequence has explanatory power—i.e., that there exists a mechanism by which state policy is shaped by the collective interest of the capitalist class. The mechanism need not be intentional design[40]—but *some* mechanism must be provided if the explanation is to be taken seriously.

Examples of the Marxist-functionalist analysis of the state abound in the German tradition of Altvater or the French manner of Poulantzas. In the United States Marxist functionalism is best represented by James O'Connor's influential *The Fiscal Crisis of the State*, from which the following passage is taken:

The need to develop and maintain a 'responsible' social order also has led to the creation of agencies and programs designed to control the surplus population politically and to fend off the tendency toward a legitimization crisis. The government attempts to administer and bureaucratize (encapsulate) not only monopoly sector labor-management conflict, but also social-political conflict emerging from competitive sector workers and the surplus population.

[39] R. Rosdolsky, *Zur Entstehungsgeschichte des Marxschen 'Kapital'* (Frankfurt: Europäische Verlagsanstalt, 1968, pp. 61–71), refers to the passages (mainly in the *Grundrisse*) where Marx develops the concept of 'capital in general'.

[40] For a survey of alternatives to intentional design see P. Van Parijs.

The specific agencies for regulating the relations between capital and organized labor and unorganized workers are many and varied. . . . Some of these agencies were established primarily to maintain social control of the surplus population (e.g. HEW's Bureau of Family Services); others serve mainly to attempt to maintain harmony between labor and capital within the monopoly sector (e.g., the Bureau of Old Age and Survivors Insurance). In both cases the state must remain independent or 'distant' from the particular interests of capital (which are very different from the politically organized interests of capital as the ruling class). The basic problem is to win mass loyalty to insure legitimacy; too intimate a relation between capital and state normally is unacceptable or inadmissible to the ordinary person.[41]

Note the implicit three-tier structure of capital interests: (1) the interest of the individual capitalist out to maximize profits come what may; (2) the interest of the capitalist class, which may have to curb the individual's greed; and (3) the interest of Capital, which may have to dissociate itself from class interests to ensure legitimacy. It is not surprising that *any* given state action can be viewed from one of these perspectives. O'Connor's scheme suggests the following methodological principle: If crude class interests will not do the explanatory job, then—but only then—invoke subtle class interests. This makes Marxism invulnerable to empirical disconfirmation, and nullifies its scientific interest.

Obviously, an alternative approach is required. Having given my views elsewhere,[42] let me summarize them briefly. (1) There are three main types of scientific explanation: the *causal*, the *functional*, and the *intentional*. (2) All sciences use causal analysis. The physical sciences use causal analysis exclusively. (3) The biological sciences also use functional analysis, when explaining the structure or behaviour of organisms through the benefits for reproduction. This procedure is justified by the theory of natural selection, according to which such beneficial effects tend to maintain their own

---

[41] *The Fiscal Crisis of the State* (St Martin's, 1973), pp. 69–70. Closely related explanations of the welfare state are given in J. Hirsch, *Staatsapparat und Reproduktion des Kapitals* (Frankfurt: Suhrkamp, 1974), p. 54, and N. Poulantzas, *Pouvoir politique et classes sociales* (Paris: Maspero, 1968), p. 310.

[42] Van Parijs, passim; also *Ulysses and the Sirens*, ch. 1.

causes. Intentional analysis, on the other hand, is not justified in biology—because natural selection is basically myopic, opportunistic, and impatient, as opposed to the capacity for strategic and patient action inherent in intentional actors. (4) The social sciences make extensive use of intentional analysis, at the level of individual actions. Functional analysis, however, has no place in the social sciences, because there is no sociological analogy to the theory of natural selection. (5) The proper paradigm for the social sciences is a mixed causal-intentional explanation—*intentional understanding* of the individual *actions*, and *causal explanation* of their *interaction*. (6) Individuals also interact intentionally. And here—in the study of the intentional interaction between intentional individuals—is where game theory comes in. The need for game theory arises as soon as individual actors cease to regard each other as given constraints on their actions, and instead regard each other as intentional beings. In parametric rationality each person looks at himself as a variable and at all others as constants, whereas in strategic rationality all look upon each other as variables. The essence of strategic thought is that no one can regard himself as privileged compared to the others: each has to decide on the assumption that the others are rational to the same extent as himself.

THE USES OF GAME THEORY IN MARXIST ANALYSIS

The basic premises of rational choice theory[43] are (1) that structural constraints do not completely determine the actions taken by individuals in a society, and (2) that within the feasible set of actions compatible with all the constraints, individuals choose those they believe will bring the best results. If the first premise is denied, we are left with some variety of structuralism—an element of which reasoning is present in Marx, and is most fully developed in French Structuralism. Although it may occasionally be true that the feasible set shrinks to a single point, a general theory to this

---

[43] A standard treatment is R. D. Luce and H. Raiffa, *Games and Decisions* (Wiley, 1957). Some nonstandard problems are raised in *Ulysses and the Sirens*, especially ch. 3.

effect cannot be defended—unless by the ptolemaic twist of counting preferences or ideologies among the constraints. True, the ruling class often manipulates the constraints facing the ruled class so as to leave it no choice, but this very manipulation itself presupposes some scope of choice for the rulers. If the second premise is denied, we are left with some variety of role theory, according to which individuals behave as they do because they have been socialized to, rather than because they try to realize some goal: causality vs. intentionality. Against this I would argue that what people acquire by socialization is not quasicompulsive tendencies to act in specific ways, but preference structures that—jointly with the feasible set—bring it about that some specific action is chosen. If the role theory was correct, it would be impossible to induce behaviour modification by changing the feasible set (e.g., the reward structure), but clearly such manipulation is an omnipresent fact of social life.[44]

Game theory is a recent and increasingly important branch of rational choice theory, stressing the *interdependence of decisions*. If all violence were structural, class interests purely objective, and class conflict nothing but incompatible class interests, then game theory would have nothing to offer to Marxism. But because classes crystallize into collective actors that confront each other over the distribution of income and power, as well as over the nature of property relations, and as there are also strategic relations between members of a given class, game theory is needed to explain these complex interdependencies. In a 'game' there are several players or actors. Each actor must adopt an action or a strategy. When all actors have chosen strategies, each obtains a reward that depends on the strategies chosen by him *and* by the others. *The reward of each depends on the choice of all.* The notion of a reward can be understood narrowly or broadly. In the narrow interpretation it signifies the material benefit received by each actor. In the broad interpretation, it covers everything in the situation of value to the actor, including (possibly) the rewards to other actors. *The reward of each depends on the reward of*

---

[44] For an elaboration of my critique of structuralism and role theory see *Ulysses and the Sirens*, ch. 3, sects. 1, 6.

all.[45] It is assumed that the actors strive to maximize their reward—to bring about a situation they prefer to other situations. When an actor chooses a strategy, he must take account of what the others will do. A strategy that is optimal against one set of strategies on the part of the others is not necessarily optimal against another set. To arrive at his decision, therefore, he has to *foresee their decisions*, knowing that they are trying to foresee his. *The choice of each depends on the choice of all.* The triumph of game theory is its ability to embrace simultaneously the three sets of interdependencies stated in the italicized sentences.[46] Nothing could be further from the truth, then, than the allegation that game theory portrays the individual as an isolated and egoistic atom.

An essential element of the situation is the *information* that the actors possess about each other. In games with perfect information, each individual has complete information about all relevant aspects of the situation. These include the capabilities of the other actors, their preferences, their information, and the payoff structure that maps sets of individual strategies into outcomes. The condition of perfect information is likely to be realized only in small and stable groups, or in groups with a coordinating instance. Also crucial

[45] This could be part of what Marx meant by his statement in the *Communist Manifesto*: 'In place of the old bourgeois society, with its classes and class antagonism, we shall have an association in which the free development for each is the condition for the free development of all.' (Another possible reading is indicated in the next note.) If 'each' and 'all' are transposed in this passage, a more adequate expression occurs. Proper understanding of the philosophical anthropology behind this statement presupposes the idea that even for the single individual, the free development of all faculties is the condition for the free development of each faculty (*The German Ideology*, in Marx and Engels, *Collected Works* (Lawrence and Wishart, 1976), v. 262). The freely-developed person is both a totality of freely-developed faculties and part of a totality of freely-developed persons. Hypertrophy is atrophy, in the individual and in society.

[46] A fourth kind of independence falls outside game theory, however. It can be summed up by saying that the *preferences of each depend on the actions of all*, by socialization and more invidious mechanisms such as conformism, 'sour grapes', etc. Game theory takes preferences as given, and has nothing to offer concerning preference formation. The transformation of a Prisoners' Dilemma into an Assurance Game (see below) must be explained by social psychology, not by game theory. We can explain behaviour intentionally in terms of preferences, but the latter themselves are to be explained causally.

is the notion of an *equilibrium point*—a set of strategies in which the strategy of each actor is optimal vis-à-vis those of the others. It is thanks to this notion that game theory can avoid the infinite regress of 'I think that he thinks that I think . . .' which plagued early attempts to understand the logic of interdependency. The notion of a *solution* can be defined through that of an equilibrium point. Informally, the solution to a game is the set of strategies toward which rational actors with perfect information will tacitly converge. If there is only one equilibrium point, it will automatically emerge as the solution—it is the only stable outcome, in the sense that no one gains from defection. If there are several such equilibria, the solution will be the one that is collectively optimal—the equilibrium point preferred by all to all the others. Not all games have solutions in this sense.

A brief typology of games may be useful. One basic distinction is between two-person and n-person games, both of which are important for Marxism. The struggle between capital and labour is a two-person game, the struggle between members of the capitalist class an n-person game. Often, however, complicated n-person games can be reduced without too much loss of generality to simpler two-person games—as games played between 'me' and 'everybody else'.[47] The simplest two-person games are zero-sum games, in which the loss of one player exactly equals the gain of the other. This is the only category of games that always have a solution. The conceptual break-through that made proof of this proposition possible was the introduction of *mixed strategies*, i.e., the choice of a strategy according to some (optimal) probability distribution. In poker, for instance, a player may decide to bluff in one half of the cases, a policy implemented by tossing a coin in each case. Here the opponent may calculate how often the player will bluff, but not whether he will do so in any particular case. In variable-sum games not only the distribution of the rewards, but also the size of the total to be

[47] For n-person versions of some of the games discussed here see A. Sen, 'Isolation, Assurance and the Social Rate of Discount', *Quarterly Journal of Economics*, 80 (1967), 112–24. For a treatment of heterogeneous preferences in n-person games, see the brilliant framework developed by T. S. Schelling, *Micromotives and Macrobehavior* (Norton, 1978).

distributed, depends on the strategies chosen. These games can be further divided into games of pure cooperation and games of mixed conflict and cooperation (whereas zero-sum games are games of pure conflict). Not all variable-sum games have a solution in the sense indicated above. They can, however, have a solution once we take the step from noncooperative to cooperative games. In cooperative games—which should not be confused with the (noncooperative) games of pure cooperation—there is joint rather than individual choice of strategies. The actors can coordinate their choices so as to avoid certain disastrous combinations of individual strategies. If there is a choice between left-hand and right-hand driving, the actors may agree to toss a coin between both driving on the right and both driving on the left—a *jointly-mixed strategy*. If they toss a coin individually, the chances are 50% that they will end up on a collision course.

The value of the cooperative approach to game theory is contested because it appears to beg the question by assuming that agreements to cooperate will be enforced. On general grounds of methodological individualism, noncooperative games are prior to cooperative games. Assuming that the actors will arrive at a cooperative solution is much like assuming that a functional need will create its own fulfilment. For this reason, and also because there are so many solution concepts for cooperative games, one will have to tread carefully when explaining the emergence of cooperative behaviour in terms of cooperative games. Properly used, however, the method can yield important results, and in any case is fruitful for the purpose of normative analysis. For n-person games, the cooperative approach does not involve universal cooperation, but rather the cooperation of some actors against the others. The theory of coalitions in n-person game theory is an increasingly important branch of game theory for economic, political, and normative analysis.[48]

[48] The most general analysis, permitting overlapping coalitions, is J. Harsanyi, *Rational Behaviour and Bargaining Equilibrium in Games and Social Situations* (Cambridge University Press, 1977). The economic theory of the core is made easily accessible by W. Hildebrand and A. P. Kirman, *Introduction to Equilibrium Theory* (Amsterdam: North-Holland, 1976). Applications to ethics include John Roemer, *A General Theory of Exploitation and*

The simplest solution concept for such games is that of the 'core'—the set of all reward distributions in which no coalition of individuals can improve their lot by breaking out and acting on their own. Once again, the cooperative approach begs the question by assuming that coalitions can be formed and maintained whenever needed. And, once again, this is more an objection to the analytical-explanatory than to the normative use of the theory.

Turning now from exposition to applications, I discuss in turn the logic of solidarity and cooperation within classes, the problem of worker-capitalist coalitions, and some static and dynamic aspects of the class struggle. These applications all presuppose that we have left behind us—if it ever existed—the capitalism of perfect competition, unorganized capital and unorganized labour. The income distribution that would emerge under perfect competition can serve as a baseline for comparison with the distributions that result when one or both of the main classes behave in an organized and strategic manner. Whether the classes will so behave is itself a question to be decided by game-theoretic analysis. I define class consciousness as the capacity of a class to behave as a collective actor. Operationally, this means the capacity to overcome the free-rider problem. This problem arises within both the capitalist and the working classes. As well explained by Mancur Olson,[49] each worker is tempted by the prospect of a free ride, of benefitting from the strikes fought by the other workers without taking part in the action himself. Similarly, capitalists face the same difficulty with regard to cartelization, wage policy, etc. If, however, we want to penetrate past these generalities to the fine grain of the problem, some distinctions must be made. I assume that each actor within the class has a choice between a *solidary strategy* (S) and an *egoist strategy* (E). In the artificial two-person game between 'me' and 'everybody else', four possibilities can be distinguished:

A. Universal cooperation: everybody uses S

Class, forthcoming from Harvard University Press [1982], and Roger Howe and John Roemer, 'Rawlsian Justice as the Core of a Game', forthcoming in the *American Economic Review* [71.5 (1982)].

    [49] *The Logic of Collective Action* (Harvard University Press, 1965), ch. 4.

B. Universal egoism: everybody uses E
C. The free rider: 'I' use E, 'everybody else' uses S
D. The sucker: 'I' use S, 'everybody else' use E.

Every individual in the society will rank these outcomes in a particular order, according to what he—in the role of 'I'—would prefer. Excluding ties, there are 24 possible rankings of these four alternatives.[50] If we disregard all that rank B before A, as we are permitted to do by the very nature of the problem under discussion, we are left with twelve cases. If we then exclude the 'masochistic' cases that have D ranked above A, we are left with eight alternatives. I shall limit myself to four cases that have a central place in the literature on collective action. I shall also limit myself to the hypothesis that each 'I' views the situation in the same way. Although mixed cases will be the rule in actual situations, the assumption of homogeneity makes for a more tractable analysis.[51]

The first case is the well-known Prisoners' Dilemma, defined by the ranking CABD and characterized by the following features. (1) Strategy E is dominant, i.e., for each actor it is the best choice regardless of what the others will do. Here, then, we need not impose any stringent information requirement for the solution to be realized. Also, it is not true here that 'the choice of each depends on the choice of all'. In a sense, therefore, it is a rather trivial game. (2) The solution to the game is universal egoism, which everybody ranks below universal cooperation. Individual rationality leads to collective disaster. (3) Universal cooperation is neither individually stable nor individually accessible: everybody will take the first step away from it, and no one the first step toward it. We can apply this to the workers' predicament. For

---

[50] For a more fine-grained typology, see A. Rapoport, M. J. Guyer, and D. G. Gordon, *The 2 x 2 Game* (University of Michigan Press, 1976). For other discussions of the relation among the preference structures analysed here see S.-C. Kolm, 'Altruismes et efficacités', *Social Science Information*, 20 (1981), 293–344, and R. van der Veen, 'Meta-Rankings and Collective Optimality', ibid. 345–74.

[51] For a brief discussion of some mixed cases see my Introduction to the articles by Kolm and van der Veen cited in the preceding note. See also Schelling.

the individual there is no point in going on strike if his fellow
workers do so, for by remaining at work he can derive the
benefit from their action *and* be (highly) paid during the
strike—and if they do not strike he has nothing to gain and
much to lose by unilateral action.

Is there a 'way out' of the Prisoners' Dilemma? Can
individuals caught in this situation overcome the dilemma
and behave cooperatively? No consensus has emerged from
the extensive literature, but I believe that in the present
context two approaches stand out as the most promising. In
the case of working-class cooperation the most plausible
explanation is by change of the preference structure. Through
continued interaction the workers become both concerned and
informed about each other. Concern for others changes the
ranking of the alternatives, and information about others
enables the actors to realize the solution of the ensuing game.
This is the 'Assurance Game', defined by the ranking ACBD
and possessing the following features. (1) There is no
dominant strategy in this game. Egoism is 'my' best reply
to egoism, solidarity the best reply to solidarity. (2) The
optimum of universal cooperation is individually stable,
but not individually accessible. (3) Universal egoism and
universal solidarity are both, therefore, equilibrium points in
the game. Because universal cooperation is preferred by all to
universal egoism, the former emerges as the solution to the
game. (4) Because there is no dominant strategy, the solution
will be realized only if there is perfect information. Imperfect
information—about preferences or information—easily leads
to uncertainty, suspicion, and play-safe behaviour. Amartya
Sen has argued that Marx's *Critique of the Gotha Programme* can
be interpreted in terms of the Assurance Game.[52] Solidarity
can substitute for material incentives. I would tend to believe
that quite generally working-class solidarity and collective
action can be understood in these terms, although I shall later
point to an alternative explanation.

Although the Prisoners' Dilemma and the Assurance Game
differ profoundly in their structure, behaviour—in cases of
incomplete information—may occur *as if* the preferences

[52] A. Sen, *On Economic Inequality* (Oxford University Press, 1973), ch. 4.

were a Prisoner's Dilemma when in fact they form an Assurance Game. In tax evasion or suboptimal use of public transportation, for instance, the observed outcome may be the result of lack of information rather than of free-rider egoism. Likewise, the Assurance Game preferences should be distinguished from those of the Categorical Imperative, although behaviourally they may be indistinguishable. The Categorical Imperative is defined by the ranking ADBC, with solidarity as a dominant strategy. The history of the working class shows, in my opinion, that cooperative behaviour typically is conditional rather than unconditional—motivated by the concern for doing one's share of a common task rather than by the spirit of sacrifice or disregard for actual consequences characteristic of the Categorical Imperative. Indeed, more harm than good sometimes ensues from heroic individual acts of revolt or disobedience, if the others are not willing to follow suit, because such acts may provide the authorities or the employers the excuse they need to crack down further on the workers. This, I believe, shows that Kant's individualistic ethic is not appropriate for collective action.[53]

The Assurance Game also provides an interpretation of Charles Taylor's notion of *common meaning*, designed to elucidate the meaning of consensus. In his polemic against methodological individualism Taylor asserts there are two forms of meaning that are irreducibly nonsubjective: the intersubjective meanings and the common meanings. Intersubjective meanings are, roughly, rules for social behaviour

---

[53] The point is that acting unilaterally on the Categorical Imperative may be downright unethical. A striking example could be unilateral disarmament, if the situation is such that other countries will rush in to fill the power vacuum. Instead of acting in a way that would lead to good results *if* everyone else did the same, one should act to promote the good on realistic assumptions about what others are likely to do. A little morality, like a little rationality, may be a dangerous thing. There is room and need for a 'moral theory of the second best', corresponding to the economic theory of the second best which shows that if out of n conditions for an economic optimum, one is not fulfilled, the optimum may be more closely approached if additional conditions are violated. (R. G. Lipset and K. Lancaster, 'The Economic Theory of Second Best', *Review of Economic Studies*, 24 (1957–8), 133–62.)

whose negation cannot be generalized without contradiction. Thus promises should be kept because the notion of a society in which promises were never kept is logically contradictory. Common meanings illustrate the Assurance Game. Taylor distinguishes common meanings from shared subjective meanings by saying that 'what is required for common meanings is that this shared value be part of the common world, that *this sharing itself be shared*.'[54] The phrase I have italicized amounts to a condition of perfect information. For a consensus to be a living force, it must be known to exist. Everybody acts in a solidary manner because of knowing that the others are going to do so as well. This way of looking at consensus enables us to refute the following claim made by Taylor:

Common meanings, as well as intersubjective meanings, fall through the net of mainstream social science. They can find no place in its categories. For they are not simply a converging set of subjective reactions, but part of the common world. What the ontology of mainstream social science lacks, is the notion of meaning as not simply for an individual subject; of a subject who can be a 'we' as well as an 'I'.[55]

Game theory provides what Taylor claims is lacking—the notion of a subject that can be a 'we' as well as an 'I'. Through the triple interdependence that game theory analyses—between rewards, between choices, and between rewards and choices—the individual emerges as a microcosm epitomizing the whole network of social relations. A similar demystification makes good sense of Sartre's notion of the 'group', even though he claims it cannot be rendered in the 'neo-positivist' language of 'analytical reason'.[56]

Arthur Stinchcombe analyses Trotsky's account of the October Revolution in terms that fit this analysis of solidarity. The key idea in Stinchcombe's explanation is the breakdown of authority in the prerevolutionary situation. The old authority

[51] C. Taylor, 'Interpretation and the Sciences of Man', *Review of Metaphysics*, 25 (1971), 31.

[55] Ibid. 31–2.

[56] J.-P. Sartre, *Critique de la raison dialectique* (Paris: Gallimard, 1960), pp. 417, 404 ff.

breaks down when new social orders become thinkable, i.e., real possibilities. The 'Revolution grows by the exploration of these possibilities, and by the communication of there being possibilities to those who would support them, "if only they knew they were really Bolsheviks".'[57] When the workers and the soldiers, especially, come to believe that change is possible, change becomes possible:

The fickleness of the masses during a revolution thus takes on a completely different interpretation. Trotsky's sarcasm about spon-taneity as an explanation of the movements is essentially an assertion that the explanations of the masses about why they are doing what they are doing are going to be reasonable, but that reasonableness is going to be based on their estimates of the probabilities that (a) this institution or authority will pursue my goals; or (b) this institution or authority is the best I am likely to find, because no alternatives are possible or because the alternatives are in the hand of the enemy. And it is these probabilities that fluctuate wildly during a revolution but are reasonably stable during times of governmental quiescence.[58]

Revolutions succeed when these probabilities cease to fluctuate wildly and settle into some new and stable pattern because uncertainty, suspicion, and play-safe thinking no longer are predominant. Tacit coordination that becomes possible when people come to trust each other is the essential condition for successful collective action. The role of the revolutionary leader is to provide the information that makes this tacit coordination possible, rather than to be a centre of command and authority. This view constitutes an alternative to the Leninist theory of revolutionary leadership. Mancur Olson,[59] following Lenin, assumes that the only possible motivational structures are the free-rider egoism of the Prisoners' Dilemma and the unconditional altruism of the Categorical Imperative. Rightly rejecting the latter as wishful thinking, and observing that the former can never bring about collective action, he concludes that strikes or revolutions can only be brought about from above, through discipline verging on coercion. But the conditional altruism of the Assurance Game is also a possible motivational structure, which may lead to collective

[57] A. Stinchcombe, *Theoretical Methods in Social History* (Academic Press, 1978), p. 54.
[58] Ibid. 41.   [59] Olson, p. 106.

action by tacit coordination, given information provided by the leaders.

The problem of capitalist class solidarity requires different tools. We can hardly assume that interaction between capitalists will make them care about each other and change their motivations. Nor can we assume that the structure of their coordination problems invariably is that of a Prisoners' Dilemma. As to the last question, we can return to the issue of labour-saving inventions, which illustrates the ranking CADB.[60] This game has the paradoxical feature that the optimum is individually accessible, but not individually stable. When everyone uses E, it is in the interest of each actor to use S, but when everyone uses S, it is in the interest of each to switch to E. The game, in fact, has no solution. If no other capitalists seek labour-saving inventions, wages can be expected to rise, which makes it rational for the individual capitalist to pre-empt the wage rise by saving on labour—but if all capitalists do this, the individual capitalist has no incentive to do so. Clearly, this inherent contradiction sets up a pressure for concerted action,[61] which may or may not be realized.

I have assumed that for the individual capitalists there are costs associated with the search for labour-saving inventions, as distinct from the search for inventions in general. If we drop this assumption, the resulting interaction structure takes the following form. Each capitalist is indifferent between A and C, but prefers both to B and D, between which he is also indifferent. This, again, offers a crucial scope for the exercise of leadership. The task of the business leaders will be to persuade the individual entrepreneurs to act in a way that is neither harmful nor beneficial from their private viewpoint, but which brings about collective benefits when adopted by all. Leadership, then, is to make use of the 'zone of indifference' of the individuals.[62]

[60] For details about this game (often called 'Chicken' after a well-known ritual of American juvenile culture), see A. Rapoport, *Two-Person Game Theory* (University of Michigan Press, 1966), pp. 140 ff.

[61] Luce and Raiffa, p. 107.

[62] I am indebted to Ulf Torgersen for this observation. See also A. Stinchcombe, *Constructing Social Theories* (Harcourt, Brace and World, 1968), p. 157 for a discussion and some further references.

These problems are hardly discussed in the literature. By contrast, there are many discussions of capitalist Prisoners' Dilemmas, mainly in the context of cartelization. For each firm the best option is to have a high output at the high prices made possible by the cartel restrictions on the output, but such free-rider behaviour will of course make the cartel break up, or its anticipation prevent the cartel from forming. Yet cartels sometimes do form without immediately breaking up. This often happens because of asymmetries among the firms. A large firm will be strongly motivated to adopt the cartel policy even if the others do not follow suit, because it can internalize more of the benefits.[63] Moreover, it will typically possess the economic power to retaliate against firms that do not follow suit. But even in competitive markets with many identical firms, cartelization may occur by voluntary and selfish action. This may be explained by the theory of 'supergames', or repeated Prisoners' Dilemmas.[64] When the same actors play a Prisoners' Dilemma over and over again, the possibility of retaliation against free riders may make it rational to cooperate. It is easy to see that this will occur only if the number of iterations is indefinite. If the actors know when the games come to an end, there will be no reason for cooperation in the very last game, because no retaliation can take place afterwards if they defect. But this means that for the purposes of decision the penultimate game can be treated as the last, to which the same reasoning applies, and so on in argument that inexorably zips back to the first game. According to John Bowman, this explains the failure of Roosevelt's National Recovery Act: 'Voluntary cooperation in the Prisoners' Dilemma is possible only when the supergame is of indefinite length. The N.R.A. had a terminal date. Thus it was in the best interests of every conditional cooperator to break the code provisions before his competitors did.'[65]

[63] Olson, pp. 29–30.
[64] For the general theory of supergames see M. Taylor, *Anarchy and Cooperation* (Wiley, 1976). For applications to competition and cooperation among firms see M. Friedman, *Oligopoly and the Theory of Games* (Amsterdam: North-Holland, 1977).
[65] 'New Deal, Old Game: Competition and Collective Action among American Capitalists, 1925–1934' (unpublished manuscript, University of Chicago, Department of Political Science, 1979).

Explanations in terms of supergames may also apply to working-class cooperation, though less plausibly. I believe anyone familiar with the history of the working class will agree that solidarity is not merely enlightened long-term selfishness. Operationally, the issue could be decided by looking at cases in which the working-class interaction was known to have a terminal date, as in the National Recovery Act, and see whether this had any stifling effects on cooperation and solidarity. For solidarity among the workers to emerge, it is crucial that they interact for some time, because otherwise the mutual concern and knowledge will not have time to be shaped. But there should be no reason to believe that solidarity requires a cooperation of indefinite length, if my account is correct. In perfectly competitive capitalism, as I have argued elsewhere, workers are doubly alienated—from the means of production and from the products of their labour.[66] Alienation from the means of production stems from the alienation of the workers from their own history, i.e., from past generations of workers who produced the means of production currently used. The alienation from the products stems from their alienation from the class to which they belong, and permits the capitalist to treat each worker as if he were 'the marginal worker', in the economic sense of that term, and to pay him according to marginal productivity. Only by overcoming this double alienation, by taking possession of their past history and by acting jointly as a class, can the workers achieve class consciousness that goes beyond wage claims to make a radical rupture with capitalist relations.

What happens if the workers overcome the alienation from their class, but not that from their history—if they see through the 'marginalist illusion', but not the 'presentist illusion'? This partial liberation distinguishes the modern capitalist societies of the social democratic variety, in which working-class organizations negotiate with employer associations over the division of the net product. Because the basic assumption behind this bargaining is that capital, as a 'factor of production' on a par with labour, has a right to some part of

[66] 'The Labor Theory of Value', *Marxist Perspectives* 3 (1978), 70–101.

the product, the only issue of the class struggle becomes the *size* of that part, not its existence. Take first the simplest case, in which we disregard the question of reinvestment out of profits. In this purely static setting, workers do not ask what use is made of ths surplus value extracted from them. If they could get the whole net product and spend it immediately, they would. But they cannot. The problem, then, is one of dividing a jointly-made product between the producers. It is, clearly, a mixed conflict-cooperation game, in which the strategies determine both the total product and how it is to be divided. Both parties have threats—strikes and lockouts— that are characteristically double-edged: they enhance the probability of getting a large share of the total, but reduce the total to be shared. In such bargaining each side has a lower limit beneath which it cannot go, e.g., subsistence for the workers and a minimal profit for the capitalists. And the sum of these limits is smaller than the total to be shared. In other words, there is a set of possible divisions that are compatible with the last-ditch demands of both classes, and over which the bargaining takes place.

There is no way the two groups can converge tacitly in a pair of demands that exactly exhaust the total product. The game has no noncooperative solution. Considerations other than purely rational calculation must, therefore, decide the outcome. Bargaining theory addresses this problem. Its general assumption is that the actors must form some psychological hypotheses about each other, even if these cannot be rationally justified. Indeed, according to some bargaining models, each actor at each step of the process believes himself to be one step ahead of the other.[67] The mutual inconsistency of these beliefs do not, however, necessarily prevent the sequence of demands and counter-demands from converging toward some division of the product, which is then the outcome of the bargaining process.

Of the many varieties of bargaining theory,[68] one has received general attention and is uniquely interesting from the

[67] A. Coddington, *Theories of the Bargaining Process* (Allen and Unwin, 1968), pp. 58 ff.

[68] For surveys see Coddington, and the articles collected in *Bargaining*, ed. O. Young (University of Illinois Press, 1975).

methodological point of view. This is the Zeuthen-Nash theory, named after the authors who proposed two radically different versions, which John Harsanyi later proved to be mathematically equivalent.[69] The Nash version offers an axiomatic method of finding the normatively justified outcome for two-person cooperative games, whereas the Zeuthen method offers a step-by-step method, taking us through claims and counterclaims to a uniquely determined outcome. Because both versions lead to the same result, we can use cooperative game theory without coming into conflict with methodological individualism. We do not, that is, simply *assume* that the cooperative outcome will be realized simply because there is a *need* for it; rather we exhibit *a causal mechanism whereby it will be achieved*. The Nash solution is determined by assuming that a certain number of conditions are fulfilled. First, it should not make any difference to the outcome whether the rewards are measured on one particular utility scale among the many scales that are positive linear transformations of each other. To explain the last expression, it should suffice to point out that the Celsius and Fahrenheit temperature scales are positive linear transformations of each other, differing only in the choice of zero and in the unit of measurement. Secondly, the outcome should be Pareto-optimal, so that it is impossible to improve the situation of one actor without harming that of another. Thirdly, it should be symmetrical, in the sense that equally powerful actors should get equal rewards. Lastly, it should satisfy the 'condition of the independence of irrelevant alternatives', stipulating that adding new alternatives to the bargaining situation can only change the outcome if the new outcome is one of the new options. The addition of a new alternative, that is, can never make a different old alternative emerge as the outcome.

Nash's theorem states there is only one division of the product that satisfies these conditions—viz., the division that maximizes the mathematical product of the rewards. From the way these rewards are measured,[70] a further feature of the

[69] For a full explanation see Harsanyi.

[70] The rewards are measured in cardinal utilities, which are constructed from the individual's preferences over alternatives some of which may be lotteries (Luce and Raiffa, ch. 2). This lends great importance to the

solution follows: it typically accords the largest portion of the jointly made product to the most powerful actor. This is the 'Matthew effect' in bargaining theory: to him that hath, shall be given. For a poor actor, even a small gain is so important that he can be made to be content with it, whereas the more affluent can say with equanimity, 'Take it or leave it.' The Matthew effect may itself be seen as a form of exploitation,[71] or at least as contrary to distributive justice, which rather demands that the least advantaged person should be given more.[72] This inequity, however, is secondary, because there is no normative basis for the capitalist class to get anything at all. In any case, the model may be behaviourally attractive even if its normative appeal is weak. Zeuthen's argument showed that it is plausible to believe that this outcome will in fact be the result of bargaining, if at each step the player whose relative loss is smaller makes a concession to the opponent.[73] This approach is important in bargaining cases that involve a once-and-for-all confrontation that does not have consequences beyond the present. If, however, the bargaining parties know they will have to bargain again later, and that the outcome of present bargaining will affect future welfare, it will not do. Wage bargaining, in fact, tends to be regular, institutionalized, sometimes even continuous. Also, the current division of the net product between wages and profit makes a big difference to the future welfare of both classes, because part of the profit is reinvested. The less the

---

attitude toward risk-taking; and typically the rich will be less risk-averse than the poor.

[71] Perhaps Marx had something like this in mind when he wrote that in some forms of international trade, the 'richer country exploits the poorer one, even where the latter gains by the exchange' (*Theories of Surplus-Value*, iii. 106).

[72] This requirement could be defended either on utilitarian grounds, because the poor generally will get more utility out of a given increase in income, or on the grounds of the 'difference principle' (J. Rawls, *A Theory of Justice* (Harvard University Press, 1971)), stating that one should maximize the welfare of the least-advantaged.

[73] 'Relative loss' means the difference between demand and offer, divided by the demand. 'Concession' means making a new demand that gives one's opponent the smallest relative loss.

capitalist class has left in profits, the smaller the prospects for economic growth and future increase in consumption.

Kelvin Lancaster proposes a model that captures this double time-dependence of bargaining.[74] He views the wage struggle between capital and labour as a 'differential game', i.e., as a continuous strategic interaction. The model, and even more the general theory behind it, constitutes an important conceptual breakthrough, with many consequences for the way in which we think about exploitation, power, and capitalism. The theory does for social democracy what Marx did for classical capitalism: it explains how class struggle evolves when the workers overcome the synchronic alienation, but not the diachronic one. Lancaster assumes that workers and capitalists confront each other as organized groups, and that there are no other social classes. He assumes, moreover, that each of the two classes controls an essential economic variable. The workers can, within certain limits,[75] determine the rate of working-class consumption out of the current net product, whereas the capitalists can control the rate of investment out of profits. The assumption regarding the capitalists' control variable is simply part of the definition of capitalism, whereas the assumption regarding the workers' control over the current consumption reflects the development of capitalism since Marx. In modern capitalist economies, especially the social democratic variety prominent in north-western Europe, the workers have the power—either directly through unions or indirectly through profit taxation—to retain for themselves virtually all of the net product, should they so desire. This statement is not easily substantiated, being counterfactual, yet it is defensible. Under early capitalism, working-class consumption was kept down to subsistence for

[74] K. Lancaster, 'The Dynamic Inefficiency of Capitalism', *Journal of Political Economy*, 81 (1973), 1092–1109. Further developments of the model include M. Hoel, 'Distribution and Growth as a Differential Game Between Workers and Capitalists', *International Economic Review*, 19 (1978), 335–50, and, importantly, A. Przeworski and M. Wallerstein, 'The Structure of Class Conflict in Advanced Capitalist Societies', paper presented at the annual meeting of the American Political Science Association, Aug. 1980.

[75] These limits are required for the game to have a solution, but they may be arbitrarily close to = and 100% respectively, and hence do not restrict the model in any substantial manner.

many reasons, including low productivity, weak working-class organizations, a high degree of capitalist cohesion, rapid population growth, and a state that championed the capitalist class. In modern capitalist economies of the social democratic variety, none of these conditions obtains. True, the capitalist class remains strong, in that it is able to discipline its own members. But its capacity for subjugating the workers has been drastically reduced, for if the workers are denied in direct wage bargaining, they can retaliate with state intervention and heavy taxation on profits.

Yet the workers do not use their power. Lancaster suggests, correctly, that this hesitancy owes to certain strategic facts of the situation and to the interest of both classes in present and future consumption. Hence the workers must leave some profit to the capitalists for reinvestment and increased future consumption. Finn Kydland and Edward Prescott suggest that the workers, therefore, should bind themselves—that the 'workers, who control the policy, might rationally choose to have a constitution which limits their power, say, to expropriate the wealth of the capitalist class.'[76] This is a new twist on the theme of abdication, performed here by the workers instead of the capitalists, as in Marx's *Eighteenth Brumaire*. Their analysis is incomplete, however, as it does not take the strategic nature of the situation into account, as Lancaster does when he observes that both the workers and the capitalists are in a dilemma. To be precise, we have:

The Workers' Dilemma: If they consume everything now, nothing will be left for investment and future increases in consumption, but if they leave something for profits, they have no guarantee that the capitalists will use this for investment rather than for their own consumption.

The Capitalists' Dilemma: If they consume the entire profits now, nothing will be left for investment and future increases in consumption, but if they invest out of profits, they have no guarantee that the workers will not retain for themselves the increase in consumption thereby generated.

Observe the assumption that capitalists desire consumption rather than profits. The rate of profit is fixed by the working

[76] 'Rules Rather than Discretion: The Inconsistency of Optimal Plans', *Journal of Political Economy*, 85 (1977), 473–92.

class, hence it cannot also be maximized by the capitalists. This argument does not deny the importance of profit maximization, for if capitalists can do even better than the rate fixed for them, they will also benefit in consumption terms. Observe, too, that the model has potential applications in many settings. Consider, for instance, the relation between a multinational firm that controls the rate of local reinvestment out of locally created profits, and the local government that controls the tax rate on profits.

A strategy, in the game set up by these dilemmas, is a time profile of values of the control variable, i.e., a continuous sequence of rates of consumption out of the net product for the workers, and a sequence of rates of investment out of profits for the capitalists. A solution, here as in general, consists of two strategies that are optimal against each other. Lancaster shows that if the two classes are assumed to maximize their consumption over some finite time period, the game has a solution. He also shows that the solution is suboptimal, in the sense of implying a smaller total consumption for each class than would be possible with different time profiles. It is also discontinuous: at one point in time both classes switch from minimal to maximal consumption. In my view these results depend too heavily on the specific assumptions of the model to be of great interest. The importance of the model is above all conceptual. It shows how the workers can hold political power, yet be powerless if the capitalists retain economic power; how the workers may control consumption, yet be powerless if the capitalists control investment; how the workers can determine the present, yet be powerless if the capitalists determine the future. The exploitation of the working class, then, does not consist only in the capitalists' appropriation of surplus-value, but also in the workers' exclusion from decisive investment choices that shape the future. Or, alternatively, the workers suffer not only exploitation, but also lack of self-determination.[77] In the capitalist countries where social

---

[77] L. Kolakowski (*Main Currents of Marxism* (Oxford University Press, 1978), 3 vols., i. 333) defines exploitation in terms of the 'exclusive powers of decision' held by the capitalist. Similarly, E. O. Wright in various works (e.g., *Class Structure and Income Determination* (Academic Press, 1979), pp. 14 ff.)

democracy is most advanced, one may argue with Ralf Dahrendorf that power rather than wealth is the crux of the class
struggle.[78]

Cooperative n-person game theory has been usefully
applied to the study of exploitation. In John Roemer's *General
Theory of Exploitation and Class* it is shown that the feudal,
capitalist, and socialist modes of exploitation can be characterized by means of notions from this theory.[79] A group of
individuals are said to be exploited if, were they to withdraw
from society according to certain withdrawal rules, they
could improve their situation. Different forms of exploitation
correspond to different withdrawal rules. Thus the serfs were
exploited in the feudal sense, because they could have done
better for themselves had they withdrawn from society with
their own land. Workers are capitalistically exploited because
they could have done better were they to withdraw with their
per capita share of society's tangible assets, i.e., capital goods.
And under socialism a group is exploited if it could do better
were it to withdraw with its per capita share of the intangible
assets, i.e., skills and talents. Whereas the last notion is
somewhat hazy, the characterizations of feudal and capitalist
exploitation are very valuable, as is also the observation that
the neoclassical view, that workers are not exploited under
capitalism, really amounts to a denial of feudal exploitation in
capitalist societies. It is also possible to arrive at specific
statements about the intensity of exploitation, by using
the framework of cooperative game theory. Consider a

adds authority to surplus extraction as a component of exploitation and
class. John Roemer (*A General Theory of Exploitation and Class*) takes the more
orthodox line that the lack of power over economic decisions is distinct from
exploitation.

[78] It should be observed at this point that even the Marxists who accept
that authority relations are a component of class restrict themselves to intra-
firm relations of command and subordination, whereas Dahrendorf extends
the notion to include authority relations in any organization.

[79] Roemer also argues, more ambitiously, that exploitation can be *defined*
in terms of hypothetical alternatives. In my contribution to a symposium on
Roemer's work (forthcoming in *Politics and Society* [11.3, (1982)]) I argue
that this proposal has counter-intuitive consequences. It remains true that
important cases of exploitation can be (nondefinitionally) characterized in
the way he proposes.

case discussed by Lloyd Shapley and Martin Shubik,[80] agricultural production where one capitalist owns the land and the workers own only their labour power. How will the product be divided between landowner and workers if coalitions can be formed between the owner and some of the peasants? Shapley and Shubik show that the outcome is worse for the workers than it is under perfect competition where no coalitions of any kind are allowed. Worker-landowner coalitions conform to a 'divide and rule' principle: the workers are weakened by landowner inducements that lead them to betray their class. Even if the workers are too weak to agree on concerted action, they may be strong enough to prevent such partial accommodations with the capitalist. Compared to collective bargaining, individual wage negotiations betray weakness; but opposed to coalition bargaining, they betoken incipient class consciousness. Coalition theory thus embraces simultaneously the problems of class solidarity and of class struggle.

The weakness of game theory, in its present state, is the lack of testable hypotheses. There are many experimental studies of gaming, within the noncooperative and the cooperative framework, but few applications to nonexperimental settings. The value of the theory, therefore, is mainly in illuminating the nature of social interaction and in creating more discriminating categories of sociological analysis. Yet I am confident that this is a transitory situation only, and that game theory will increasingly help us understand social and historical problems. My reasons for this belief are somewhat *a priori*. If one accepts that interaction is of the essence of social life, then I submit that the three, interlocking, sets of interdependencies set out above capture interaction better than does any alternative. Game theory provides solid microfoundations for any study of social structure and social change. Yet the problems of aggregation and statistical analysis still confound us when it comes to complex real-life cases. This is not an argument for abandoning the search for microfoundations, but a compelling reason for forging better links between aggregate analysis and the study of individual behaviour.

[80] 'Ownership and the Production Function', *Quarterly Journal of Economics*, 80 (1967), 88–111.

For Marxism, game theory is useful as a tool for under-standing cases of mixed conflict and cooperation: cooperation in producing as much as possible, conflict over dividing up the product. Game theory can help understand the mechanics of solidarity and class struggle, without assuming that workers and capitalists have a common interest and need for cooperation. They do not. The interest of the working class is to suppress the capitalist class—and itself qua wage-earners—not to cooperate with it. Within the alienated framework of capitalism, however, this interest is easily misperceived. For there is the appearance of a common interest, such that working-class action will follow lines like those sketched here. Only through proper analysis of the mechanism of this reformist class struggle can one understand how to transform it into one that aims at abolishing the capitalist system.

REPLY TO ELSTER ON 'MARXISM, FUNCTIONALISM, AND GAME THEORY'

G. A. COHEN

Jon Elster and I each worked sympathetically on Marxism for a long time, and each of us independently came to see that Marxism in its traditional form is associated with explanations of a special type, ones in which, to put it roughly, consequences are used to explain causes. In keeping with normal practice, Elster calls such explanations *functional* explanations, and I shall follow suit here.[1] He deplores the association between Marxism and functional explanation, because he thinks there is no scope for functional explanation in social science. It is, he believes, quite proper in biology, because unlike social phenomena, biological ones satisfy the presuppositions that justify its use. Elster therefore concludes that the Marxist theory of society and history should abandon functional explanation. He also thinks that it should, instead, draw for its explanations on the resources of game theory.

I do not think that course is open to historical materialism. I believe that historical materialism's central explanations are unrevisably functional in nature, so that if functional

From *Theory and Society*, 11 (1982), pp. 483–95. Reprinted by permission of Kluwer Academic Publishers.

[1] For reasons given in my 'Functional Explanation, Consequence Explanation, and Marxism' (*Inquiry*, 1982) I am not certain that explanations of causes by consequences should be considered functional explanations, but that issue is irrelevant to Elster's article, so I shall here fall in with the standard practice of regarding what I would call *consequence* explanations as functional explanations. Much of this reply has already appeared in the *Inquiry* article mentioned above, and I am grateful to the editor of that journal for allowing it to be reproduced here.

explanation is unacceptable in social theory then historical materialism cannot be reformed and must be rejected. But I do not think functional explanation is unacceptable in social theory. My judgement that historical materialism is indissolubly wedded to functional explanation naturally reflects my conception of the content of historical materialist theory. To display, then, the grounds of that judgement, I shall expound what I think historical materialism says. I shall provide a résumé of the theory that I attribute, on a textual basis, to Marx, and that I explicate and defend in my book *Karl Marx's Theory of History*.[2]

In my book I say, and Marx says, that history is, fundamentally, the growth of human productive power, and that forms of society rise and fall according as they enable and promote, or prevent and discourage, that growth. The canonical text for this interpretation is the famous 1859 'Preface' to *A Contribution to the Critique of Political Economy*, some sentences of which we shall look at shortly. I argue (in section 3 of Chapter 6) that the 'Preface' makes explicit the standpoint on society and history to be found throughout Marx's mature writings, on any reasonable view of the date at which he attained theoretical maturity. In attending to the 'Preface', we are not looking at just one text among many, but at that text which gives the clearest statement of the theory of historical materialism. The presentation of the theory in the 'Preface' begins as follows:

In the social production of their life men enter into definite relations that are indispensable and independent of their will, relations of production which *correspond* to a definite stage of development of their material productive forces. The sum total of these relations constitutes the economic structure of society, the real *basis, on which arises* a legal and political superstructure. (italics added)

These sentences mention three ensembles, the productive forces, the relations of production, and the superstructure, among which certain explanatory connections are asserted. Here I say what I think the ensembles are, and then I describe the explanatory connections among them. (All of what follows

---

[2] G. A. Cohen, *Karl Marx's Theory of History* (Oxford and Princeton, 1978): henceforth referred as as *KMTH*.

is argued for in *KMTH*, but not all of the argument is given in what follows, which may therefore wrongly impress the reader as dogmatic). The productive forces are those facilities and devices used in the process of production: means of production on the one hand, and labour power on the other. Means of production are physical productive resources; e.g., tools, machinery, raw materials, and premises. Labour power includes not only the strength of producers, but also their skills, and the technical knowledge (which they need not understand) they apply when labouring. Marx says, and I agree, that this subjective dimension of the productive forces is more important than the objective or means of production dimension; and within the more important dimension the part most capable of development is knowledge. In its higher stages, then, the development of the productive forces merges with the development of productively useful science.

Note that Marx takes for granted in the 'Preface', what elsewhere he asserts outright, that 'there is a continual movement of growth in productive forces.'[3] I argue (in section 6 of Chapter 2 of *KMTH*) that the relevant standard for measuring that growth in power is how much (or, rather, how little) labour must be spent with given forces to produce what is required to satisfy the inescapable physical needs of the immediate producers.[4] This criterion of social productivity is less equivocal than others that may come to mind, but the decisive reason for choosing it is not any such 'operational' advantage, but its theoretical appropriateness: if kinds of economic structure correspond, as the theory says they do, to levels of productive power, then this way of measuring productive power makes the theory's correspondence thesis more plausible.[5] (I do not say that the only explanatory feature of productive power is how much there is of it: qualitative features of productive forces also help to explain the character of economic structures. My claim is that

---

[3] *The Poverty of Philosophy*, in Marx and Engels, *Collected Works*, vi (Lawrence and Wishart, 1976), 166.

[1] As opposed, for example, to their socially developed needs, reference to which would be inappropriate here (though not, of course, everywhere).

[5] For a set of correspondences of relations to forces of production see *KMTH*, p. 198.

insofar as quantity of productive power is what matters, the key quantity is how much time it takes to reproduce the producers.)

We turn to relations of production. They are relations of economic power, of the economic power[6] people enjoy or lack over labour power and means of production. In a capitalist society relations of production include the economic power capitalists have over means of production, the limited but substantial economic power workers (unlike slaves) have over their own labour power, and the lack of economic power workers have over means of production. The sum total of production relations in a given society is said to constitute the economic structure of that society, which is also called—in relation to the superstructure—the basis, or base, or foundation. The economic structure or base therefore consists of relations of production only: it does not include the productive forces. The 'Preface' describes the superstructure as legal and political. So it at any rate *includes* the legal and state institutions of society. It is customary to locate other institutions within it too, and it is controversial what its correct demarcation is: my own view is that there are strong textual and systematic reasons for supposing that the super-structure is a lot smaller than many commentators think it is.[7] It is certainly false that every noneconomic social phenomenon is superstructural: artistic creation, for example, is demonstrably not, as such, superstructural for Marx. In these remarks I shall discuss the legal order only, which is uncontroversially a part of the superstructure.

So much for the identity of the three ensembles mentioned in the 'Preface'. Now relations of production are said to *correspond* to the level of development of the productive forces, and in turn to be a *foundation* on which a superstructure rises. I think these are ways of saying that the level of development of the productive forces explains the nature of the production

---

[6] I call such power 'economic' in virtue of what it is power over, and irrespective of the means of gaining, sustaining or exercising the power, which need not be economic. See *KMTH*, pp. 223–4.

[7] The common practice of overpopulating the superstructure is criticized in my review of Melvin Rader's *Marx's Interpretation of History* (Oxford University Press, 1979), in *Clio*, 10. 2 (1981), 229–33.

relations, and that they in turn explain the character of the superstructure co-present with them. But what kind of explanation is ventured here? I argue that in each case what we have is a species of functional explanation.

What sort of explanation is that? It is, very roughly, an explanation in which an event, or whatever else, if there is anything else that can have an effect, is explained in terms of its effect. But now let us be less rough. Suppose we have a cause, e, and its effect, f. Then the form of the explanation is not: e occurred because f occurred—that would make functional explanation the mirror image of ordinary causal explanation, and then functional explanation would have the fatal defect that it represented a later occurrence as explaining an earlier one. Nor should we say that the form of the explanation is 'e occurred because it caused f'. Similar constraints on explanation and time order rule that candidate out: by the time e has caused f, e has occurred, so the fact that it caused f could not explain its occurrence. The only remaining candidate, which I therefore elect, is: e occurred because it *would* cause f, or, less tersely but more properly, e occurred because the situation was such that an event of type E would cause an event of type F.[8] So in my view a functional explanation is an explanation in which a dispositional fact explains the occurrence of the event-type mentioned in the antecedent of the hypothetical specifying the disposition. I called the laws justifying functional explanations *consequence laws*. They are of roughly this form: $(E \to F) \to E$ (a more precise specification of their form is given in section 4 of Chapter 9 of *KMTH*). If this account of what functional explanations are is correct, then the main explanatory theses of historical materialism are functional explanations. For superstructures hold foundations together, and production relations control the development of productive forces: these are undeniable facts, of which Marx was aware. Yet he asserts that the character of the superstructure is explained by the nature of the base, and that the base is explained by the

---

[8] Small letters represent phrases denoting particular events, and capital letters represent phrases denoting types of event. Where the letters are the same, the particular event belongs to the type in virtue of the meanings of the phrases denoting them.

nature of the productive forces. If the intended explanations are functional ones, we have consistency between the effect of A on B and the explanation of A by B, *and I do not know any other way of rendering historical materialism consistent.*

I now expound in greater detail one of the two functional explanatory theses, that which concerns base and super-structure. The base, it will be recalled, is the sum total of production relations, these being relations of economic power over labour power and means of production. The capitalist's control of means of production is an illustration. And the superstructure, we saw, has more than one part, exactly what its parts are is somewhat uncertain, but certainly one *bona fide* part of it is the legal system, which will occupy us here. In a capitalist society capitalists have effective power over means of production. What confers that power on a given capitalist, say an owner of a factory? On what can he rely if others attempt to take control of the factory away from him? An important part of the answer is this: he can rely on the law of the land, which is enforced by the might of the state. It is his legal right that causes him to have his economic power. What he is effectively able to do depends on what he is legally entitled to do. And this is in general true in law-abiding society with respect to all economic powers and all economic agents. We can therefore say: in law-abiding society people have the economic powers they do because they have the legal rights they do.

That seems to refute the doctrine of base and superstructure, because here superstructural conditions—what legal rights people have—determine basic ones—what their economic powers are. But although it seems to refute the doctrine of base and superstructure, it cannot be denied. And it would not only seem to refute it, but actually would refute it, were it not possible, *and therefore mandatory* (for historical materialists), to present the doctrine of base and superstructure as an instance of functional explanation. For we can add, to the undeniable truth emphasized above, the thesis that the given capitalist enjoys the stated right because it belongs to a structure of rights, a structure that obtains because it sustains an analogous structure of economic power. The content of the legal system is explained by its function, which is to help sustain an economy of a particular kind. People do usually get their powers from their rights, but in a manner that is not only allowed but demanded by the way historical materialism explains superstructural rights by reference to basic powers. Hence the effect of the law of property on the economy is not, as is often supposed, an embarrassment to historical materialism. It is something that historical materialism is committed to emphasizing, because of the particular way it explains law in terms of economic conditions. Legal structures rise and fall according as they sustain or frustrate forms of economy that, I now add, are favoured by the productive forces. The addition implies an explanation why whatever economic structure obtains at a given time does obtain at that time. Once more the explanation is a functional one: the prevailing production relations prevail because they are relations that advance the development of the productive forces. The existing level of productive power determines what relations of production would raise its level, and relations of that type consequently obtain. In other words: if production relations of type R obtain at time t, than that is because R-type relations are suitable to the development of the forces at t, given the level of their development at t.[9]

Now to say that A explains B is not necessarily to indicate *how* A explains B. The child who knows that the match burst into flame because it was struck may not know how the latter event explains the former (because he is ignorant of the relationship between friction and heat, the contribution of oxygen to combustion, and so on).[10] In this sense of 'how', we can ask: how does the fact that the economic structure promotes the development of the productive forces (or that the superstructure protects the base) explain the character of the economic structure (or the superstructure)? Consider an analogy: to say, correctly, that the species giraffe developed a long neck because of the utility of that feature in relation to the

[9] For a detailed account of the nature of the primacy of the forces see sect. 5 of ch. 6 of *KMTH*, which also discusses the transitional case where relations of production fetter the development of the productive forces.

[10] In a widely favoured idiom, he may not know the *mechanism* linking cause and effect, or, as I prefer to say, he may be unable to *elaborate* the explanation. I use both forms of expression in the sequel.

diet of giraffes (acacia tree leaves) is not to say how the utility of that feature accounted for its emergence or persistence. To that question Lamarck gave an unacceptable answer and Darwin an excellent one. To the corresponding questions within historical materialism no one has given excellent answers. I make some unexcellent attempts in Chapter 10 of my book. This seems to me an important area of future research for proponents of historical materialism, because the functional construal of the doctrine cannot be avoided.

Let me now summarize my argument for the thesis that the chief explanatory claims of historical materialism are functional in form. Historical materialism's central claims are that

1. The level of development of the productive forces in a society explains the nature of its economic structure, and
2. its economic structure explains the nature of its super-structure.

I take 1 and 2 to be functional explanations, because I cannot otherwise reconcile them with two further Marxian theses, namely that

3. the economic structure of a society promotes the development of its productive forces, and
4. the superstructure of a society stabilizes its economic structure.

3 and 4 entail that the economic structure is functional for the development of the productive forces, and that the superstructure is functional for the stability of the economic structure. These claims do not by themselves entail that economic structures and superstructures are *explained* by the stated functions: A may be functional for B even when it is false that A exists, or has the character it does, *because* its existence or character is functional for B. But 3 and 4, *in conjunction with 1 and 2*, do force us to treat historical materialist explanation as functional. No other treatment preserves consistency between the explanatory primacy of the productive forces over the economic structure and the massive control of the latter over the former, or between the explanatory primacy of the economic structure over the superstructure and the latter's regulation of the former. I did

not come to associate historical materialism with functional explanation because I thought functional explanation a good thing and I therefore wanted Marxism to have it. I began with a commitment to Marxism, and my attachment to functional explanation arose out of a conceptual analysis of historical materialism. I do not see how historical materialism can avoid it, for better or for worse. Contrast Jon Elster's attitude to Marxism and game theory. He wants Marxism to liaise with game theory because he admires game theory and thinks Marxism can gain much from the match. He wants to put Marxism and game theory together. I would not say that I want to put together Marxism and functional explanation, because I think functional explanation is inherent in Marxism.

At the beginning of his article Elster complains that Marxist social analysis has been contaminated by the principles of functionalist sociology. I am sure that claim is both historically and conceptually incorrect. Marxists do not indulge in functional explanation because they are influenced by the bad bourgeois science of functionalist sociology, and it is not open to them to use the better bourgeois science of game theory instead. They indulge in functional explanation because they are committed to historical materialism. Because functional explanation cannot be removed from the centre of historical materialism, game theory cannot be installed there in its stead. But it might be thought that game theory could also figure at the centre of historical materialism, not as a replacement but as an addition. Yet that, too, I argue, is false. Game theory may be, as Elster says, 'tailor-made for Marxist analysis',[11] but it is irrelevant to historical materialism's central theses, which are propositions 1 and 2. Its relevance, as I now explain, is to theses immediately peripheral to 1 and 2.

Elster makes deft use of game theory in a discussion of the dialectics of class struggle that I greatly admire. And it is not surprising that game theory illuminates class behaviour. But Marxism is *fundamentally* concerned not with behaviour, but with the forces and relations constraining and directing it. When we turn from the immediacy of class conflict to its long-

[11] Jon Elster, *Ulysses and the Sirens* (Cambridge University Press, 1979), p. 34.

term outcome game theory provides no assistance, because that outcome, for historical materialism, is governed by a dialectic of forces and relations of production that is background to class behaviour, and not explicable in terms of it. Game theory helps to explain the vicissitudes of the struggle, and the strategies pursued in it, but it cannot give a Marxist answer to the question why class wars (as opposed to battles) are settled one way rather than another. The Marxist answer is that the class that rules though a period, or emerges triumphant from epochal conflict, does so because it is the class best suited, most able and disposed, to preside over the development of the productive forces at the given time.[12] That answer may be untenable, but I cannot envisage a game-theoretical alternative to it that would qualify as historical materialist.

Elster says that 'game theory is invaluable to any analysis of the historical process that centres on exploitation, struggle, alliances, and revolution.' But for Marxian analysis those phenomena are not primary but, as it were, immediately secondary, on the periphery of the centre: they are, in the words of the 1859 'Preface', the 'forms in which men become conscious of the conflict [between forces and relations of production] and fight it out'. To put the point differently, we may say that the items on Elster's list are the actions at the centre of the historical process, but for Marxism there are also items more basic than actions at its centre.[13] By 'revolution' Elster must mean the political phenomenon of transfer of state power, as opposed to the transformation of economic structure political revolution initiates or reflects. Many facts about political revolutions are accessible to game-theoretical explanation, but not the world-historical facts that there was a bourgeois revolution and that there will be a proletarian one. Elster urges that game theory bears on strategic questions of great importance to Marxists. I accept that contention, which is amply supported by the excellent illustrations in his article. When faced with a strategic problem, such as how to transform society, we need strategic, not functionalist,

[12] See *KMTH*, pp. 148–9.

[13] Hence to say, as some Marxists do, that 'class struggle is the motor of history', is to abandon historical materialism.

thinking. But when Marx called on the workers to revolutionize society he was not asking them to bring about what would explain their doing so: the exhaustion of the progressive capacity of the capitalist order, and the availability of enough productive power to install a socialist one.

The concepts exercised in the previous sentence take us away from game theory to the fundamental context of historical materialism, that of forces and relations of production. There exists a splendid unpublished essay by Jon Elster entitled 'Forces and Relations of Production'. The essay makes no use of game theory. That is striking confirmation of my view that it is irrelevant to the foundational claims of Marxism: it shows that Elster himself agrees, in practice, with that view. Having constructed a rigorous theory of contradiction between forces and relations of production, Elster says that 'the great weakness of the theory is that it is very difficult to link it to action.' Now despite my insistence on the centrality in historical materialism of things that are not actions, I do appreciate that actions are prominent proximate causes of social effects. If links with action cannot be forged, if the question *how* the functional explanations of historical materialism explain cannot even in principle be answered, then that would have lethal significance for historical materialism. And this brings me to Elster's critique of functional explanation.

I remarked earlier that even when A is functional for B, A's existence or character need not be *explained* by that fact. Thus to confer credibility on the claim that B functionally explains A one must supply evidence in excess of that needed to show that A *is* functional for B. Elster and I disagree about what sort of further evidence is necessary. He demands that the claim that B functionally explains A be supported by a plausible story that reveals *how* B functionally explains A. I think that is sufficient, but not necessary. For I think one can support the claim that B functionally explains A even when one cannot suggest what the mechanism is, if instead one can point to an appropriately varied range of instances in which, whenever A would be functional for B, A appears.[14] This is an

[14] That is the simplest way of confirming a functional explanation without establishing a mechanism. For more complicated ways see *KMTH*, ch. 9, sect. 5, 7.

application to functional explanatory claims of a general truth about explanatory claims. There are always two ways of backing them up. Suppose, for example, that Elster and I notice a dead body in the library of the country house the morning after the dinner party, and that we hypothesize that its owner died because of something he ate the night before. Further research can take either of two forms. We might open him up to see whether there are any poisons in him, which would be analogous to what Elster thinks we must do to back up functional explanations, or we might find out what he ate, what other guests ate, and which other guests took ill or died, and that would be analogous to the way I say we can proceed with functional explanations. In my procedure we look for appropriately consonant and discrepant parallel instances. In Elster's we rely on pre-existing knowledge about parallel instances at a more basic causal level and we look for a mechanism in the given case that is consonant with that knowledge.

I can illustrate what is at stake by reference to the case of Lamarck and Darwin. Darwin showed how functional facts about the equipment of organisms contribute to explaining why they have it: the answer lies in the mechanism of chance variation and natural selection. Now I claim, and Elster denies, that, before Darwin thereby advanced the science of natural history, the belief that the useful characters of organisms are there because they are useful was already justified, by the sheer volume of evidence of adaptation. The belief was certainly widely held, by people who had no idea how to elaborate it and by others, such as Lamarck, who had what proved to be an unsatisfactory idea of how to elaborate it. And I contend, and Elster denies, that it was a justified belief. This debate is pursued elsewhere, and I shall not take it further here.[15]

[15] See the exchange between Elster and myself referred to in his n. 5, especially pp. 126, 133–4, and the *Inquiry* article mentioned in my n. 1. One result reached in the latter article bears mention here. I show that if Elster is right about what functional explanation is (he says what it is in *Ulysses and the Sirens*), then he is wrong that natural selection is necessary to sustain functional explanations in biology. It follows that he is also wrong in the corresponding claims about sociological functional explanation at pp. 51, 65.

Now because I concede that Marxists have not yet produced good elaborations of their functional explanatory theses, I concede that historical materialism is *at best* in a position like that occupied by natural history before Darwin transformed the subject. But I am not convinced that it has got even that far. For whereas Elster and I disagree strongly about what would confirm functional explanations, we disagree less about whether Marxists have actually produced well-confirmed functional explanations. The essays in Marxist functional explanation which he discusses are sadly representative, and I have no desire to defend them against his criticisms. Here we can make common cause. Many Marxist exercises in functional explanation fail to satisfy even the preliminary requirement of showing that A *is* functional for B (whether or not it is also *explained* by its function(s)).[16] Take, for example, the claim that the contemporary capitalist state functions to protect and sustain the capitalist system. Legislation and policy in the direct interest of the capitalist class can reasonably be regarded as confirming it. But what about putative counter-examples, such as social welfare provision and legal immunities enjoyed by trade unions? These too might be functional for capitalism in an indirect way, but that is something which needs to be argued with care, not just asserted. But those who propound the general claim about the state rarely trouble to say what sort of evidence would falsify or weaken it, and therefore every action of the state is treated as confirmatory, because there is always some way, legitimate or spurious, in which the action can be made to look functional. Methodological indiscipline is then compounded when, having established to his own satisfaction that state policy is functional, the theorist treats it, without further argument, as also functionally explained. He proceeds from 'A is functional for B' to 'B functionally explains A' without experiencing any need to justify the step,

---

[16] Elster does not always distinguish this criticism from the one I make in the next paragraph: see, for example, his comments (p. 57) on the passage from the *Eighteenth Brumaire*. If he is right, both criticisms apply, but he does not properly separate them.

if, indeed, he notices that he has taken a step from one position to a distinct and stronger one.[17]

Most Marxists are methodologically unselfconscious. If they were more sophisticated, they might provide a better defence of the functional explanations they offer. And then, again, they might not. I do not know how to be confident about this, one way or the other. But I maintain my insistence, first, that historical materialism cannot shed its commitment to functional explanation, and, second, that there is nothing inherently suspect in it. Elster's philosophical criticisms of historical materialist functional explanation still strike me as without force, by contrast with his polemic against particular essays in functional explanation. Our philosophical disagreement is pursued in *Political Studies* and *Inquiry*. In n. 8 of his present contribution Elster offers two new objections to my own theory of functional explanation, both of which are misguided. His first objection is that even when it is true that whenever A would have favourable consequences for B, A appears, A might not be explained by its possession of such consequences, because a third factor, C, might both cause A to have favourable consequences for B, and cause A to appear, without causing the latter as a result of causing the former. That is so, but it is not an objection to my theory.[18] The form of an ordinary causal law is: whenever A occurs, B occurs. Once again, this might be caused by a third factor, C, so related to A and B that A does not qualify as causing B. But there are tests which, when appropriate results are forthcoming, render the hypothesis that there exists such a C implausible, and suitably analogous tests may be conducted in the case of consequence laws.[19] Elster's second fresh objection rests on the premise that I do not mention time in my characterization of consequence laws. It is true that I do

[17] And sometimes it is unclear that a step has been taken from a statement of functionality to a functional explanation, and, therefore, it is correspondingly unclear that a fallacy has been committed. Thus, for example, I do not share Elster's confidence that Marx's use of the word 'means' in the quotation from vol. 3 of *Capital* on p. 457 proves that Marx is offering a functional *explanation*, and I am sure that he is wrong when he claims (p. 456) that Marx subscribed to 'the main functional paradigm'.

[18] It is, indeed, a point I made myself: see *KMTH*, pp. 267 ff.

[19] See, further, 'Functional Explanation'.

not mention particular amounts of time when describing the form of such laws in general terms, just as one does not when one describes the form of ordinary causal laws as 'whenever A occurs, B occurs'. But causal laws are not therefore 'vacuously confirmable', because particular causal laws include appropriate temporal specifications. All that need be said in general terms about consequence laws and time will be found on pp. 260–1 of *KMTH*.

I now take up two issues in the part of Elster's article in which he successfully conjoins Marxism and game theory. In a highly original account of the ideology and practice of social democratic capitalism, Elster sets the stage by describing the dissolution of the marginalist illusion, and the action unfolds along lines scripted by Zeuthen and Nash on the one hand and Lancaster on the other. I have two criticisms of this treatment. The first is that Elster misidentifies the illusion that survives after the marginalist one has been dissolved. He calls it 'the presentist illusion' [p. 78 above] and attributes it to 'diachronic alienation' [p. 82 above]. Workers are alienated 'from their own history, i.e., from past generations of workers who produced the means of production currently used', and they overcome that alienation 'by taking possession of their history' [p. 78 above]. Elster would agree that unrevolutionary workers believe that the capitalist is entitled to a return because he is the morally legitimate owner of the means of production. He thinks the presentist illusion explains why they think the capitalist's ownership is legitimate. But in what does the illusion consist? In a false belief that the means of production were not produced by workers in the past? But workers know better than that. They know, if they reflect on the matter, that means of production were produced by earlier workers, but just as they believe that their own employer is entitled to a return, so, in parallel, they think the employer of earlier workers was; whence, in particular, employers of workers producing means of production came to possess them legitimately and passed them on, directly or indirectly, through market exchange and gift (especially inheritance), to the employers of today. If there exists any kind of presentist illusion, why should workers not project it backwards when they think about their predecessors?

My second criticism of the game-theoretical part of Elster's article concerns his remarks on the locus of exploitation. He writes that 'the exploitation of the working class . . . does not consist *only* in the capitalists' appropriation of surplus-value, but also in the workers' exclusion from decisive investment choices that shape the future.' [p. 84 above, my emphasis] Much the same sentence occurs in an earlier version of Elster's article, except that the word 'mainly' occurs where the word 'only' appears in this final version. This reply was originally composed in response to that earlier version. Having read my response, Elster changed 'mainly' to 'only', thereby partly spoiling some criticisms I had made of the original version. I shall nevertheless enter the following paragraph of criticism of his original formulation (the one with 'mainly') here, not only out of vanity but also because it still applies, if with reduced force, against his revised formulation, and most importantly because I think it is useful to try to identify rather precisely what exploitation consists in.

I do not doubt that workers are excluded from investment decisions, but I deny that they are thereby *exploited*. If someone robs me of the power to control my own life, he does not *ipso facto* use me unfairly to his own advantage, which is what, very roughly, exploitation is. Authoritarian parents do not, by virtue of being authoritarian, qualify as exploiters of their children, and authoritarian parenthood is a good analogue to the relationship Elster highlights here, which is one of subordination, not exploitation. That subordination is, moreover, a consequence of exploitation in the traditional sense, which is therefore not displaced by (what is anyway wrongly considered) a further form of exploitation. It is because capitalists appropriate surplus value that they are able to decide what to do with it, to consume and invest in whatever proportions they choose. And the exploitation of the worker lies in the appropriation, not in the subsequent disposal over what has been appropriated. Part of what moved Elster to make his (original) statement was the fact, which he emphasizes elsewhere, that only a small proportion of total social product remains for capitalist consumption after workers' income and capitalist investment have absorbed their shares.[20] But because there are relatively few capitalists, that small proportion enables them to enjoy a life of comfort and freedom inaccessible to workers. The difference in *per capita* personal income remains massive, and it matters a great deal to the self-perception and sense of dignity of working people. Working-class existence, even in America, is full of strain unknown to wealthy people. Elster's (original) formulation overlooks that sheer difference in standard of living between the classes remains a major part of the injustice of capitalism.

My present view about the matters in contention between Elster and myself is as follows: (1) Functional explanation lies at the heart of historical materialism. (2) Game theory therefore cannot replace functional explanation within Marxist social analysis. (3) Nor is there a place for game theory at the heart of historical materialism, alongside functional explanation. (4) But game theory is very helpful in relation to claims near, but not quite at, historical materialism's heart. (5) There is no methodological error in historical materialism's functional explanatory theses. (6) But Marxists have not done much to establish that they are true. If Marxian functional explanation remains as wanting in practice (as opposed to high theory) as it has been, the foundational claims of historical materialism might need to be severely modified. Positions of great traditional authority might have to be abandoned. One of Elster's achievements is that he has shown how fruitfully what would remain of the doctrine we have inherited can be enriched and extended.

[20] See 'Exploring Exploitation', *Journal of Peace Research*, 15 (1978), 12, where he concludes that 'in modern capitalist economies the notion of exploitation should be linked to the lack of power over investment decisions rather than to the fact (or to the possibility) of capitalists having a high level of consumption at the expense of workers.'

4

ANTHONY GIDDENS:
A CONTEMPORARY CRITIQUE

ALEX CALLINICOS

By way of apology for the title of this chapter, I should point out that it refers not merely to Anthony Giddens's recent *A Contemporary Critique of Historical Materialism*, but also to the fact that I am discussing an enormously energetic and prolific writer responsible over the last few years for a prodigious outpouring of books that develop, and sometimes modify, a coherent set of views on social theory. To attempt to summarize and subject to criticism such an œuvre is a little like trying to catch quicksilver.

My reasons for nevertheless making the attempt are twofold. First, the sheer erudition and intellectual range of Giddens's work[1] commands our attention. A writer who draws on such a wide variety of thinkers—Marx, Weber, Durkheim, Mead, Heidegger, Wittgenstein, Schutz, Foucault, Derrida, to name but a few—to develop his own distinctive theory deserves serious consideration, especially in the light of the deeply parochial nature of so much British intellectual culture. The two books under view, *A Contemporary Critique of Historical Materialism*, an ambitious reworking of social theory, *Profiles and Critiques in Social Theory*, a collection of essays that

From *Theory and Society*, 14 (1985), pp. 133–66, copyright © 1985 by Elsevier Science Publishers B. V. Reprinted by permission of Kluwer Academic Publishers.

[1] I have used abbreviations when citing the following books by Anthony Giddens: *The Class Structure of the Advanced Societies* (2nd edn., London: Hutchinson, 1981), *CSAS*; *New Rules of Sociological Method* (London: Hutchinson, 1976), *NRSM*; *Central Problems in Social Theory* (London: Macmillan, 1979), *CPST*; *A Contemporary Critique of Historical Materialism* (London: Macmillan, 1981), *CCHM*; *Profiles and Critiques in Social Theory* (London: Macmillan, 1982), *PCST*.

illustrate this reworking mainly through the criticism of others' views, offer an admirable opportunity to assess the direction and coherence of Giddens's project.

Secondly, *A Contemporary Critique of Historical Materialism*, as the title suggests, itself expounds Giddens's substantive theory in the form of an appraisal of Marxism. The criticisms it offers represent a direct challenge to those, such as myself, of a Marxist persuasion, a challenge to which I feel obliged to respond. But, in doing so, I am fully in agreement with Erik Olin Wright that 'the book is a serious engagement with Marxism, and deserves a serious reading by both Marxists and non-Marxists.'[2] Giddens is too intelligent and sympathetic a critic of Marx simply to be brushed aside.

What, then, is the nub of Giddens's critique of Marxism? Brutally summarized, it is that Marx himself in the bulk of his mature writings, and, much more so, his successors, adopted a one-sided and economically reductive account of human conduct. They consequently developed an evolutionary theory of historical development that explained social change in terms of the growth of the productive forces, denying human agents any significant role in the reproduction and trans-formation of societies. As a result, Marxism has been largely insensitive to the diversity and irreducibility of power-relations, blindly believing that national, racial, and sexual oppression were merely the epiphenomena of class exploitation. The hopeless inadequacy of such an intellectual framework has been decisively proved in recent years with the evolution of 'really existing socialism' along lines quite unanticipated by Marx, and the emergence of autonomous social movements such as feminism.

To Giddens's views thus baldly stated, one might respond 'So what else is new?' An alternative conceptualization of society to Marxism that stresses the variety and permanency of power-relations is implicit in Nietzsche's thought, was developed systematically by Weber, and has recently been revived with a fashionably 'post-structuralist' twist by Foucault and Deleuze, and, rather more accessibly, by Frank Parkin in

[2] E. O. Wright, 'Giddens's Critique of Marxism', *New Left Review* 138 (1983), 12.

his Weberian critique of neo-Marxist class theory.[3] Is not Giddens's work merely a variation, no doubt erudite and sophisticated, but nevertheless still a variation on a rather well-worn theme?

Giddens thinks not. In the 1979 postscript added to the second edition of his *The Class Structure of the Advanced Societies*, first published in 1973, Giddens rejects descriptions of that book as 'Weberian' or 'neo-Weberian', insisting that 'the position I developed in the book owes considerably more to Marx than to Weber.'[4] He furthermore subjects Parkin's *Marxism and Class Theory* to virulent criticism for its negative and dismissive attitude towards Marxism.[5] And he explicitly declares, 'I do not seek to replace Marx by Nietzsche.'[6]

Giddens's work can best be represented as a very ambitious attempt to effect a synthesis of distinct and opposed traditions in social theory. Thus, at the methodological level he seeks to preserve the stress laid by 'interpretive sociology' (Weber, Schutz, ethnomethodology) on social relations as the result of the intentional activity of human agents, while at the same time acknowledging the importance, asserted strongly by Marxists, Parsonian sociologists, and structuralists alike, of social structures in shaping human conduct. Again, substantively, Giddens is concerned to evolve an account of society that accords primacy to the phenomenon of power, maintaining that 'power was never satisfactorily theorized by Marx',[7] while treating Marx's analysis of capitalism as a limited but largely correct account of one case of this general phenomenon.

The attempt to construct syntheses is undoubtedly a worthwhile intellectual activity. Indeed, Hegel's dialectic treats it as the characteristic form of theoretical progress, the

[3] See, for example, M. Foucault, *Power/Knowledge* (Brighton: Harvester, 1980), G. Deleuze and F. Guattari, *Mille Plateaux* (Paris: Minuit, 1980), and F. Parkin, *Marxism and Class Theory* (London: Tavistock, 1979).

[4] *CSAS*, p. 296.

[5] A. Giddens, 'Classes, Capitalism, and the State', *Theory and Society*, 9. 6 (1980), reprinted in *PCST*. The same issue contains Parkin's equally bitter 'Reply to Giddens'.

[6] *CCHM*, p. 3. See also A. Giddens, 'From Marx to Nietzsche?', in *PCST*, esp. p. 229.

[7] *CCHM*, p. 30.

concept of *Aufhebung* expressing how opposites are cancelled
and preserved in a new unity. It is not wholly inaccurate
to describe historical materialism as such a synthesis of
Hegel and Ricardo. But, as this example suggests, genuinely
innovative syntheses are rare and difficult to arrive at.
Too often attempted syntheses amount merely to banality,
incoherence, or eclecticism.

I am reluctant to ascribe any of these three qualities to
Giddens's work, brilliant and stimulating as it often is. But I
wish to argue that his attempt to transcend the rival traditions
he hopes to synthesize is a failure. I shall try to prove my case
by considering two of the main features of Giddens's general
approach: his theory of structuration and his account of
power. I shall then go on to consider in detail some of his
criticisms of Marxism, showing them to be largely mistaken
and resting on a highly selective reading of its productions. I
shall conclude with some general reflections on the nature of
Giddens's project. I am well aware that in pursuing this
course I shall not pay due tribute to the many exciting and
suggestive passages especially in *A Contemporary Critique* in
which Giddens discusses a variety of theoretical and historical
issues. My failure, however, to match his erudition and range
may still lead to gains in clarity.

THE THEORY OF STRUCTURATION

A central theme of Giddens's two main methodological
treatises, *New Rules of Sociological Method* and *Central Problems in
Social Theory*, is what he calls the 'dualism of agency and
structure'.[8] By this he means the following. A variety of
philosophical traditions, notably hermeneutics and post-
Wittgensteinian analytical philosophy, have developed highly
sophisticated accounts of human conduct as intentional
action, any explanation of which makes irreducible reference
to the intentions, beliefs, and desires of the agent ascertainable
primarily through the medium of language. They have,
however, 'paid little attention to, or have found no way of

---

[8] See, for example, *CPST*, pp. 49 ff.

coping with, conceptions of structural explanation or social causation.'[9] On the other hand, those intellectual traditions that have developed such conceptions have ignored the subject. For example,

in both Althusserian Marxism and Parsonian sociology the reproduction of society occurs 'behind the backs' of the agents whose conduct constitutes that society. The involvement of actors' own purposive conduct with the rationalization of action is lacking in each case . . . hence the teleology of the system either governs . . . or supplants . . . that of the actors themselves.[10]

Giddens's aim is to overcome this pervasive dualism of agency and structure through the theory of structuration. His starting point is one very close to the hermeneutic and Wittgensteinian traditions:

The *production of society* is a skilled performance, sustained and 'made to happen' by human beings. It is indeed only made possible because every (competent) member of society is a practical social theorist; in sustaining any sort of encounter he draws upon his knowledge and theories, normally in an unenforced and routine way, and the use of these practical resources is precisely the condition of the production of the encounter at all.[11]

'Knowledgeable human agents' do not, however, make society in circumstances of their own choosing. '*The realm of human agency is bounded*', 'the production of constitution of society is a skilled accomplishment of its members, but one that does not take place under conditions that are wholly intended or wholly comprehended by them.'[12]

It is here that social structures enter the scene, as the 'unacknowledged conditions and unanticipated consequences' of human conduct. Giddens distinguishes sharply between these structures and social systems, by which he means human collectivities persisting in time and space. The persistence of a social system can only be accounted for by invoking structure, which is itself 'non-temporal and non-spatial . . . *a virtual order of differences* produced and reproduced in social interaction as its medium and outcome'.[13] Every

[9] Ibid. 49.   [10] Ibid. 112.
[11] *NRSM*, pp. 15–16.   [12] Ibid. 160, 102.
[13] *CPST*, p. 3.

social system possesses a set of '*structural principles*', the 'structural elements that are most deeply embedded in the space-time dimensions of social systems' and that 'govern the basic institutional alignments of a society'.[14] Giddens distinguishes between three main dimensions of structure: signification, in which agents communicate and rationalize their actions by means of interpretive schemes; domination, arising from asymmetries in the distribution of resources; and legitimation, through which different forms of conduct are sanctioned by means of norms. Structural principles, according to Giddens, typically involve social contradictions, in the sense that they 'operate in *terms of each other* but at the same time *contravene one another*'.[15]

I cannot dwell here on the many felicities of Giddens's detailed account of structure—its anti-functionalism, for example, based on the 'guiding tenet: don't look for the functions social practices fulfil, look for the contradictions they embody',[16] or his conceptualization of structures as enabling as well as constraining, so they do not simply limit the scope of human conduct, but make certain forms of activity possible. More relevant for present purposes is the fact that for Giddens the existence of structures does not in itself explain the persistence of social systems. The belief to the contrary he regards as 'the decisive error in functionalism'.[17] According to a thesis that Giddens calls 'the *duality of structure*', 'structure is both medium and outcome of the reproduction of practices.'[18] In other words, although structure shapes the conduct of human agents, it is only through that conduct that it itself possesses any effectivity, and it may itself be modified by the activity of which it is the unacknowledged condition and unanticipated consequence.

Giddens illustrates this argument by invoking the case of language. The rules of a language constitute *langue*, the underlying structures that govern *parole*, speakers' actual usage. But it is only by virtue of being applied in speech that these rules become operative; without *parole*, *langue* would not exist. Furthermore, it is always possible that usage will alter

[14] *CPST*, p. 106.   [15] Ibid. 141.
[16] Ibid. 131.   [17] Ibid. 211.
[18] Ibid. 5.

the rules of language; indeed, language is constantly changing as a result of shifts of usage. Similarly, it is through the conduct of 'knowledgeable human agents' that structures are produced, reproduced, and transformed.

The 'duality of structure' thus formulated serves to conceptualize social systems as the outcome of an interaction between underlying structures and intentional conduct. Giddens is obviously sensitive to the arguments advanced especially by structuralism and post-structuralism that the subject can no longer be conceived, as it has been since Descartes, as the autonomous source of meaning. Yet he hopes to accommodate these arguments within a position that does not simply turn the subject into a mere 'bearer' of anonymous structures, as Althusser, for example, did. 'A de-centring of the subject must at the same time *recover* that subject as a reasoning, acting being.'[19] As Fred R. Dallmayr observes: 'Giddens has seen himself faced with a momentous challenge: . . . the task of moving beyond subjectivist metaphysics *without* relinquishing some of its insights, and especially without lapsing into objectivism and determinism.'[20]

The attractions of such a position are obvious, avoiding as it does the extremes of a functionalism or structuralism that denies any scope to the human subject, and a hermeneutics that can find no place for social structure. Or rather, it would be attractive had Giddens successfully avoided these extremes. I wish to argue that he has not, and that his commitment to the notion that human agents produce society gives rise to a tendency to collapse into the hermeneutic pole of the two extremes.

Part of the difficulty lies in Giddens's identification of social structures with *rules*. 'Rules', he tells us, 'generate—or are the medium of—the production and reproduction of practices.'[21] Such a treatment of rules as constitutive of social practice, suggested already by his invocation of an analogy with language, is, of course, far from peculiar to Giddens. It was, indeed, typical of much Anglo-American philosophy in

[19] A. Giddens, 'Hermeneutics and Social Theory', in *PCST*, p. 8.
[20] F. R. Dallmayr, 'The Theory of Structuration: a Critique', in *PCST*, p. 19.
[21] *CPST*, p. 67.

the 1950s and 1960s under the influence of a certain reading of the work of the later Wittgenstein. Winch's *Idea of a Social Science* represented the apotheosis of this trend, as applied to social theory. Now Giddens wishes to distance himself from social science à la Winch, if only because he believes that structure involves, as well as rules, resources whose unequal distribution gives rise to power-relations.[22] Nevertheless, the conception of social practice as rule-governed is crucial to his theory of structuration.

There seem to me two reasons for questioning this approach. First, it involves generalizing from the case of language to social practice as such. Such a treatment of language as paradigmatic of social life is again not peculiar to Giddens—apart from in linguistic philosophy of the post-war Oxford school, it is also be found in Lévi-Strauss's structural anthropology, in Habermas's recent work, and in deconstructionists of the Derrida sort.

Of course, these various approaches embody, on the whole, very different conceptions of language—compare the Derridean treatment of discourse as inherently heterogenous and self-subverting, and Habermas's discovery, implicit in every speech-act, of a tendency toward rational consensus. Nevertheless, they share a proneness to what Perry Anderson has recently called the '*exorbitation of language*', the identification of the structures of language with those of society.[23] But, as Anderson persuasively argues, 'language is no fitting model for any other human practice': linguistic structures change very slowly, are not subject to the constraints of natural scarcity, and exist through individual rather than collective agents.[24] Anderson shows how the overextension of language has led in the case of post-structuralism to a point where neither history nor indeed reality itself have any standing outside the endless play of signifiers.

These are, however, general considerations. There is a second reason for quarrelling with Giddens's identification of structure with rules. Recent discussion, notably by Saul

---

[22] For these and other criticisms of Winch see *NRSM*, pp. 44–51.
[23] P. Anderson, *In the Tracks of Historical Materialism* (London: Verso, 1983), pp. 40–2. See ibid. 60–7 for a discussion of the similarities, and differences, between Habermas and post-structuralism.   [24] Ibid. 43–5.

Kripke,[25] of the passages in the *Investigations* and *Remarks on the Foundations of Mathematics* where Wittgenstein examines the notion of following a rule suggests that in these texts, far from conceiving social practice as rule-governed, he sets out to attack the idea that, as John McDowell puts it, 'the rules mark out rails along which correct activity within the practice must run.'[26]

The difficulty with rule-following thus conceived is well stated by P. F. Strawson in this limpid summary of Kripke's reading of Wittgenstein:

It is natural to suppose that when we use a word or symbol of our language, we are guided in its use by our grasp of its meaning, or of the concept which it expresses, or of the rules or instructions for its use which we have mastered; that these are what tell us that it is correct to use the expression in such-and-such a way; to apply it to *this* case (if it is a descriptive term) or to compute with it in *this* way (if it is a mathematical symbol). So we appear to invoke some fact about our mental life to explain our confidence in the correctness of our current use of the expression. But if we take this conception seriously, it seems that there can be no guarantee that what we now take ourselves to mean by the expression is the same as what we meant by it in the past. For our practice is consistent with our having meant by it something quite different . . . the point . . . should be obvious to any reader of Nelson Goodman: perhaps by 'green' in the past I meant *grue* (where anything green seen before now and anything seen blue from now is *grue*).[27]

The conclusion of this sort of sceptical consideration is what Wittgenstein describes as the following paradox: 'no course of action could be determined by a rule, because every course of action can be made to accord with it.'[28] Rather than

[25] See S. Cavell, *The Claim of Reason* (Oxford University Press, 1979), S. M. Holtzmann and C. M. Leich (eds.), *Wittgenstein: to Follow a Rule*, (London, Boston and Henley: Routledge and Kegan Paul, 1981), and S. Kripke, *Wittgenstein on Rules and Private Language* (Oxford: Basil Blackwell, 1982).

[26] J. McDowell, 'Non-Cognitivism and Rule-Following', in Holtzmann and Leich, op. cit. 144.

[27] P. F. Strawson, 'Sense and Consensus', *Times Literary Supplement*, 11 Feb. 1983.

[28] L. Wittgenstein, *Philosophical Investigations* (Oxford: Basil Blackwell, 1968), I, para. 201.

grounding social practice, rules depend for their applicability on the shared responses of members of a community. It is on the basis of this interpretation of rule-following that Wittgenstein argues, in the later parts of the *Investigations*, that a private language, i.e., one that in principle only one speaker could use, is impossible, since the only criterion of correct usage is that provided by the common action of members of a society.

If this argument is valid, and it has still to be shown that it is not, then Giddens cannot appeal to the notion of rules as the basis of his account of social structure. Rather than generating practices, rules collapse into them. This is no great worry if one accepts, as I do, a much stronger sense of structure than that proposed by Giddens. It merely provides persuasive backing for my opposition to generalizing from the case of language. But, for Giddens, who wishes to preserve the hermeneutic tradition's sensitivity to the interpreting and acting subject while recognizing the structural aspects of social practice, it is a serious difficulty.

Giddens shows no sign of being aware of this difficulty. This is especially surprising in the light of the fact that he is evidently acquainted with the issues raised by Wittgenstein's discussion of rule-following. Indeed, he writes that 'the knowledgeability involved in practical consciousness conforms generally to the Wittgensteinian notion of "knowing a rule" or "knowing how to go on." '[29] Yet, in the exchange with Dallmayr published in *Profiles and Critiques*, Giddens ignores the former's demand for 'further argument . . . to pinpoint the status of rules in the process of structuration'.[30]

Dallmayr goes on to argue that, although Giddens has 'told us repeatedly that he wants to move beyond the so-called subject-object dichotomy' in the theory of structuration, 'he reverts again to the subject-object dualism of actors constituting and being constituted.'[31] That this is so, that there is a persisting dualism of agency and structure in Giddens's writings despite his claim to have overcome it, can be illustrated by his discussion of two issues. In each he tends

[29] A. Giddens, 'Action, Power and Structure', in *PCST*, p. 31.
[30] Dallmayr, 'Theory', p. 22.   [31] Ibid. 27.

to treat agents and structures as separate from, and external to each other, and to accord primacy to the former.

The first is the question of resistance by subordinate groups. Giddens attacks Foucault's notion of 'history without a subject' on the grounds that 'human beings are always and everywhere knowledgeable human agents, though acting within historically specific bounds of the unacknowledged conditions and unaccepted consequences of their acts.'[32] He proceeds to criticize Foucault's notion of society as constituted by a pervasive and omnipresent apparatus of 'power-knowledge' by arguing that 'Foucault's "archaeology"', in which human beings do not make their own history but are swept along by it, does not adequately acknowledge that those subject to the power of dominant groups are themselves knowledgeable human agents, who resist, blunt or actively alter the conditions of life that others seek to thrust upon them.'[33]

Now this argument is closely related to the well-known difficulty in Foucault's recent work that, although resistance is always supposedly immanent in power-relations, he never provides any basis for this resistance.[34] Giddens seeks to provide such a basis by invoking the concept of 'knowledgeable human agents'. This is a completely ahistorical approach. There is no discussion of the historically specific conditions that lead oppressed groups to resist and that provide their resistance with sources of organization and power. It is merely a general property of 'knowledgeable human agents' that they 'resist, blunt or actively alter' their 'conditions of life'. The strategy recalls Edward Thompson's counter-position in *The Poverty of Theory* of the creativity and humanity of social agents to the structural conditions of their activity. Perry Anderson's response to Thompson seems to me applicable to Giddens as well: the scope for agency (and hence resistance) in history varies according to the specific circumstances in which people

[32] *CCHM*, p. 171. See generally ibid. 157–81 and Giddens, 'From Marx to Nietzsche?' p. 32.

[33] *CCHM*, p. 171.

[34] See N. Poulantzas, *State, Power, Socialism* (London: NLB, 1978), pp. 146–53 and P. Dews, '*Nouvelle Philosophie* and Foucault', *Economy and Society* 8. 2 (1979).

find themselves.[35] Giddens's preference for a philosophical invocation of subjects' capacity to resist rather than for a historical examination of the variable conditions of action is indicative of his privileging of the pole of agency as against that of structure in the theory of structuration.

Support for this view is provided by a highly symptomatic misreading of Foucault on Giddens's part. He writes: 'Discipline, Foucault says, disassociates power from the body . . . At the same time, the emphasis is placed on the "interiorization" of power.'[36] Foucault, of course, says no such thing. The rise of the disciplines in early nineteenth-century Europe indeed represents a shift from the form of power characteristic of absolutism, involving the spectacular use of violence in public executions. But the new form of power, in which individuals are subjected to general norms within the context of institutions such as prisons, according to Foucault, also acts on bodies. In this case, however, it serves to constitute them as subjects, providing them with a set of motives governing their actions. Giddens's talk of 'the "interiorization" of power' reveals his own presupposition that structures act on independently formed subjects. But, for Foucault, in the disciplines, power does not penetrate the consciousness of a pre-formed subject; rather, these disciplines *create* the subject.

The same presupposition underlies Giddens's critique of Harry Braverman's *Labour and Monopoly Capital*.[37] Giddens quite correctly points to the weakness of Braverman's account of scientific management and the deskilling of labour, namely that it treats workers as passive objects apparently incapable of effective organization and resistance. However, this criticism is theoretically grounded in the assertion that 'to be a human agent is to have power', so that 'the most seemingly "powerless" individuals are able to mobilize resources whereby they carve out "spaces of control"' giving rise to 'a dialectic of control'.[38]

---

[35] P. Anderson, *Arguments within English Marxism* (London: NLB, 1980), ch. 2.

[36] Giddens, 'From Marx to Nietzsche?' p. 220. .

[37] A. Giddens, 'Power, the Dialectic of Control and Class Structuration', in *PCST*.

[38] Ibid. 197–8.

All this is true enough, but it short-circuits the analysis of different modalities of resistance in different social formations. The scope for resistance of, for example, a slave in the Athenian silver mines at Laureion, while no doubt real enough, was surely much narrower than that of, say, the auto-workers at Ford Halewood studied by Huw Beynon. A Marxist would argue that the difference between the two can only be understood by examining what Erik Olin Wright has called the structural capacities of particular classes—in other words, the distinctive powers that they derive from their position in historically specific relations of production.[39] Thus the shortcomings of Braverman's analysis of the modern labour-process is closely related to his failure to grasp that workers' position within this process endows them with a capacity for collective organization and resistance.[40] Unfortunately, Giddens's preoccupation with an abstract account of human subjectivity prevents him from following through the consequences of his own insight into the way in which social structures enable as well as constrain.

A second index of Giddens's underlying preference for an account of society centring on the subject is his discussion of 'time-space distanciation'. One of the most interesting and innovative aspects of Giddens's recent work is his insistence on integrating the spatial and temporal dimensions of human life into social theory. Recent work in human geography, for example, should be treated, not as part of a separate discipline from sociology, but as an intrinsic part of the study of social formations.[41]

I have neither the competence nor the desire to question Giddens's often exhilarating discussions of these matters, merely to draw attention to one feature of the conceptual framework he uses. He draws on Heidegger and Derrida in order to argue that 'all social interaction intermingles presence and absence.'[42] Human beings have direct contact with each other as present in space and time. However, they also have access to those distant in time through oral

---

[39] E. O. Wright, *Class, Crisis and the State* (London: NLB, 1978), pp. 98 ff.

[40] Giddens himself makes this point against Foucault: 'From Marx to Nietzsche?', pp. 222–3.

[41] See *CPST*, ch. 6; *CCHM*, chs. 1, 3, 4.   [42] *CCHM*, p. 38.

tradition, writing, and other such storage devices, and to those distant in space by various communications systems. Social structures serve to bind practices together in time and space through their contribution to the constitution and reproduction of systems of social interaction. Giddens goes on to distinguish between societies on the basis of the degree of their 'presence-availability'. In 'societies or communities of high presence availability . . . interaction is predominantly of a face-to-face kind.'[43] Such societies are to be found, for example, among hunter-gatherers. Giddens argues that history is characterized by a process of '*time-space distanciation*', such that 'societies are "stretched" over longer spans of time and space.'[44] This occurs as both communications and storage devices become more sophisticated, so that people interact with those with whom they are not in face-to-face contact. The culmination of this process is the emergence of the capitalist world-system.

I shall discuss this analysis, insofar as it supposedly contradicts Marxism, below. I wish merely to note here that Giddens's argument differs significantly from the conception of Being as presence-absence developed by Heidegger and Derrida. For the latter argue that the condition of 'high-presence availability' that Giddens attributes to band-societies is impossible. They do so for general philosophical considerations: namely, they wish to deny that a state of *parousia* or absolute presence in which we have direct access to reality can exist. We can only relate to such a state as necessarily absent, something that we have lost or may still hope to (re)gain. This is the point of Derrida's concept of *différance*, of a constant play of presence and absence in which we are obliged to postulate, but never to attain, presence.

Of course, Giddens is perfectly entitled to appropriate and modify other people's concepts. But it is the nature of the modification that is interesting. One of the points of the concept of *différance* was precisely to dislodge from his sovereign place the Cartesian subject, having direct access to the contents of his consciousness (in other words, being 'self-present'), and providing a basis on which our knowledge of

[43] *CPST*, p. 103.   [44] *CCHM*, p. 90.

the world (and indeed on some versions the world itself) could be constituted. Giddens does not reinstate the Cartesian self: rather it is the subject of social interaction, engaging in face-to-face contact with other subjects in the manner analysed by Goffman, which reigns in the condition of 'high presence-availability'.[45] History becomes, as Derrida argues it must necessarily be, the story of the loss of presence, of the 'high presence-availability' characteristic of hunter-gatherer societies. Once again, 'knowledgeable human agents' triumph over structures.

These two cases—Giddens's discussion of resistance and his account of 'time-space distanciation'—suggest that he has failed to overcome the duality of agency and structure. The reason for this failure is not a contingent one—it is not a matter of Giddens being inconsistent. Rather, in my view, its source lies in the very conception of structure as the unacknowledged condition and unanticipated consequence of human actions.

Let us consider structure in its two aspects. Conceiving structure as the unanticipated consequence of human action does not involve any challenge to the primacy of agents over structures. On the contrary, such a conception of structure has usually been held precisely as a means of securing this primacy. This is most obviously so in the case of methodological individualism. If social structures arise as the unintended consequences of individual actions, then it is with these actions, and the beliefs, desires, and intentions that produce them, that we must start in order to account for the existence of structures and of the practices bound up with them. Jon Elster, who recently urged that methodological individualism can provide the 'microfoundations of Marxist social theory',[46] has, in line with this approach, developed an account of social contradiction as unintended consequence.[47]

That Giddens is committed to a stronger notion of structure than Elster's is suggested by his critique of the latter's theory

[45] *CPST*, pp. 201–6.
[46] J. Elster, 'Marxism, Functionalism and Game Theory: The Case for Methodological Individualism', *Theory and Society*, 2.4 (1982) [pp. 48–87 above].
[47] J. Elster, *Logic and Society* (London: John Wiley & Sons, 1978).

of contradiction.[48] And, indeed, the concept of structure as the unacknowledged condition of human action seems to go much further than any account in terms of unintended consequences, especially when Giddens talks of structure as both constraining and enabling. But when we consider the detail of Giddens's account, structure is once again reduced to a secondary role. Structures are, let us recall, rules and resources. Even though Giddens does not fully grasp the import of Wittgenstein's arguments about rule-following, he does recognize rules' dependence on the practices that they supposedly govern.[49] So rules only 'generate' practice in a very weak sense.

The other aspect of structure is resources, which are either authoritative or allocative, depending on whether they give command over persons or objects respectively. I shall have more to say about them when I come to discuss Giddens's account of power. What I wish to stress here is that he describes resources as 'media' or 'means' that are 'utilized' by agents seeking their own ends, and thereby (unintentionally) reproducing society.[50] Structure thus understood in no way constitutes social action. It is conceived instrumentally, as a tool used by agents in order to realize their wants.

Surprisingly, since Giddens often belabours Marx for identifying human practice with the material work of transforming nature,[51] his is a remarkably economic conception of practice, in which agents use scarce resources to achieve their ends. There seems to me no way of genuinely distinguishing this position from Popper's, whose methodological individualism is precisely a generalization of neo classical economics' model of rational action.

Habermas's recent comments on Giddens go to the heart of the matter. Giddens's 'concept of practice', Habermas writes,

is supposed to be related to the constitution of action-complexes and to their reproduction. I do not think that this choice of conceptual strategy is a fortunate one, because the basic epistemological concept of 'constitution', which refers to the formation of object-domains, causes confusion in social theory. It suggests that speaking and acting subjects 'produce' their social life-context in a way similar to that in

---

[48] *CPST*, pp. 139–41.   [49] Ibid. 59–69.
[50] Ibid. 92.   [51] For example, *CCHM*, p. 53.

which they make products of instrumental action [i.e., labour] . . .
The over extension of action-concepts in a theory of constitution
remains stuck in metaphors; the basic concept of the philosophy of
Praxis gives at best an anthropomorphistic concept of society.[52]

Habermas has put his finger on the central fault in Giddens's
theory of structuration. The way in which Giddens concep-
tualizes structure means that it can only function as a
secondary aspect of social practice, subject to the creative
interventions of 'knowledgeable human agents'. The result, as
Habermas points out, is 'an anthropomorphistic concept of
society', in which the subject reigns supreme, producing
society as labour produces use-values. Far from overcoming
the dualism of agency and structure, Giddens is stuck firmly
at the pole of agency. The much-invoked 'duality of structure'
amounts to little more than a substitution of two letters—a
verbal change.

THE PARALOGISMS OF POWER

Similar conceptual sleight of hand characterizes Giddens's
account of power. The concept of power is central to his
critique of Marxism. Thus,

a fundamental component of my arguments is that the articulation
of space-time relations in social systems has to be examined in
conjunction with the generation of *power*. A preoccupation with
power forms a leading thread of this book. I maintain that power
was never satisfactorily theorized by Marx, and that this failure is at
the origin of some of the chief limitations of his scheme of historical
analysis.[53]

There are three main steps in Giddens's conceptualization of
power. First, he argues that 'the notion of "action" . . . is
logically tied to that of power . . . Action intrinsically involves the
application of "means" to achieve outcomes, brought about
through the direct intervention of an actor in a course of
events.'[54] 'Power' is understood here as 'the transformative

---

[52] J. Habermas, 'A Reply to my Critics', in J. B. Thompson and D. Held
(eds.), *Habermas: Critical Debates* (London: Macmillan, 1982), p. 286.
[53] *CCHM*, p. 3.   [54] *NRSM*, p. 110.

capacity of human agency', that is, as 'the capability of the
actor to intervene in a series of events so as to alter their
course; as such it is the "can" which mediates between
intentions and wants and the actual realization of the
outcomes sought after.'[55]

The second step involves introducing a 'narrower, relational
sense' of 'power' as a 'property of interaction', 'power as
domination'.[56] It arises 'where transformative capacity is
harnessed to actors' attempts to get others to comply with their
wants'.[57] The result is 'structures of domination' which
'involve *asymmetries of resources employed* in the sustaining of
power-relations in and between systems of interaction'.[58]
Giddens distinguishes between two main forms of domination,
allocation and authorization, depending on which type
of resource is unequally distributed. Allocative resources
comprise 'material features of the environment', 'material
means of production/reproduction', and 'produced goods'.
Giddens's account of authoritative resources, which consist in
the 'organization of social time-space', 'production/reproduction
of the human body', and 'organization of human life-chances',
is a good deal less perspicuous: these resources are something
of a residual category.[59] Nevertheless, the gist is clear enough:
allocation is essentially economic domination, authorization
politico-ideological.

The third step is to use these concepts to offer a theory of
historical development. Giddens claims that power and
domination are inherent in human social life.[60] The chief
variation is in the form of domination. Prior to capitalism,
Giddens argues, authorization was the prevailing form. He
distinguishes between class-divided and class societies. In
both categories classes, i.e., 'the sectional forms of domination
created by private ownership of property',[61] are to be found.
However, in a class-divided society 'class analysis does
not serve as a basis for identifying the basic structural
principles of organization of that society.'[62] Class-divided
societies compromise all 'non-capitalist civilizations'—city

---

[55] *NRSM*, p. 111.   [56] Ibid.   [57] *CPST*, p. 43.   [58] Ibid.
[59] *CCHM*, pp. 51–2.   [60] Ibid. 28–9.   [61] Ibid. 107.
[62] Ibid. 108.

states, empires, and feudal societies. The structures of domination in these societies depend upon the distribution of authoritative resources. 'In class-divided societies, as opposed to class society, *authorization has primacy over allocation.*'[63] Capitalism is the only case of a class society; here alone does allocation prevail. The only limited validity historical materialism possesses is in its analysis of capitalism, where economic factors do predominate over ideological and political ones.

I wish to criticize this account of power, but let me first stress its virtues. Giddens's is not a harmonistic theory of society. At its centre is contradiction, power, and struggle. This is its merit, compared with those of Parsons and Habermas, for whom power serves primarily to integrate social systems, and to dampen down social conflict.[64] Giddens's is a view of society having much in common with Weber's, and, as I shall try to show, it is with Weber that he is best compared, despite his assertions to the contrary.

A crucial element in Giddens's strategy is the shift from the broad to the restricted conceptions of power, from power as transformative capacity to power as domination. He is quite explicit in insisting that it is the broad concept of power that grounds the claim that domination is inherent in social life. For example,

all social interaction involves the use of power, as a necessary implication of the logical connection between human action and *transformative capacity.* Power within social systems can be analyzed as
relations of autonomy and dependence between actors in which
these actors draw upon and reproduce structural properties of domination.[65]

Similarly, 'transformative capacity . . . forms the basis of human action—the "could have done otherwise" inherent in the concept of action—and at the same time connects action to domination and power.'[66]

---

[63] *CPST*, p. 162.
[64] See A. Giddens, ' "Power" in the Recent Writings of Talcott Parsons', in Giddens, *Studies in Social and Political Theory* (London: Hutchinson, 1977) and 'Labour and Interaction', in *PCST*.
[65] *CCHM*, pp. 28–9.   [66] Ibid. 53.

If we are to take these passages as suggesting that one may infer from the 'logical connection' between transformative capacity and action to domination as a persisting feature of social interaction—and that is what expressions such as 'necessary implication' would lead us to believe—then Giddens is guilty of an obvious fallacy. I doubt if anyone would wish to question whether 'action' is 'logically tied' to 'transformative capacity', but recognition of the involvement of power thus understood in human action does not commit one to very much. For 'transformative capacity' understood as 'the capability . . . to intervene in a series of events so as to alter their course' is a property of *all* causal agents, not merely human ones. Indeed, 'transformative capacity' seems in reality to be merely another expression for 'causal powers', since such powers consist precisely in the ability to bring about some alteration in the course of the world.[67] It is true that Giddens makes much of 'the "could have done otherwise" inherent in the concept of action', presumably referring to the unique property of human beings to reflect upon and choose between alternative interventions. But this consideration does not bear on the *nature* of 'transformative capacity' but rather on human agents' peculiar ability consciously to control and monitor the exercise of their causal powers.

It is one thing to attribute to human beings this 'transformative capacity'. It is quite another to infer from this true but rather trivial proposition the much more interesting, but controversial (and, in my view, false) thesis that power in the sense of domination is intrinsic to human life. There is no necessary connection between the two concepts of power. Further premises would be required to justify the inference from transformative capacity to domination. Interestingly enough, a similar point has been made recently by Foucault. He distinguishes between 'objective capacity', 'which is exerted over things and gives the ability to modify, use, consume, or destroy them', and 'power, which brings into play relations between individuals (or between groups)'. 'Objective capacities' and 'power-relations', Foucault insists,

[67] See, for example, R. Harré and E. Madden, *Causal Powers* (Oxford: Basil Blackwell, 1975).

'should not . . . be confused'.[68] Although Giddens distinguishes carefully between the broad and restricted sense of power, it is difficult not to feel that when he claims that 'transformative capacity . . . connects action to domination and power', he is guilty of an equivocation. The result is a paralogism, in which the same word, 'power', is used in different senses in the premise and conclusion of the same argument.

It does not seem to me, for reasons that I will make clear shortly, that this elementary logical mistake is necessarily fatal for Giddens's account of domination. But since he makes so much of the notion of 'transformative capacity' it is worth pointing out how little use of this concept commits one to. This brings out a common feature of Giddens's writings, namely, that they are prolific of neologisms and, more frequently, of redefinitions of familiar words, without these new concepts, and the complex typologies often accompanying them, usually offering much gain in clarity or empirical reach. *Central Problems in Social Theory* is especially guilty of this, an arid treatise heaping definitions and diagrams on the bewildered reader's head. From this point of view *A Contemporary Critique* is especially to be welcomed, since here Giddens cashes his conceptual cheques, putting the typologies of *Central Problems* to work in order to provide an account of historical development different from Marx's.

It is here that one might quite reasonably say in Giddens's defence that his analysis of domination can stand on its own legs, without the support of 'transformative capacity'. The test of its validity will then turn on whether it explains a series of phenomena that Marxism cannot. This argument is a cogent one, and can only be answered by turning, at last, to the concrete detail of Giddens's critique of Marx.

MARXISM AND EVOLUTIONISM

The Marxism that Giddens seeks to transcend is an evolutionist one, in which social change is an outcome of the level of development of the productive forces. Such a view of historical

[68] M. Foucault, 'The Subject and Power', afterword to H. L. Dreyfus and P. Rabinow, *Michel Foucault* (Brighton: Harvester, 1982), pp. 217–18.

development is characteristic of Marxism in general: 'Marxist authors are virtually everywhere committed to evolutionism in one guise or another.'[69] Only in those sections of the *Grundrisse* where he discusses pre-capitalist social formations (the so-called *Formen*) does Marx himself adopt a different approach: 'rather than implying that the forces of production have their own internal dynamic, as in his evolutionary view, Marx seems in the *Formen* to give primacy to "ecological" factors (dispersal or concentration of populations) and to war in stimulating social transformation.'[70]

Giddens seeks to disprove Marx's evolutionary theory and substantiate his own theory of domination by providing an account of historical development in which it is the distribution of authoritative resources that has primacy until the development of capitalism. We have already seen that he believes history to be a process of time-space distanciation in which the high presence-availability of tribal societies is progressively lost. These changes are highly significant for the manner in which societies are integrated. Giddens distinguishes between societal and system integration. Societal integration involves the relationships between individual social actors; systems integration concerns the connections between social groups and collectivities.[71] In tribal societies the two forms of integration are fused, so that system-integration, the relations between groups, is dependent on the face-to-face contacts between individuals·and the traditions and kinship networks with which these contacts are intimately bound.

The two forms of integration are separated with the emergence of class-divided societies. Societal integration still depends on kinship and tradition, and small localized communities continue to form the basis of these societies. However, system-integration depends increasingly on the power of the state, and the authoritative resources that it is able to mobilize. The extraction of surplus-labour from these communities depends on the intervention of the state, and takes the form of deductions—taxation, rent, etc.—leaving much of their daily life unaffected. The necessary authoritative

[69] *CCHM*, p. 20.   [70] Ibid. 80.
[71] Ibid. 161–66; *CPST*, pp. 76 ff.

resources to mount such control over local communities required the development of new forms of 'information storage', such as writing, that in turn depended on the emergence of the city. It is the rise of the city, 'the generator of the authoritative resources out of which state-power is created and sustained',[72] not the development of the productive forces, that is the decisive factor in the emergence of classes.

Capitalism, like 'class-divided societies', separates societal and system integration. However, the content of these two forms of integration is radically changed. The extraction of surplus-labour comes to depend, not on the direct intervention of coercive power, but rather on economic mechanisms, the pressures, analysed by Marx in *Capital*, that force workers to sell their labour-power. Capitalism is thus characterized, as Giddens has earlier stressed in *The Class Structure of the Advanced Societies*, by 'a "separation" between economy and policy such that there is at least a substantial scope for the play of market mechanisms independent of active political control'.[73] But he now accounts for the 'insulation' of economy and policy on the grounds that 'only with the advent of capitalism does an exploitative class relation become part of the very mechanism of the productive process'.[74]

The other side of the separation of state and market is the transformation of the state into 'a much more intrusive and comprehensive set of institutions in capitalist than in class-divided societies, so far as those subject to its administration "internally" are concerned'.[75] No longer is societal integration left to kinship and tradition. The dependence of the capitalist economy upon the capacity of producers continually to increase their output requires an enormous expansion of state-directed apparatuses of surveillance, by which Giddens means both the accumulation of information, and what Foucault calls the disciplines, the systematic supervision and regulation of the activities of those involved in a variety of institutions— factories, armies, prisons. Consequently, the 'crucible of power' is no longer the city, but the nation-state, a phenomenon

---

[72] *CCHM*, p. 145.   [73] *CSAS*, p. 134.
[74] Ibid. 298 (1979 Postscript).
[75] *CCHM*, p. 165.

whose significance Giddens believes Marxism largely to have ignored.[76]

Nevertheless, I suspect that most people, confronted with this account of historical development, would be puzzled as to why it should be regarded, with all its stress on changing modes of surplus-extraction, as in any sense critical of, or an alternative to Marxism. Giddens's reply would presumably be that Marxism accords primacy to the productive forces, attributing to them an 'internal dynamic' that is the source of all historical change. Now it is true that such is one version of Marxism, most eloquently defended recently by G. A. Cohen in his *Karl Marx's Theory of History: a Defence*. It is not, however, the only version of Marxism, nor is it, as I have argued elsewhere, the most adequate.[77] Furthermore, I think it can be shown that it is a view that Marx himself progressively abandons.[78]

However, as Erik Olin Wright persuasively argues, rejection of evolutionist Marxism does not require the abandonment of *any* notion of historical evolution.[79] The crucial distinction, he suggests, is that between teleological versions of historical materialism that conceive social formations as evolving towards a predetermined goal, and those that adopt a weaker and unobjectionable evolutionary theory. Wright urges that all such a theory must claim is that 'there is some process, however weak and sporadic, which imparts a directionality to movements from one form to another.'[80] Indeed, he suggests, Giddens's own account of history as a process of time-space-distanciation, in which time and space are progressively stretched, and 'the immediacy of presence'[81] gradually lost, meets the conditions for an evolutionary theory: 'Because of the link between conflict, power, resources and distanciation, there will be at least some impulse for increasing space-time distanciation.'[82]

[76] Ibid. 147.
[77] See A. Callinicos, *Is there a Future for Marxism?* (London: Macmillan, 1982), pp. 142–7 and id., *Marxism and Philosophy* (Oxford: Clarendon Press, 1983), pp. 110–13.
[78] See Callinicos, *Marxism and Philosophy*, ch. 2.
[79] Wright, 'Giddens's Critique of Marxism', pp. 25–34.
[80] Ibid. 26.   [81] *CCHM*, p. 157.
[82] Wright, 'Giddens's Critique of Marxism', p. 31.

Giddens cannot in any case dispense with the notion of the development of the productive forces as easily as he would like. Writing, which Giddens believes to have developed 'as a means of recording information relevant to the administration of societies',[83] may have in fact originated in the clay tokens used by Neolithic farmers to keep track of their food stores.[84] More generally, time-space distanciation crucially depends on technological innovations—improvements in transport, new systems for transmitting information, etc. The stretching of space and time is in no sense a process autonomous of the development of the productive forces.

To argue in this manner is not, however, to accord causal primacy to the productive forces. Their development is best understood, in my view, as a necessary, but not sufficient condition of changes in social relations. Furthermore, the scope for developing the productive forces is determined by the prevailing relations of production. These relations are best conceived as a specific mode of appropriation of surplus-labour, which in turn depends upon the distribution of the means of production. Forces and relations mutually limit one another, rather than the one exerting primacy over the other.[85]

Now the relations of production thus conceived seem to me perfectly capable of accounting for the shift from authoritative to allocative domination on which Giddens places such stress. Marx himself provides such an explanation in his crucial chapter. 'Genesis of Capitalist Ground-Rent' in *Capital* volume 3.[86] There he argues that

in all forms in which the direct labourer remains the 'possessor' of the means of production and labour-conditions necessary for the production of his own means of subsistence, the property relation-ship must simultaneously appear as a direct relation of lordship and servitude, so that the direct producer is not free; a lack of freedom which may be reduced from serfdom with enforced labour

[83] *CCHM*, p. 95.
[84] D. Schmandt-Besserat, 'The Earliest Precursor of Writing', in *Prehistoric Times: Readings from* Scientific American, ed. B. M. Fagan (San Francisco: W. H. Freeman and Co., 1983).
[85] See, Callinicos, *Future*, chs. 6 and 7.
[86] K. Marx, *Capital*, iii (Moscow: Progress, 1971), pp. 782–813.

to a mere tributary relationship. The direct producer, according to our assumption, is found here in possession of his own means of production, the necessary material labour conditions required for the realization of his labour and the production of his means of subsistence . . . Under such conditions the surplus-labour for the nominal owner of the land can only be extorted from them [the direct producers] by other than economic means.[87]

As a conceptualization of feudal relations of production this account is not wholly unproblematic.[88] Nevertheless, it has provided the basis of at least one major empirical study of late feudalism.[89] And it does provide a means for accounting for the apparent primacy of 'authoritative domination' in pre-capitalist social formations. Surplus-labour can be appropriated by a ruling class where the direct producers themselves control the labour-process only through the systematic use of the means of coercion. By contrast, the complete separation of the direct producers from the means of production under capitalism accords primacy to economic mechanisms in the extraction of surplus-labour. As Marx puts it, 'the silent compulsion of economic relations sets the seal on the domination of the capitalist over the worker. Direct extra-economic force is still of course used, but only in exceptional cases.'[90]

Now Giddens is perfectly well aware of this analysis. Indeed his own account of the differences between class-divided and class societies depends crucially upon it, as he acknowledges.[91] Some of the most suggestive parts of *A Contemporary Critique*, for example his demonstration of how the mechanisms of 'surveillance' described by Foucault can only be understood in the light of the mode of surplus-extraction peculiar to capitalism,[92] are best taken as a development of Marx's own account. Why, then, does Giddens believe that his version of historical development is an alternative to Marx's?

---

[87] K. Marx, *Capital*, iii (Moscow: Progress, 1971), pp. 790–1.

[88] See B. Hindess and P. Hirst, *Precapitalist Modes of Production* (London: Routledge and Kegan Paul, 1975).

[89] G. Bois, *Crise du feodalisme* (Paris: Presses de la Fondation Nationale des Sciences Politiques, 1976).

[90] K. Marx, *Capital*, i (Harmondsworth: Penguin, 1976), p. 899.

[91] *CCHM*, p. 122. See generally ibid. 107–28.   [92] Ibid. 157–81.

There seem to be at least three reasons. The first is Giddens's persisting methodological commitment, as I have shown earlier in this article, to a .version of interpretive sociology, which gives the subject primacy over structures, and treats power in the sense of domination as intrinsic to social life. I shall have a little to say about this at the end of this section. Secondly, Giddens, as we have seen, misinterprets Marxism, treating it as necessarily evolutionist, that is, as an interpretation of history as inevitable progress toward a predetermined goal.

It is, however, the third reason to which I wish first to devote some attention. This is Giddens's tendency to identify the relations of production with market-relationships. This is most obvious in the case of *The Class Structure of the Advanced Societies*, where he argues, for example, that 'classes are *large-scale* groupings' whose existence depends upon 'the formation of market-relationships'.[93] He concludes, not surprisingly, that neither feudalism nor what he chooses to call 'state socialism' are class societies. Moreover, in capitalism itself 'the system of exploitation operates through differentials in market capacity.'[94] On this basis, Giddens distinguishes between three classes in capitalism—the bourgeoisie, owning the means of production, manual workers, owning labour-power, and an intermediate class today composed largely of white-collar workers whose greater skill than manual workers enhances their 'market capacity'.

While Giddens's analysis of class-relations is considerably more sophisticated in *A Contemporary Critique*, as well as (because?) closer to Marx, he continues to identify class with market relations. Thus he argues that in class-divided societies, class is less important than under capitalism because the main form of private property, land, is alienable only to a limited degree, if at all.[95] The salience of class and the development of the market are directly related.

With Marx, however, the existence of classes depends upon the monopolization of the means of production by a minority and their consequent ability to appropriate surplus-labour. It is entirely a secondary matter whether these means of

[93] *CSAS*, p. 84. [94] Ibid. 131.
[95] *CCHM*, pp. 113–17.

production are commodities that may be purchased and sold on the market. (Even under capitalism land is a very peculiar sort of commodity.) The relations of production may well contradict the apparent organization of society, what I have called elsewhere a social formation's form of articulation. Thus, in the case of feudalism, the dependence of surplus-extraction on coercion means that the relations of production 'appear as a direct relation of lordship and servitude'. Social stratification consequently takes the form of a status hierarchy, the division of society into estates, that contradicts the underlying class-relationships. Similarly, under capitalism the relations of production take the form of market relation-ships, of apparently equal and reciprocal relations between commodity-owners. In the crucial chapter of *Capital* volume 1, 'The Sale and Purchase of Labour-Power', Marx stresses the disjunction between this apparent equality and the underlying inequality between the capitalist who owns the means of production and the worker who has nothing but his or her labour-power.[96]

Yet when we turn to Giddens we find that the main lesson he takes from Marx is that of 'the centrality of the *labour-contract* to the capitalist system'.[97] It is not, however, the labour contract, but the distribution of the means of production underpinning it that is crucial for Marx. Giddens's discussion of class and capitalism can be said to suffer from two serious weaknesses. First, it tends to overemphasize the importance of commodity production for capitalism. This is reflected, for example, in his introduction of the notion of a commodification of time under capitalism, which raises issues too complex to be discussed here, but which seems to me to be both overstated and misleading.[98] (The difficulties Giddens experiences here are in my view bound up with his rather unsteady grasp on Marx's economic theory. Of his discussion of Marx's theory of money, for example, where Giddens says that for Marx 'money becomes a commodity only because it represents or symbolizes the exchange-value of all other commodities'[99]—the exact reverse of Marx's own view, the less said the better.) Secondly, there is a tendency to confuse

---

[96] Marx, *Capital*, i. 270–80.　　[97] *CSAS*, pp. 298–9 (1979 Postcript).
[98] *CCHM*, pp. 130 ff.　　　　　[99] Ibid. 116.

juridical property forms, such as the labour-contract, with the relations of production. What Marx is concerned with is not legal entitlement but effective possession.[100]

Giddens is, in my view, insufficiently aware of the fact that, for Marx, the relations of production and class are analytical concepts rather than descriptive categories. In other words, they are intended to uncover underlying relationships precisely because the latter's nature is not directly observable. Giddens consequently commits what Whitehead called the fallacy of misplaced concreteness, supposing that it is only when the division of society into economic classes is directly visible, as under capitalism, that historical materialism can be said to be valid.

Marx had in a sense already responded to Giddens's 'contemporary' critique when he answered in *Capital* volume 1 a 'German-American publication' that had argued that the materialist conception of history 'is all very true for our own times, in which material interests are preponderant, but not for the Middle Ages, dominated by Catholicism, nor for Athens and Rome, dominated by politics'. Marx replied that 'one thing is clear: the Middle Ages could not live on Catholicism, nor could the ancient world on politics. On the contrary, it is the manner in which they gained their livelihood which explains why in one case politics, in the other case Catholicism, played the chief part.'[101] The role of the concept of the relations of production is precisely to explain the changes in the forms of domination.

One might recast the points I have just made in slightly more formal terms, drawing on recent work in the philosophy of science. Imre Lakatos distinguished between a scientific research programme's heuristic, the set of privileged propositions forming its 'hard core' and specifying procedures for resolving problems, and the 'protective belt' of revisable and empirically falsifiable auxiliary hypotheses surrounding the

[100] See K. Marx and F. Engels, *Collected Works*, 50 vols. (London: Lawrence and Wishart, 1975–   ), vi. 197 and xxxviii. 99, Hindess and Hirst *passim*, and G. A. Cohen, *Karl Marx's Theory of History: a Defence* (Oxford: Clarendon Press, 1978), pp. 217–5.

[101] Marx, *Capital* i. 176 n.

heuristic.[102] Progress within a research programme depends, Lakatos argued, on the empirically successful modification and elaboration of auxiliary hypotheses along lines suggested by the heuristic. One could say, in the case of Marxism, that its heuristic consists in the basic concepts and propositions of historical materialism, while the auxiliary hypotheses are analyses of specific modes of production, social formations, and conjunctures.[103] Much of the point of auxiliary hypotheses is to account for phenomena that apparently contradict the factual claims made in the heuristic. An example of such recalcitrant phenomena in the case of Marxism are the pre-capitalist societies in which authoritative rather than allocative domination seems to prevail. Giddens, because he fails to distinguish between the different theoretical levels of a scientific research programme, believes that the mere existence of these societies counts as a refutation of historical materialism.

It is an implication of this argument that the proof of the pudding is in the eating. Is historical materialism capable of providing empircally satisfactory analyses of pre-capitalist societies? The work of Marxist historians suggests that it is. One example must do. G. E. M. de Ste Croix's *The Class Struggle in the Ancient Greek World* is notable, not only for the wealth of scholarship, and ethical and political passion that it displays, but because it is, as Perry Anderson says, 'one of the most strenuously theoretical works of history ever to be produced' in Britain.[104] Of particular importance is the manner in which Ste Croix uses Marx's theory of class in effect as a heuristic, that is, as the basis on which to formulate empirical propositions concerning the social structure of Antiquity. Rather than concentrate on the description of visible status differences, in the manner of M. I. Finley, Ste

[102] I. Lakatos, *Philosophical Papers*, 2 vols. (Cambridge: Cambridge University Press, 1978), esp. i, ch. 1.

[103] For a similar use of the distinction between heuristic and auxiliary hypotheses see A. Gilbert, *Marx's Politics* (Oxford: Martin Robinson, 1981), pp. 5–13 and 'The Storming of Heaven: Politics and Marx's *Capital*', in J. R. Pennock and J. W. Chapman (eds.), *Marxism* (*Nomos XXVI*, New York: New York University Press, 1983), pp. 151–61.

[104] P. Anderson, 'Class Struggle in the Ancient World', *History Workshop*, 16 (1983), 58.

Croix uses the basic concepts of historical materialism both to anatomize classical society, and to provide a dynamic explanation of its development.[105] His book is a formidable challenge to Giddens's claim that Marxism offers insight only into the workings of capitalism.

Let me now return to the two reasons for Giddens's rejection of historical materialism other than his misunderstanding of Marx's theory of class—namely, his methodological commitment to interpretive sociology, and his identification of Marxism with evolutionism. One might imagine a connection between the two. I have already mentioned Giddens's vigorous objection to functionalism. Not unnaturally, he tends to associate evolutionism with the use of functional explanations, since both tend to treat society as a self-reproducing organism with its own needs.[106] Now Giddens might argue that any Marxism that continues to accord primacy to structures over subjects must necessarily rely on the tacit or open use of functional explanations that effectively reduce agents to the 'supports' of structures. The thought would be that however much Marxists such as Wright and myself might like to repudiate evolutionist and functionalist Marxism, that is all the Marxism there is.

Giddens could appeal for support to G. A. Cohen. Rejecting Jon Elster's proposal that historical materialism be reconstructed along methodological individualist lines, Cohen correctly insists that 'Marxism is *fundamentally* concerned not with behaviour, but with the forces and relations [of production] constraining and directing it', but asserts also that the constraining and directing role of these forces and relations can only be explicated by means of functional explanations: 'if functional explanation is unacceptable in social theory then historical materialism cannot be reformed and must be rejected.'[107]

---

[105] G. E. M. de Ste Croix, *The Class Struggle in the Ancient Greek World* (London: Duckworth, 1981), ch. 2.

[106] See especially the critiques of functional explanation in J. Elster, *Ulysses and the Sirens* (Cambridge: Cambridge University Press, 1979) and id., 'Marxism, Functionalism and Games Theory'.

[107] G. A. Cohen, 'Reply to Elster on "Marxism, Functionalism, and Game Theory"', *Theory and Society*, 11. 4 (1982), 489, 483 [pp. 96, 89 above].

This line of thought is not compelling. It is perfectly possible to follow Giddens in rejecting functional explanation, while continuing to accord primacy to structures over agents. The key lies in Giddens's own conceptualization of structures as both enabling *and* constraining. Thus we may accept one of the standard accounts of action made available by contemporary analytical philosophy, conceiving agents' behaviour as proximately caused by their intentions, beliefs, and desires, while treating the powers instantiated in this behaviour as to a large extent structurally determined. In other words, what agents can collectively or individually do depends to a significant degree on their position in the relations of production. The objection to the philosophies of action formulated within the analytical or hermeneutic traditions would then be not so much that such theories are false, or part of a 'problematic of the subject', as that they are *empty*, lacking as they do an empirical account of the historically variable structural determinants of action.

Obviously these remarks are more hand-waving than a properly formulated argument. Nevertheless, they serve to suggest that the dilemma between functionalism and hermeneutics, to which Giddens offers the theory of structuration as a solution, does not exhaust the available alternatives.

CAPITALISM, SOCIALISM, AND THE STATE

Let me turn now to consider some rather surprising criticisms of Marxism that Giddens makes towards the end of *A Contemporary Critique*. These centre on the role of the state and violence. He writes, for example, that 'Marxism has no tradition of theorizing violence either as an integral and chronic feature of repression, or of the "world violence" of the contemporary system of power blocs and nation-states.'[108] This is related to the historical claim that the development of capitalism was bound up with the formation of a European power-system dominated by the great absolutist states, so that 'capitalism developed within a military "cockpit" in which the

[108] *CCHM*, p. 250.

expansion of industrial production very soon came to be seen by all ruling groups as the *sine qua non* of national survival.'[109] 'The conjunction between the rise of capitalism and the absolutist state system produced a system of nation-states that, far from being ephemeral, is integral to the world capitalist economy—which is at one and the same time a world military order.'[110]

I describe these criticisms as 'surprising' because many of the statements I have just cited, which Giddens clearly believes to be damaging criticisms of Marxism, are from the standpoint of Marxism platitudinous. The notion, for example, of the state as constituted by violence, by the existence of what Lenin called 'special bodies of armed men', is a central theme of such texts as *The Civil War in France*, *The Origin of the Family, Private Property and the State*, and *The State and Revolution*. The more usual criticism of Marxist writing on the state is that it overestimates the role of violence as 'an integral and chronic feature of repression'.

Again, to take the case of absolutism, Marx in his writings on France traces the origins of the modern capitalist state to the absolute monarchies of the *ancien régime*. The role of the quasi-absolutist Tudor state in promoting the development of capitalism through the systematic use of coercion, and of the world power struggle between the European states in contributing to the 'primitive accumulation' of capital are well-known themes of part eight of *Capital* volume 1.

Then there is the matter of the 'world capitalist economy'. Giddens writes as if this were a concept discovered a few years ago by Immanuel Wallerstein, rather than being a theme of Marx's own economic writings, which assumed central importance for those who sought to develop the analyses they contain. It was precisely on the capitalist world-system that the two generations of Marxists after Marx focused their attention. The result was numerous texts by Kautsky, Hilferding's *Finance Capital*, Luxemburg's *The Accumulation of Capital*, Lenin's *Imperialism*, and Bukharin's *Imperialism and World Economy* and *The Economics of the Transformation Period*. Lenin and Bukharin in particular stress that with the emergence of

---

[109] Ibid. 190.   [110] Ibid. 198.

imperialism competition between capitals increasingly took the form of military competition between nation-states.

I do not wish to claim that this body of writing on the state and the world system is wholly satisfactory or adequate. But it exists. It is true that the whole body of work to which I have referred was vulgarized and integrated into a highly evolutionist form of Marxism with the triumph of Stalinism. Moreover, the various schools of Western Marxism were largely, though by no means wholly, uninterested in the type of economic and political analysis characteristic of classical Marxism.

But even at the height of Stalinism's grip on Marxism evolutionism did not go unchallenged. For example, Giddens lays great stress on the concept of 'time-space edges', by which he means 'the simultaneous inter-connected existence of different types of society. This helps to free us from the tendency of evolutionary thought to analyse societal development in terms of "stages", and from the influence of "unfolding models" of change.'[111] Compare this, with, for example, the opening chapters of Trotsky's *History of the Russian Revolution*, where central importance is given to 'the law of *combined development*—by which I mean a drawing together of the different stages of the journey, a combining of separate steps, an amalgam of archaic with more contemporary forms'.[112] Trotsky uses the concepts of uneven and combined development to explain why socialist revolution occurred first in Russia, rather than, as evolutionist Marxism had predicted, in the more advanced capitalist countries. (Incidentally, Giddens himself had earlier offered a highly evolutionist explanation of this revolution, arguing that 'the [manual] working class is most likely to achieve a high degree of revolutionary class consciousness in the initial phase of the industrialization process.')[113]

---

[111] *CCHM*, p. 83.

[112] L. Trotsky, *The History of the Russian Revolution*, 3 vols. (London: Sphere, 1967), i. 23. See G. Novack, *Understanding History* (New York: Monad, 1972), B. Knei-Paz, *The Social and Political Thought of Leon Trotsky* (Oxford: Clarendon Press, 1978), pp. 62–107, and M. Löwy, *The Politics of Combined and Uneven Development* (London: NLB, 1981), chs. 1–3.

[113] *CSAS*, p. 153.

The revival of Marxist theory in the past decade and a half has seen a significant return to the classical focus on the world-system and the state. Giddens cites, but does not discuss Poulantzas's last book, *State, Power, Socialism*, which is concerned precisely with the essential role of the organized violence of the state in both the constitution and the reproduction of the relations of production.[114] Giddens describes Perry Anderson's *Lineages of the Absolutist State* as 'a fundamental source',[115] but does not address the central thesis of that book, which is that the absolutist state must be understood as a form of feudal class rule. Although it is true to say that much of the 'state-derivation' debate among German Marxists has been sterile and formalistic in the extreme, nevertheless a number of contributions to that and connected debates, notably those by Claudia von Braumuhl, Colin Barker, and Cesare Luporini, have focused on a theme that Giddens appropriates as his own, namely the claim that capitalism involves a system of competing nation-states whose origins are to be found in the absolutist era.[116] These texts all deal with the centrality of war to that system, as do Anderson in his discussion of absolutism, and the theorists of the permanent arms economy (T. N. Vance, Michael Kidron, and Christ Harman) in their analyses of contemporary capitalism.[117]

The interesting question to arise from all this is why so erudite, and, in many ways, so friendly a critic of Marxism as Giddens, should come to ignore so large and important a body of writing. There are, I think, at least two reasons. The first has to do with sociology's general failure to confront Marxism as a political tradition. With the very important exception of Marx himself, classical Marxism is not discussed by Giddens.

[114] *CCHM*, p. 279 n. 16.   [115] Ibid. 275 n. 5.

[116] See C. von Braumuhl, 'The Analysis of the Nation-State within the World Market Context', in *State and Capital*, eds. J. Holloway and S. Picciotto (London: Arnold, 1978), C. Barker, 'The State as Capital', *International Socialism*, 2. 1 (1978), and C. Luporini, '"Politique" et "Étatique"', in E. Balibar *et al.*, *Marx et la critique de la politique* (Paris: Maspero, 1979).

[117] See T. Vance, *The Permanent Arms Economy* (Berkeley, 1970), M. Kidron, *Western Capitalism since the War* (Harmondsworth: Penguin, 1970), and C. Harman, *Explaining the Crisis* (London: Bookmarks, 1984).

Lenin, Hilferding, and Gramsci each appear once in the index of *A Contemporary Critique*, Engels, Luxemburg, Trotsky, and Bukharin not at all. Althusser and Poulantzas, on the other hand, receive generous attention.

Why does this matter? Because the theoretical writings of the classical Marxists have an irreducibly political orientation. Their intellectual activity bore an intrinsic connection to their participation as revolutionary socialists in working-class movements. This active involvement in politics explains why what Perry Anderson calls the 'areas most central to the classical traditions of historical materialism' were 'scrutiny of the economic laws of motion of capitalism as a mode of production, analysis of the political machinery of the bourgeois state, strategy of the class struggle necessary to overthrow it'.[118] The political orientation of classical Marxism has, however, made it a difficult tradition for academic social science to engage with. It is, for example, only in the past few years, and largely as a result of the radicalization produced in the late 1960s and early 1970s, that serious studies of the political thought of Marx and Lenin have appeared.[119] On the whole, sociologists have found it easier to address those Marxists, such as the Frankfurt school and Althusser and his followers, whose theoretical preoccupations are largely detached from political activity, and are therefore much more readily assimilable to a purely academic discourse. Although there is a political undercurrent to Giddens's work (*A Contemporary Critique* is the first in a two-volume attempt to rethink socialist theory),[120] he shares this common failure to grasp the distinctive nature of classical Marxism.

The second reason for Giddens's highly selective reading of Marxism has to do with his latent Weberianism. When he says that 'Marxism has no tradition of theorizing violence' he may mean, not so much that Marxism ignores the

[118] P. Anderson, *Considerations on Western Marxism* (London: NLB, 1976), pp. 44–5.

[119] See, for example, H. Draper, *Karl Marx's Theory of Revolution*, 2 vols. (New York: Monthly Review Press, 1977 and 1978), A. Gilbert, *Marx's Politics* (Oxford, 1981), T. Cliff, *Lenin*, 4 vols. (London: Pluto, 1975–9), N. Harding, *Lenin's Political Thought*, 2 vols. (London: Macmillan, 1977 and 1981).

[120] *CCHM*, pp. 3, 24–5.

phenomenon of violence, as that it has no satisfactory explanation of it. Marxism, Giddens might say, recognizes the existence of violence; it even seeks to explain it—for example, in the way that Engels and Lenin do, in terms of class exploitation and the specific political structures to which it gives rise. But, Giddens might argue, these explanations will not do. Why will they not do? In part, because of the weaknesses specific to these explanations; and indeed Giddens subjects recent Marxist writing on the state to critical examination.[121]

But there is also, I think, an undercurrent to Giddens's arguments that suggests that any attempt to explain violence in terms of other factors is doomed to failure. Formulations such as 'an overwhelmingly obvious and chronic trait of human affairs—recourse to violence and war'[122] seem to imply that this 'trait' is an irreducible feature of social life. Any theory of violence that, like Marxism, treats it, at least in its more organized and destructive forms, as specific to certain forms of society (namely, those in which classes exist) is, from this perspective, necessarily mistaken. Such a line of argument, if present in Giddens's writings, is surely connected to his tendency to assimilate the two senses of power—transformative capacity and domination. For a theory of action implying that relations of domination are an essential characteristic of social formations can easily be made to issue in an account of violence that treats it as an equally 'chronic' and irreducible 'trait of human affairs'. The kinship between such a view of society and what Giddens himself acknowledges to be Weber's Nietzschean stress on power, conflict, and violence[123] is obvious.

The Weberian drift of Giddens's argument is evident when we consider one of his other criticisms of Marxism. He argues that Marx, by focusing on the extraction of surplus-labour, offered too narrowly economic an account of exploitation, which should properly be understood simply as 'domination *which is harnessed to sectional interests*'.[124] Giddens is then

[121] Ibid., ch. 9.
[122] Ibid. 177.
[123] Giddens, 'From Marx to Nietzsche?', p. 218.
[124] *CCHM*, p. 161.

able to identify forms of exploitation that Marxism has failed
to account for:

(*a*) exploitative relations between states, where these are strongly
influenced by military domination; (*b*) exploitative relations between
ethnic groups, which may or may not converge with the first; and
(*c*) exploitative relations between the sexes, sexual inequality . . .
These are major 'absences' in Marxist theory.[125]

What does it mean to talk here of ' "absences" in Marxist
theory'? If Giddens means that Marxism has consistently
ignored, or denied the existence of, say, racial and sexual
inequalities, then he is surely wrong. We can point to, for
example, Engels's *Origin of the Family*, the debates in the
Second International on the national question, and recent
Marxist work on racial oppression in South Africa. If Giddens
is saying that Marxism has failed to come up with a
satisfactory theory of phenomena such as nationality, then
I'm inclined to agree with him (though it's not clear that
orthodox social science has done any better). If, however, the
claim is that Marxism cannot provide such a theory, then
more argument is required in its support than Giddens gives.

Let me elaborate the last point by returning to the
distinction drawn above between the heuristic and the
auxiliary hypotheses of a scientific research programme.
The heuristic of historical materialism, consisting as it
does of concepts such as forces and relations of production,
exploitation, class, etc., does not make any reference to sexual,
ethnic, and inter-state relations. This is, however, in no sense
a decisive objection to Marxism. For the work of the heuristic
is done precisely in generating auxiliary hypotheses that must,
inter alia, provide empirical explanations of phenomena such
as racial inequality. The relative failure of classical Marxism
to come up with adequate theories of racial and sexual
oppression in comparison with the considerable body of
economic and political analyses to which I have already
referred arguably has less to do with any immanent 'class-
reductionist' logic than with political priorities that encouraged
the development of historical materialism in other directions.

This is in no sense an invitation to Marxists complacently

[125] *CCHM*, p. 242.

to ignore the many inadequacies of their theories. But it is to say that the mere existence of apparently aberrant phenomena does not refute historical materialism. What makes Marxism, despite its many 'crises', still the most powerful and challenging research programme in the social sciences is precisely the strength and implausibility of its basic claim, namely, that the variety and complexity of social life is to be explained ultimately in terms of the prevailing forces and relations of production. Intuitively this is no more credible a claim than was Galileo and Newton's aspiration to mathematize nature in the seventeenth century. Modern physics' success in accounting for phenomena that seem to refute it sets a model for Marxism's own ambition. Giddens, however, seems to believe that the very failure to build into the heuristic of historical materialism forms of 'exploitation' other than the extraction of surplus-labour counts against it. In doing so, he implicitly counterposes to Marxism what Erik Olin Wright calls 'a contingent causal pluralism',[126] in which inter-state conflict, and racial and sexual inequalities are of equal explanatory importance to class exploitation. His objection is thus indicative more of his own presumptions about what a true social theory would be like than of any inherent defect in Marxism.

Giddens's final objection to Marxism is also more revealing of his own views than it is of those he criticizes. The evolution of 'state socialism', he claims, shows that 'Marx's thought supplies precious few clues indeed about the continuing significance of power in socialist society.'[127] It all depends, of course, on what you mean by socialism. Giddens's main discussion of state socialism, not, to my knowledge, subsequently repudiated, is in *The Class Structure of the Advanced Societies*, where it is defined as '*any economic order in which the means of production is formally socialized in the hands of the state*'.[128] It follows from the premises of Giddens's theory of class that state socialism thus conceived cannot be a class society. For such a society requires the insulation of economy and polity that will permit market forces unrestrainedly to allocate

[126] Wright, 'Giddens's Critique of Marxism', p. 32.
[127] *CCHM*, p. 244.
[128] *CSAS*, p. 155.

people to their position in society. However, in state socialism, 'the forms of differentiation in market capacity which operates in capitalist societies are considerably modified'.[129] Consequently, 'the institutional mediation of power created by the integration of economy and polity . . . does provide an escape route from class society.'[130] However, the state socialist societies clearly involve a high degree of social and economic inequality and political oppression. Since Marx explained phenomena of this sort in terms of the division of classes on the basis of exploitive relations of production, the existence of state socialism must count as a refutation of historical materialism.

An adequate reply to this argument would take too long, and would involve tramping over very well worn ground.[131] Let us simply note that this conclusion follows from Giddens's premises, not Marx's. In the first place, as we have seen, Marx does not ground class in market-relations, but rather on the distribution of the means of production. These depend, not on juridical property-forms, but on relations of effective possession. Secòndly, it is clear from *The Civil War in France* and his other political writings, that for Marx the decisive step in the transition to a classless society came not with the introduction of state ownership of the means of production, but with the replacement of the repressive state apparatus by new forms of workers' power based on a popular militia and the election and recall of public officials. This theory may or may not be mistaken, but it offers quite a different account of socialism to that provided by Giddens in refutation of Marx. It has been pointed out by Marxists from Engels and William Morris onward that state ownership of the means of production is quite compatible with the persistence of class exploitation, and that private capitalism could under certain conditions be replaced by state capitalism. Giddens is unable to envisage such a possibility, partly I think because of his tendency to identify capitalism with the prevalence of commodity production. Once again, a misreading of Marxism prevents him from engaging with the real issues.

[129] *CSAS*, p. 230.
[130] Ibid. 282.
[131] See especially T. Cliff, *State Capitalism in Russia* (London: Pluto, 1975).

THE RHETORIC OF SYNTHESIS

In conclusion, I wish to offer some remarks about the nature of Giddens's project. Since the 1960s a number of younger sociologists have sought to integrate some elements of Marxism into their thinking, prompted to do so by a variety of reasons, notably the inability of what Giddens calls the 'orthodox consensus' to handle the phenomenon of social conflict, and the burgeoning of such conflict in the world outside sociology departments.[132] Often such pillaging of Marxism is accompanied by its disdainful dismissal. Giddens's own work is a version of this approach, albeit methodologically far more sophisticated, and always respectful of, and increasingly sympathetic to Marxism.

Let us note what such an attempt to arrive at a synthesis of mainstream sociology and Marxism implies. It supposes that the interpretive sociology of Weber, to name the most intellectually powerful and suggestive of the mainstream traditions, itself a brilliant synthesis of hermeneutics, historicism, Nietzsche's genealogy of power, and marginalist economics, can be rendered compatible with elements at least of historical materialism. It seems to me that there are general grounds for doubting this to be so: the two traditions are so fundamentally opposed in method, substance, and political implications that the outcome of any attempt to combine them can only be incoherence, eclecticism, or the denaturing of one or both. As evidence for this claim I would cite the way in which Giddens continues to give primacy to certain fundamental Weberian premisses—the priority of subject over structure, and the omnipresence of domination.

The result is a highly unstable system, since Giddens is clearly genuinely sympathetic to Marxism, owes it many insights, and wishes to find a place for it in his synthesis. This central difficulty—Giddens's underlying commitment to interpretive sociology combined with his openness towards Marxism—helps to explain his bitter hostility to Parkin's *Marxism and Class Theory*. For Parkin is concerned above all to

[132] Giddens, 'Hermeneutics and Social Theory', pp. 1–3.

demonstrate the incompatibility of Marxism and Weberian sociology, and to advocate the superiority of the latter. Giddens rejects this claim, yet shares the same fundamental premises as Parkin—above all, they both believe relations of domination and subordination and social conflict to be ineradicable features of human existence.[133] No wonder that Giddens attacks Parkin so vehemently, for the latter is merely pointing out the simple but unwelcome truth that he cannot have his cake and eat it.

The attempt to strike an equipoise between Marxism and mainstream sociology seems to me not only impossible, but to lead often to an intellectually rather dubious approach to empirical questions. This is most evident, not in Giddens's work itself, but in a book by John Scott, *Corporation, Classes and Capitalism*,[134] which is clearly considerably influenced by him. The book is an examination of the thesis that twentieth-century capitalism is characterized by the separation of ownership and control. Scott contrasts two opposing theories, the 'theory of industrial society' (Berle and Means, Bell, Aron), which asserts this thesis, and the 'theory of capitalist society' (i.e. Marxism), which denies it. After showing conclusively that the thesis is false, Scott claims that both theories are mistaken! He is able to do so because he identifies the 'theory of capitalist society' with clearly inadequate Soviet accounts of state monopoly capitalism. Nevertheless the evidence he cites demonstrates the basic Marxist proposition than an economically dominant class continues to exist in late capitalism, and draws considerably on the research of non-Soviet Marxists. A position is thus attained *au dessus la melée*, which puts both Marxism and orthodox sociology in its place, but only at the price of grossly misrepresenting the former. Giddens's 'contemporary critique' seeks a similar vantage-point by means of such a misrepresentation of Marxism.

We may say, in conclusion, that despite Giddens's often brilliant intellectual fireworks, Marxism remains to be transcended. Both its theoretical and political revival, and the economic crises and social conflicts of the past fifteen years demonstrate its continued relevance. It is, I suppose, some

---

[133] Compare *CSAS*, p. 283 and Parkin, *Marxism*, pp. 187–92.
[134] London, 1979.

sort of tribute that Marxism is considered worthy of inclusion in a grander synthesis by someone as talented as Giddens. Unfortunately, it may not prove very easy to digest.[135]

[135] Since this article's first appearance, I have pursued its main themes further in *Making History* (Cambridge: Polity, 1987), especially chs. 2 and 4. Anthony Giddens responded to its criticisms in 'Marx's Correct Views on Everything', *Theory and Society* 14 (1985).

5

RECONSIDERING HISTORICAL MATERIALISM

G. A. COHEN

I

I called my book on Karl Marx's theory of history a *defence*,[1] because in it I defended what I took to be Karl Marx's theory of history. I believed the theory to be true before I began to write the book, and that initial conviction more or less survived the strain of writing it. More recently, however, I have come to wonder whether the theory which the book defends is true (though not whether, as I claimed, it was affirmed by Karl Marx). I do not now believe that historical materialism is false, but I am not sure how to tell whether or not it is true. Certain considerations, to be exhibited below, constitute a strong challenge to historical materialism, but while they plainly do represent a serious *challenge* to the theory, it is unclear what kind and degree of revision of it, if any, they justify.[2]

That is unclear because we still have only a rather crude conception of what sort of evidence would confirm or disconfirm historical materialism. I tried, in *KMTH*, to make the theory more determinate, and thereby to clarify its confirmation conditions, but it will be apparent from the

Reprinted by permission of New York University Press from *Marxism: NOMOS XXVI*, edited by J. Roland Pennock and John W. Chapman, copyright © 1983 by New York University.

[1] *Karl Marx's Theory of History: A Defence* (Oxford and Princeton, 1978). This work is henceforth referred to as *KMTH*.

[2] I propose what I think is an appropriate revision which, so I also think, preserves the spirit of the original, in ch. 9 of my *History, Labour, and Freedom* (Oxford, 1988).

challenge to be described in this chapter that substantial further clarification is required.

Some people may think that, in raising a challenge to historical materialism, I am letting the side down. So let me emphasize that my belated reservations about the theory do not weaken my belief that it is both desirable and possible to extinguish existing capitalist social relations and to reorganize society on a just and humane basis. The political significance of retreat from historical materialism should not be exaggerated. An appreciation of the principal evils of capitalism, which are its injustice, its hostility to the development of the faculties of the individual, and its voracious ravaging of the natural and built environment, does not depend on ambitious theses about the whole of human history. Nor does the claim that it is possible to establish a society without exploitation which is hospitable to human fulfilment require, or perhaps even follow from, those theses. So scepticism about historical materialism should leave the socialist project more or less where it would otherwise be. There are, it is true, Marxist claims about how society works whose falsehood would make supersession of capitalism and installation of socialism less likely. But one can maintain those claims without believing, as I am still sure that Marx did, that the fundamental process in history is the material one of the growth of human productive power.[3]

---

[3] The political applicability of historical materialism is limited, since it is a theory about *epochal* development, and the time horizon of political action necessarily falls short of the epochal. (The epochal scope of historical materialism is something which people are inclined to forget. The late Harry Braverman's *Labour and Monopoly Capital* is often invoked against the *KMTH* thesis that productive forces are explanatorily more fundamental than production relations, since Braverman claimed that the way the forces develop under capitalism is determined by the class antagonism between potentially insurgent workers and capitalists who forestall insurgency by introducing technologies which deskill and demean the workers. But Braverman would not himself have objected to the primacy thesis in this fashion, since he realized that historical materialism was about epochs: 'The treatment of the interplay between the forces and relations of production occupied Marx in almost all his historical writing, and while there is no question that he gave primacy to the forces of production in the long sweep of history, the idea that this primacy could be used in a formulistic way on a day-to-day basis would never have entered his mind'. (*Labour and Monopoly*

2

The epigraph of *KMTH* reproduces the final sentence of *The Little Boy and his House*,[4] which was my favourite book when I was a child. The sentence is as follows:

For what they all said was, 'It depends . . . It all depends . . . It all depends on where you live and what you have to build with.'

I thought that sentence was a charming way of communicating a central thesis of my book: that forms of society reflect material possibilities and constraints. But while my book was in press, or perhaps, I confess, a little earlier, I was rereading *The Little Boy and his House*, and I came to see that my use of its final sentence was to some extent exploitative. When the sentence is abstracted from its context what it seems to mean makes it a very suitable epigraph for the book. Seen in context, however, the sentence can be a point of departure for formulating the challenge to historical materialism that I want to discuss here.

Let me, then, supply the context. The story concerns an unnamed little boy who, at the outset, has no house to live in. In winter he is too cold, in summer he is too hot, when it rains he gets wet, and when it is windy he is nearly blown away. So he goes to see his uncle, who is sympathetic. They agree that the little boy needs something to live in. His uncle then explains that there exist many different kinds of dwelling, and that it would be wise for the little boy to examine some of them before deciding what he wants for himself. There follows a world tour, in which nine types of accommodation are examined, in nine different countries. But the boy finds each kind of dwelling either inherently unappealing (for example, because it is a Romany gypsy's tent too low to stand up in, or because it is an unpleasantly damp Spanish cave) or, however appealing, unattainable in his circumstances (for example, because it is a house made of stones which lie around the Irish

Capital, p. 19.) It would follow that the pattern of development of productive power in relatively restricted time periods is not probative with respect to historical materialist theses.)

[4] By Stephen Bone and Mary Adshead.

fields, and none lie around the fields where he lives, or because it is an igloo, and igloos would not last long in the little boy's climate). Returning to wherever they started from—the book does not say but linguistic evidence suggests that it is England—the boy sighs and says, 'What a lot of different ways of building houses!', whereupon, somewhat surprisingly, he and his uncle set about building a small red-brick bungalow. Having finished building, they invite their nine new friends to see the result, and the friends come with their wives and animals and they are so impressed that they go home determined to build houses just like the little boy's house. But when they get home they change their minds. And now I shall quote the last couple of pages of the book, which end with the sentence I used as an epigraph:

And they all went home determined to build brick houses like the Little Boy had built.

But when they all got home again, Don Estaban thought that after all it *was* very convenient to have a cave all ready made for you, and Johnnie Faa and Big Bear thought how convenient it was to have a house you could carry about wherever you wanted to go, and Wang Fu thought it was even more convenient to have a house that would carry *you* about. And E-took-a-shoo saw that where he lived he would *have* to built with ice and snow because there was nothing else, and M'popo and M'toto saw that they would *have* to build with grass and mud because they had nothing else, and Mr. Michael O'Flaherty thought that if you have a lot of stones lying about the fields it was a shame not to use them, and Lars Larsson thought the same about the trees in the forest.

So
what
do
you
think
they
did?
THEY ALL WENT ON
BUILDING JUST AS THEY'D
ALWAYS DONE.
FOR
WHAT THEY
ALL SAID
WAS . . .

'It depends . . .
    It all depends . . .
        It all depends on WHERE YOU LIVE
and WHAT YOU HAVE TO BUILD WITH'.

3

Let us think about why the little boy's friends decide not to build red-brick bungalows. In at least most cases, they are said to change their minds for reasons which *appear* accessible to historical materialism: they reject bungalow-building after reflecting on features of their physical circumstances. But their reasons for carrying on as before could appear favourable to historical materialism without actually being so. The next to last sentence says: they all went on building just as they'd always done. And I now see that, notwithstanding their sincere materialist-sounding avowals, they went on building as they'd always done partly just *because* they *had* always build in that way, and they consequently recognized themselves in the ways of life that went with their dwellings. This is a non-materialist reason for architectural conservatism, but it can come to appear materialist, because one way that a culture consolidates itself is by misrepresenting the feasible set of material possibilities as being smaller than it is in fact. Culturally disruptive material possibilities are screened out of thought and imagination: in certain contexts people prefer to think that they have no choice but to take a course to which, in fact, there are alternatives.

Big Bear thought it convenient to have a house (i.e., a tepee) that he could carry about, whereas Wang Fu thought it more convenient to have one (i.e., a houseboat) that would carry him about, but I do not think they reached these contrasting judgements because they made different technical calculations. I think they were led to them by the potent force of familiarity, which determined where they felt at home; and 'to be at home', unlike 'to be housed', is not a materialist property. It is the dialectic of subject finding itself in object that explains, at least in part, why Big Bear and Wang Fu conceived convenience differently. (I say 'at least in part' because I need not deny that houseboats are more likely to appear in territory dense with waterway, and tepees are more likely on riverless plains. But even if their respective ancestors developed their different housings under pressure of such material determinations, it is entirely implausible to think that Big Bear and Wang Fu stuck to custom not at all because it was custom, but just because the plains remained riverless and the rivers hadn't dried up.)

If, then, it all depends on where you live and what you have to build with, the importance of where you live is not purely materialist. The way of life where you live counts, as well as what you have to build with there. And people's need for shelter is in no clear sense greater than their need for traditions which tell them who they are.

And now I shall leave the story behind, but I shall presently return to the issue which I think it raises.

4

Marx produced at least four sets of ideas: a philosophical anthropology, a theory of history, an economics, and a vision of the society of the future.

There are connections among these doctrines, but before we consider some of them, I would like to point out that, despite great differences in their domains of application, the four doctrines have something important in common. In each doctrine the major emphasis, albeit in a suitably different way, is on the *activity of production*, and each of the four is, partly for that reason, *a materialist doctrine*.

The philosophical anthropology says that humans are essentially creative beings, or, in standard sexist Marxist language: man is an essentially creative being, most at home with himself when he is developing and exercising his talents and powers.

According to the theory of history, growth in productive power is the force underlying social change.

In the economic theory magnitude of value is explained not, as in rival accounts, at least partly in terms of desire and scarcity, but wholly in terms of labour, and labour is 'essentially the expenditure of human brain, nerves, muscles and sense organs',[5] the using up of a certain amount of human material substance: labour time, the immediate determinant of value, is but a measure of, or a proxy for, the quantity of living matter consumed in the process of production.

Finally, the main indictment of capitalism is that it crushes people's creative potentials, and the chief good of communism is that it permits a prodigious flowering of human talent, in which the free expression of the powers inside each person harmonizes with the free expression of the powers of all. Communism is the release of individual and collective productive capacity from the confinement of oppressive social structure.

5

I now believe that the philosophical anthropology suffers severely from one-sidedness. This has evident consequences for the vision of the desirable future, since that vision comes from the anthropology (see section 8). It should have no consequences for the economic theory, which answers questions about which the anthropology should be silent. Its consequences for the theory of history are, as we shall see (in sections 9–11), hard to judge.

6

My charge against Marxist philosophical anthropology is that, in its exclusive emphasis on the creative side of human nature, it neglects a whole domain of human need and aspiration, which is prominent in the philosophy of Hegel. In *KMTH* I said that for Marx, by contrast with Hegel, 'the ruling interest and difficulty of men was relating to the *world*, not to the *self*'.[6] I would still affirm that antithesis, and I now want to add that, to put it crudely, Marx went too far in the materialist direction. In his anti-Hegelian, Feuerbachian

[5] *Capital* (Harmondsworth: Penguin, 1976), p. 164; see also p. 274.
[6] *KMTH*, p. 22.

affirmation of the radical objectivity of matter,[7] Marx focused on the relationship of the subject to an object which is in no way subject, and, as time went on,[8] he came to neglect the subject's relationship to itself, and that aspect of the subject's relationship to others which is a mediated (that is, indirect) form of relationship to itself. He rightly reacted against Hegel's extravagant representation of all reality as ultimately an expression of self, but he over-reacted, and he failed to do justice to the self's irreducible interest in a definition of itself, and to the social manifestations of that interest.

I refer to the social manifestations of the interest in self identification because I think that human groupings whose lines of demarcation are not economic, such as religious communities, and nations, are as strong and as durable as they evidently are partly because they offer satisfaction to the individual's need for self identification. In adhering to traditionally defined collectivities people retain a sense of who they are.

I do not say that Marx denied that there is a need for self definition,[9] but he failed to give the truth due emphasis, and Marxist tradition has followed his lead. The interest in defining or locating oneself is not catered for by 'the development of human powers as an end in itself',[10] which is

[7] One of Feuerbach's achievements, according to Marx, was 'his opposing to the negation of the negation, which claims to be the absolute positive, the self-supporting positive, positively based on itself' (*Economic and Philosophic Manuscripts of 1844*, in Karl Marx and Frederick Engels, *Collected Works*, iii (London: Lawrence and Wishart, 1975), p. 328).

[8] For he is less guilty of that neglect in the 1844 *Manuscripts* and in the associated 'Comments on James Mill (ibid. iii. 211–28), where the need to affirm one's identity is interpreted as a need for a fulfilling kind of social labour in community with others: see 'Comments', 225–6.

[9] The expression 'self definition', especially, perhaps, when it is hyphenated ('self-definition'), suggests reference to a process in which the self defines itself, in which, that is, the self is not only what gets defined but also what does the defining. I shall not employ the hyphenated form, since, when I speak of the need for self definition, I mean the self's need not for the process but for the result, and I do not mean its need to define itself, but its need to be defined, whatever may, or must, do the defining. If self definition, even as I intend the phrase, is necessarily due to the activity of the self, and if the self needs that activity as well as its result, then so be it, but what especially matters here is the self's need to end up defined.

[10] *Capital*, iii. 959.

what the good Marx and Marxist emphasize. For, to begin
with, the creative activity characterized by the quoted phrase
need not provide a sense of self, and it is thought of as good in
large part independently of any self-understanding it may
afford: the perfection and employment of a person's gifts is an
attractive idea apart from any grasp of himself that may
result. And even when a person does gain an understanding
of himself through creative activity, because, as Marxist
tradition says, he recognizes himself in what he has made,
then he typically understands himself as possessed of a certain
kind of capacity: he is not necessarily thereby able to locate
himself as a member of a particular human community.

A person does not only need to develop and enjoy his
powers. He needs to know who he is, and how his identity
connects him with particular others. He must, as Hegel saw,
find something outside himself which he did not create, and to
which something inside himself corresponds, because of the
social process that created him, or because of a remaking of
self wrought by later experience. He must be able to identify
himself with some part of objective social reality: spirit, as
Hegel said, finds itself at home in its own otherness as such.[11]

A word about how the need for identity asserts its causal
power. Whereas the need for food has causal importance
because it drives people to seek to acquire food, by producing
and/or by appropriating the fruits of production, the impact of
the need for identity on action is more indirect. The need for
identity does not, standardly, drive people to seek to achieve
an identity, and that is so for two reasons. The first is that
people do not usually lack an identity: they receive an identity
as a by-product of the rearing process. The right thing to say,
in most cases, is not that people are motivated by their *need* for
identity, but that they are motivated by their *identity*, for which
they have a strong need, and the motivating power of identity
reflects the strength of the need identity fulfils. Quebecois do
not have a need for identity which drives them to become
Quebecois. Since they are raised as Quebecois, their need for
identity is readily satisfied. Quebecois are motivated not to

[11] I quote from memory, and I am afraid that I have lost my record of
where Hegel says this (or nearly this).

acquire an identity but to protect and celebrate the identity they are given.

Now it is true that creation and enrichment, and change, of identity can also result from a person's initiatives, from chosen engagements with which he comes to identify. But, even then, it is not usually a matter of a deliberate attempt to forge a (new) identity for oneself: apart from special cases, that would be self-defeating, since, on the whole, one's identity must be experienced as not a matter for choice—and that is the second reason why people do not set themselves the project of achieving an identity. What rather happens is that people engage themselves with people and institutions *other* than to secure an identity, and then the engagement persists when whatever its original rationale was has gone, so that it becomes an identification ungrounded in further reasons. The reason for abiding in some connections is that one has invested oneself in them and consequently finds oneself there (which does not, again, mean that the purpose of the investment was to find oneself there), and a person is incomplete without connections of that perhaps non-rational, but certainly not irrational, kind.

I claim, then, that there is a human need to which Marxist observation is commonly blind, one different from and as deep as the need to cultivate one's talents. It is the need to be able to say not what I can do but who I am, satisfaction of which has historically been found in identification with others in a shared culture based on nationality, or race, or religion, or some slice or amalgam thereof. The identifications take benign, harmless, and catastrophically malignant forms. They generate, or at least sustain, ethnic and other bonds whose strength Marxists systematically undervalue, because they neglect the need for self-identity satisfied by them.[12]

[12] I agree with Frank Parkin that what I would call divisions of identity are as deep as those of class, and that they cannot be explained in the usual Marxist way. But I think he is wrong to suppose that this weakness in Marxism casts doubt on its treatment of domination and exploitation as centring in class conflict. Parkin commits a category mistake when he maintains that domination or exploitation is predominantly racial in one society, religious in another, and of a class nature in a third. For racial exploitation and class exploitation are not two species of one genus. Racial exploitation is (largely) relegation to an exploited class because of race. And

To prevent misapprehension, I enter two caveats. First, I have not said that there exists a human need for religion, or for nationalism, or for something rather like them. The need I affirm is to have a sense of who I am. I say that the forms of consciousness just mentioned have, in past history, offered to satisfy that need, and have thereby obtained much of their power, but I advance no opinion about what features a form of consciousness must have to be a possible satisfier of the need I have emphasized.[13]

And the second caveat is that, in speaking of the need for an understanding of oneself, I mean 'understanding' in the sense in which false understanding is an example of it. I do not deny that many of the self-portrayals from which people draw satisfaction display a large measure of distortion and illusion. And religion and nationalism may, of course, be cases in point: nothing said here is intended to contradict the

if, as Parkin thinks, Protestants exploit Catholics in Northern Ireland, then the exploitation is economic, and not in a comparable sense religious. Catholics are denied access to material values, not religious ones.

So while I think that Marxism lacks an explanation of the potency of identities as bases of allocation to classes, I do not think that it is also mistaken in refusing to put religious and racial exploitation on a par with economic exploitation. It is false that 'closure on racial grounds plays a directly equivalent role to closure on the basis of property'. Unlike racism, property is not, in the first instance, a means of protecting privilege. It *is* privilege, although, like any privilege, it offers those who have it ways of protecting what they have. (See Frank Parkin, *Marxism and Class Theory* (London: Tavistock, 1979), esp. pp. 94, 114.)

[13] And I accept Alan Carling's criticism of my failure to cite gender, alongside nationality, race, and religion, as a powerful source of self-identification: 'Is it not beyond question that gender is a rather early and significant point of reference for "who I am"? Do I not share a culture with people of my gender as well as, and probably before, I share one with people in my slice of the amalgamated union of nationality, race, and religion?' ('Rational Choice Marxism', *New Left Review*, 160 (1986), 57.)

That rebuke is justified, but I cannot also endorse Carling's objections (ibid. 58–61) to my criticisms of Frank Parkin in the last footnote, which ride roughshod over nuances in my statements. Footnote 12 does not, *pace* Carling, deny that there exists in Northern Ireland something aptly called 'religious exploitation' but only that it 'plays a directly equivalent role' to economic exploitation. I allowed that, as the power of ethnicity attests, 'divisions of identity are as deep as those of class', and n. 12 is a contribution to delineating the different ways in which they are fundamental, *inter alia* with respect to exploitation.

proposition, with which I sympathize, that their more familiar forms constitute immature means of securing self identification, appropriate to a less than fully civilized stage of human development.

7

Let us turn to the vision of the future, which I discussed in *KMTH* (see chapter 5, section 7) under the heading 'Communism as the Liberation of the Content'. At the level of the individual, the liberation of the content is the release of his powers: he escapes location within a social role thought of as confining them. But I now suggest that Marx's desire to abolish social roles reflects a failure to appreciate how the very constraints of role can help to link a person with others in satisfying community.

'In a communist society', says Marx, 'there are no painters but at most people who engage in painting among other activities.'[14] I argued that this means two things: first, and obviously, that no one spends all of his active time painting. But, less obviously and more interestingly, it also means that there are not even part-time *painters*, where to be a painter is to be identified as, and to identify oneself as, one whose role it is to paint (even if one has other roles too). Under communism people now and then paint, but no one assumes the status painter, even from time to time.

I now wonder why roles should be abolished, and even why, ideally, people should engage in richly various activies. Why should a man or woman *not* find fulfilment in his or her work as a painter, conceived as his contribution to the society to which he belongs, and located within a nexus of expectations connecting him to other people? And what is so bad about a person dedicating himself to one or a small number of lines of activity only? There is nothing wrong with a division of labour in which each type of work has value, even though no one performs more than, say, two types of work, so that many

---

[14] *The German Ideology*, in Marx and Engels, *Collected Works*, v (London: Lawrence and Wishart, 1976), p. 394.

talents in each individual perforce lie underdeveloped.[15] Marx wanted the full gamut of each person's capacity to be realized: ' "free activity" ', he said, 'is for the communists the creative manifestation of life arising from the free development of *all* abilities.'[16] Now, whether or not that ideal is desirable, it is certainly unrealizable, as you will see if you imagine someone trying to realize it, in a single lifetime. But it is not even desirable, in every case, to realize it as much as possible. There is often a choice between modest development of each of quite a few abilities and virtuoso development of one or very few, and there is no basis for asserting the *general* superiority of either of these choices. What constitutes the free development of the individual in a given case depends on many things, and his *free* development is never his *full* development,[17] for that is possible only for beings which are sub- or superhuman. A society in which everyone is free to develop in any direction is not the same as a society in which anyone is able to develop in every direction: that kind of society will never exist, because there will never be people with that order of ability.[18]

Marx's ideal is properly called materialist because of its demand that the living substance within the individual be allowed to grow and emerge in, as he puts it in the phrase just quoted, a 'creative manifestation of life'. Elsewhere he says that to be free 'in the materialistic sense' is to be 'free not through the negative power to avoid this or that, but through the positive power to assert [one's] true individuality', and one's individuality, when asserted, is 'the vital manifestation

[15] It also bears remarking that a single demanding speciality can call upon a wide range of powers: see Lawrence Haworth, 'Leisure, Work and Profession', *Leisure Studies*, 3. 2 (1984), p. 329.

[16] *The German Ideology*, p. 225.

[17] Marx too casually juxtaposes the two when he looks to the 'full and free development of every individual' in 'a higher form of society': see *Capital*, i. 739. See also the revealing phrase 'the free development of the individual as a whole' and its context, at *The German Ideology*, 256.

[18] It might be suggested, on Marx's behalf, that the full development of a person's power need not be, as I have supposed, the development of his full (= all of his) power, but just a development of his power than which there could not be a greater development. But this saving manœuvre cannot be sustained, since Marx so often speaks of the individual developing *all* of his powers.

of [one's] being'.[19] His ideal qualifies as materialist because it is semi-biological, and it is certainly materialist in the sense of the opposition between the material and the social defended in chapter 4 of *KMTH*. It is true that for Marx the liberation of the human material is possible only in community with others, since 'only within the community has each individual the means of cultivating his gifts in all directions',[20] but here society is required, as Marx puts it, as a *means*, to an independently specified (and, I argued, absurd) goal. It is not required, less instrumentally, as a field for that self-identification the need for which is unnoticed in Marx's vitalistic formulations.

I have criticized Marx's ideal both for being too materialist and for requiring an impossibly total development of the individual. I think these are connected excesses, but I acknowledge that I have not articulated the connection between them. The idea that the human substance within should be nourished and expressed need not, it is true, imply a demand for that *plenary* development which I claim is impossible. But I do think, even if I cannot show, that the materialism encourages the wish to draw forth everything in the individual, and I note that no corresponding error is naturally associated with an emphasis on the importance of self definition. There is no temptation to think that one has a satisfactory identity only when one identifies with everything that can be identified with.

I argued that Marx's anthropology misses one great side of human need and aspiration, and I have now criticized an

---

[19] *The Holy Family*, in Marx and Engels, *Collected Works*, iv (London: Lawrence and Wishart, 1975), p. 131. I believe that the ideal figured forth in the following much-quoted passage also deserves to be called materialist: 'when the limited bourgeois form is stripped away, what is wealth other than the universality of individual needs, capacities, pleasures, productive forces, etc., created through universal exchange? The full development of human mastery over the forces of nature, those of so-called nature as well as of humanity's own nature? The absolute working out of his creative potentialities . . . which makes this totality of development, i.e. the development of all human powers as such the end in itself, not as measured on a *pre-determined* yardstick?' (*Grundrisse*, trans. Martin Nicolaus (Harmondsworth: Penguin, 1973), p. 488).

[20] *The German Ideology*, p. 78.

extreme version of the ideal of creativity the anthropology
exalts, by urging that the *full* development of the individual is
an ill-considered notion. To prevent misunderstanding I
should therefore add that I do not, of course, reject the ideal
of creativity as such, which remains a valuable part of
the Marxist inheritance and which has, as we shall see in
section 12, important political applications.

8

The vision of the future inherits the one-sidedness of the
anthropology, but the limitations of the anthropology should
not influence one's attitude to the labour theory of value,
which should never have been defended, as it sometimes has
been, on anthropological grounds. The question persists of the
bearing of the anthropology on the theory of history, and it is a
particularly difficult one.

Now there are phenomena, such as religion and nationalism,
whose importance historical materialism *seems* to underrate,
and which are intelligible in the light of the self's need for
definition. But even if the theory of history really does
undervalue what a more Hegelian anthropology would
honour, it does not follow that it is because the theory of
history depends upon an un-Hegelian anthropology that the
undervaluation occurs, for, as I shall argue in section 10, *it is
unclear that historical materialism is attached to the materialist
anthropology I have criticized.* First, though, a brief discussion of
the two phenomena just mentioned.

A certain cliché of anti-Marxist thought is probably true,
namely that Marx misjudged the significance of religion and
nationalism. He saw and exposed the class uses to which such
ideologies are put. But he did not pursue the consequences of
what he sometimes acknowledged, that they have origins far
removed from class struggle. The power they have when they
are used for particular class purposes is applied to those
purposes, not derived from them. They might, in consequence,
have a social and historical weight beyond their role within
the schema of base and superstructure.

Marx's awareness that religion's source is deep in human

need is evident in his statement that it is the opium of the people. He did not mean that priests devise it on behalf of exploiters and dispense it to the people to keep them in order. What priests do helps to keep the people still, but religion does not come from priests. It is, instead, 'the sigh of the oppressed creature, the soul of a heartless world, just as it is the spirit of a spiritless situation. It is the opium of the people.'[21]

Participation in religion is a form of alienation. It is a search on an illusory plane for what is unavailable in life itself. If religion is the spirit of a spiritless situation, one might expect that it will disappear only when there is spirit in life itself. It would then follow that, since there is no religion under communism, there will be a spirit in the free association of individuals. But where does Marx say anything about it?

Let us turn from religion to nationalism. Two passages in the *Communist Manifesto* warrant mention here. The first is the statement that working men have no country,[22] which expressed an expectation that the various national proletariats would rapidly transcend particularism in favour of international solidarity. It is hard to repel the suggestion that the workers refuted this when they marched to the trenches of World War I. Consider too what the *Manifesto* says about nationality and culture:

In place of the old local and national seclusion and self-sufficiency, we have intercourse in every direction, universal inter-dependence of nations. And as in material, so also in intellectual production. The intellectual creations of individual nations become common property. National one-sidedness and narrow-mindedness become more and more impossible, and from the numerous national and local literatures, there arises a world literature.[23]

Now if Marx means just that locally produced cultural objects become globally available through improved education and communication, then of course he is absolutely right. But I think his remarks go beyond that. I think they reflect a belief

---

[21] Introduction to *A Contribution to the Critique of Hegel's Philosophy of Law*, in Marx and Engels, *Collected Works*, iii. 175 (translation amended).

[22] *The Communist Manifesto*, in Marx and Engels, *Collected Works*, vi (London: Lawrence and Wishart, 1976), p. 502. Note how false the predictions made at this point in the *Manifesto* are.

[23] Ibid. 488.

and hope that men and women will relate to other men and women as fellow human beings, and on a world scale, not in addition to but instead of finding special fellowship in particular cultures. Against that I would say that literatures are national, or in some other way parochial, because their makers are, as they must be, connected with particular sets of people. Like everybody else they need to, and do, participate in concrete universals. Marxist universalism suffers from the abstractness of the Enlightenment universalism criticized by Hegel. The Enlightenment was wrong because the universal can exist only in a determinate embodiment: there is no way of being human which is not *a* way of being human.

I do not deny that the literature of one nation can be appreciated by the people of another, and they need not think of it as foreign literature to do so. When people from different cultures meet, they get things they do not get at home. But I think Marx is guilty of the different idea that people can, should, and will relate to each other just as people, an idea that ignores the particularization needed for human formation and human relationship. He complained that 'in bourgeois society a general or a banker plays a great part, but man pure and simple plays a very mean part.'[24] I am not on the side of the generals and bankers, but I do not think they are unattractive because the characterizations they satisfy are too specific, and that man pure and simple is what everyone should try to be.

I have expressed a positive attitude to ties of nationality, so I had better add that I lack the Hegelian belief that the state is a good medium for the embodiment of nationality.[25] It is probably true that whenever national sentiment fixes itself, as it usually does, on the state, there results a set of preposterous illusions and infantile emotions on which manipulating political rulers opportunistically play. But even if that claim is too strong, it is evident that, unlike literature, the state is a terribly dangerous vehicle of self-expression, and it is a good thing that in our own time people are developing

[24] *Capital*, i. 135.
[25] No one was keener on nationality than Johann Gottfried Herder, and yet he hated states: see Isaiah Berlin's 'Herder and the Enlightenment' in his *Vico and Herder* (London: Hogarth Press, 1976), pp. 158–65, 181.

identifications of more local kinds, and also international ones, identifications which cut within and across the boundaries of states.[26]

9

Two questions remain, only the second of which will be pursued here (in sections 10 and 11). Chapter 9 of *History, Labour, and Freedom* is to a large extent a response, if not precisely an answer, to the first question.

That first question is: how much damage to historical materialism is caused by the fact that the phenomenon of attachment to ways of life that give meaning to life is not materialistically explainable? Is the force of that attachment great enough to block or direct the development of the productive forces, or influence the character of economic structures, in ways and degrees which embarrass the theory of history? This is the question I said at the outset I found it hard to answer, because the confirmation conditions of the theory of history remain unclear. It may seem obvious that the human interest I have emphasized makes historical materialism unbelievable, but it is not obvious in fact. That people have goals that are as important, or even more important, to them than development of the productive forces need not contradict historical materialism, since even if 'people have other goals which are always preferred to productive development whenever they conflict with it', the conflict might never determine the direction of events at critical junctures and might therefore never assume pivotal significance.[27]

[26] Marx was not alone in his tendency to underestimate the strength of national bonds. For a brilliant evocation of general intellectual failure on that score, see Isaiah Berlin's essay on 'Nationalism' in his *Against the Current* (London: Hogarth Press, 1979): there is a good summary statement on p. 337.

[27] The quotation is from Allen Wood, to whom I am here indebted, but I have modified his point, since he says that the conflict might be too infrequent to threaten historical materialism, and the crucial question is not how many times it occurs, but whether, as I have said, it assumes pivotal significance. (See Allen Wood, *Karl Marx* (London: Routledge and Kegan Paul, 1981), p. 30.)

10

The second question is whether Marxism's one-sided anthropology is the source of historical materialism's lack of focus on the phenomenon referred to in the first question, however damaging or otherwise to historical materialism that lack of focus may be.

It is natural to think that the anthropology and the theory of history are closely related, since each has the activity of production at its centre. Yet they seem on further (if not, perhaps, in the final) analysis, to have little to do with one another. Hence, although I think that the anthropology is false, and also that historical materialism *may* be false because it neglects what the anthropology cannot explain, I also think that *if* historical materialism is false then we probably have parallel errors here, rather than one error giving rise to another: although historical materialism does not depend on the philosophical anthropology, considerations which appear to refute the anthropology might also, but independently, refute historical materialism.

Production in the philosophical anthropology is not identical with production in the theory of history. According to the anthropology, people flourish in the cultivation and exercise of their manifold powers, and they are especially productive— which in *this* instance means creative—in the condition of freedom conferred by material plenty. But, in the production of interest to the theory of history, people produce not freely but because they have to, since nature does not otherwise supply their wants; and the development in history of the productive power of *man* (that is, of man as such, of man as a species) occurs at the expense of the creative capacity of the *men* who are the agents and victims of that development. They are forced to perform repugnant labour which is a denial, not an expression, of their natures: it is not 'the free play of their own physical and mental powers'.[28] The

---

[28] *Capital*, i. 284. It is, in fact, 'only through the most tremendous waste of individual development that the development of humanity in general is secured and pursued', at least 'in that epoch of history that directly precedes the conscious reconstruction of human society' (ibid. iii. 182). See *Theories of*

historically necessitated production is transformation of the world into a habitable place by arduous labour, but the human essence of the anthropology is expressed in production performed as an end in itself, and such production differs not only in aim, but, typically, in form and in content, from production which has an instrumental rationale.[29]

When Marx says that 'people have history because they must *produce* their life'[30] the 'must' derives not from their creative natures but from their circumstances. The necessity to produce in history is not the necessity to produce under which Marx thought Milton wrote *Paradise Lost*, for the *historical* necessity to produce is not at all a necessity to express one's being. Marx said that Milton 'produced *Paradise Lost* for the same reason that a silk worm produces silk. It was an activity of *his* nature.'[31] But the necessity under which people produce their lives goes against, not with, the grain of their natures.

If 'people have history *because* they must produce their life', it follows that there will be no history when they do not have to produce their life, because, for example, their natural environment is unusually hospitable. And this consequence is affirmed by Marx. He calls the earth 'too lavish' when she supplies means of survival without human assistance, for she then

'keeps man in hand, like a child in leading-strings'. She does not make his own development a natural necessity. . . . It is the necessity of bringing a natural force under the control of society, of economizing on it, of appropriating it or subduing it on a large scale by the work of the human hand, that plays the most decisive role in the history of industry.[32]

Surplus Value (London: Lawrence and Wishart, 3 vols., 1964–72), ii. 118 for a similar statement; and for a very grim formulation of the point, see the remarkable climax to Marx's 'Future Results of British Rule in India', in Marx and Engels, *Collected Works*, xii (London: Lawrence and Wishart, 1979), p. 222.

[29] I do not say that the two categories of production cannot overlap, and it may be that their potential intersection is greater than Marx allowed himself to hope: see *KMTH*, pp. 324–5.

[30] *The German Ideology*, p. 41.

[31] *Theories of Surplus Value*, i. 401.

[32] *Capital*, i. 649.

and hence, we may add, in history *sans phrase*. Where the fruit falls from the tree into humanity's lap there is no history because there is no *need* for history. History, one might say, is a substitute for nature: it occurs only when and because nature is niggardly.

If people produce, historically, not because it belongs to their *nature* to do so, but for the almost opposite reason that it is a requirement of survival and improvement in their inclement *situation*, then it follows that the Marxist theory of human nature is, as I contend, an inappropriate basis on which to found historical materialism. The appropriate premisses in an argument for historical materialism feature, instead, the situation of scarcity in which history-making humanity is placed, together with the intelligence and rationality which enables people to ameliorate, and, ultimately, to extricate themselves from, that situation.[33] The argument would not benefit from a premiss which says that humanity is by nature productive in the sense that human fulfilment lies in some kind of productive activity, for such a premiss is irrelevant to the questions how and why humanity is productive in history.

To show how easy it is, and how wrong, to elide the distinction between historical materialism and the Marxist conception of human nature, I quote and criticize Allen Wood:

Historical progress consists fundamentally in the growth of people's abilities to shape and control the world about them. This is the most basic way in which they develop and express their human essence. It is the definite means by which they may in time gain a measure of freedom, of mastery over their social creations.[34]

Wood's first sentence is ambiguous because of the phrase 'people's abilities', which may denote either abilities inherent in individuals or the Ability of Man, of humanity as such, and only under the latter interpretation is the sentence true to Marx, who thought that the growth of the productive power of humanity proceeded in tandem with confinement of the creative capacity of most humans. It follows that Wood's second sentence is false: people do not develop and express

[33] See *KMTH*, pp. 152 ff.   [34] *Karl Marx*, p. 75.

their human essence in activity which thwarts that essence.
The third sentence, taken out of context, might still be
true, since an essence-frustrating cause could have essence-
congenial effects, but if we take it to mean that humanity
engages in self-denying labour *in order* 'in time' to achieve self-
fulfilment, then it is false, since it is false—it could not be
true—that the whole of history has a purpose which humanity
sets and pursues, and in his more sober moments Marx
ridiculed just such claims.[35] (In the most ambitious of those
readings of historical materialism in which humanity is an
agent with a purpose, the historical production whose
character is dictated by circumstance is undertaken in order
to realize a conquest of nature after which production need no
longer be dictated by circumstance: under communism
essence-governed creativity is possible for the first time.[36] In a
slightly less extravagant reading, there exists no purpose of
facilitating creative expression independently of and prior to
history, but, once production begins under the imperative of
survival, the latent powers of humanity are roused,[37] and the
project of attaining a creative existence is founded.)

Since the production of history frustrates human nature, it
does not occur because it is human nature to be productive.
The theory of history does not, accordingly, derive from the
anthropology. But the two doctrines do not contradict one
another,[38] and since, as I noted a moment ago, essence-

---

[35] For an unsober moment see the passage in Marx's article on Friedrich
List's *Nationales System* in which he flirts with the suggestion that humanity
undertakes production in history so that it can one day engage in production
as an end in itself. (Marx and Engels, *Collected Works*, iv (London: Lawrence
and Wishart, 1975), p. 281).

[36] Or possible, that is, for people in general, since it is false that essence-
based creativity is never exhibited in history: one person who exhibited it
was, as we have seen, John Milton. On creativity before and after the advent
of communism see *KMTH*, p. 205. (By the way: would a communist Milton
lack the historical Milton's singleness of vocation? Would he function not as
a *writer* but as one who engages in writing 'among other activities' (see sect.
7 above)? The idea is neither attractive nor plausible.)

[37] It is adversity which 'spurs man on to the multiplication of his needs,
his capacities, and the instruments and modes of his labour' (*Capital*, i. 649).

[38] A tension between the two doctrines, but one which falls short of being
a contradiction between them, is explored in *History, Labour, and Freedom*, ch.
9, sect. 9.

frustrating causes can have essence-congenial effects, it is possible to conjoin the two theories: one could say that humanity is essentially creative, but that its historical creativity, this side of communism, is governed not by its essence but by its circumstances, so that there is a frustration of the human essence which only communism, the ultimate result of essence-frustrating activity, will relieve.

The feasibility of this conjunction throws no doubt on the separability of historical materialism and Marxist anthropology: what we have here is truly a conjunction, rather than, as it were, a fusion. It is the anthropology, and not historical materialism, which grounds the description of historical production as essence-frustrating, that being a notion foreign to the historical materialist vocabulary. And the independent contribution to the conjunction of the theory of history is plain from the coherence of the following fantasy: one might, at a pinch, imagine two kinds of creature, one whose essence it was to create and the other not, undergoing similarly toilsome histories because of similarly adverse circumstances. In one case, but not the other, the toil would be a self-alienating exercise of essential powers.

11

I deal here with objections to the claims of section 10.

It might be argued that the anthropology supplies *part* of the explanation of the reworking of the world in history, since, even if the thesis that humanity is by nature creative is irrelevant to the human *interest* in transforming the environment, it is needed to explain why and how people are *able* to pursue that interest. The fact that humanity is by nature productive enables it to do what intelligence and rationality induce it to do against the rigour of scarcity. That people *can* transform the world, it might be said, is an implicit premiss in the argument of chapter 6 of *KMTH*.

But this argument for the relevance of the anthropology to the theory of history is mistaken. For the relevant implicit premiss of the theory of history is not that humanity is *essentially* productive, but just that, whether or not this is an essential truth about them, human beings can produce, and perhaps, indeed, in a sense of 'produce' different from that in which, according to Marx, producing belongs to their essence.

One might, however, say that historical materialism requires the anthropology as a basis for its forecast of how human beings will occupy themselves under communism. But I have wanted here to separate the vision of the future from the theory of the past, and I have meant by 'historical materialism' the theory of the dialectic of forces and relations of production which comes to an end with the achievement of communism. Historical materialism here is the theory of what Marx called *prehistory*,[39] and the present objection is therefore out of order.

The claim that historical materialism does not contradict the anthropology could also be challenged. For, according to historical materialism, people produce because of scarcity, because they have to, while the thesis that humanity is by nature creative entails that people would produce even when they do not have to produce, when, indeed, they do not have to do anything. Yet, as I emphasized in *KMTH*, Marx represents people as not producing in the Arcadian conditions which stimulate no historical development.[40]

To deal definitively with this objection one would need to be more clear about the concept of human essence than I am at the moment. But a rather simple distinction will, I think, get us somewhere. Here are two contrasting principles about essence, neither of which is absurd:

E: If an activity is essential to a being, then the being does not *exist* (and, *a fortiori*, does not flourish) unless it performs it.

F: If an activity is essential to a being, then the being does not *flourish* (though it might exist) unless it performs it.

If our understanding of essence includes principle *E*, then the objection stated above succeeds, unless Marx thought, as perhaps, indeed, he did, that people in Arcadian conditions are, in virtue of their underdevelopment, pre-human. This last saving suggestion might seem to offer only temporary relief,

---

[39] See the reference to prehistory in Marx's Preface to *A Contribution to the Critique of Political Economy* (London: Lawrence and Wishart, 1971), p. 22.

[40] *KMTH*, pp. 23–4; and see sect. 10 above.

since the objector could then say that non-Arcadians *are*
human for Marx, and even though they do produce—so that
the objection does not apply in its original form—they do not
produce in a way that manifests their essence, as the *E*
conception of essence would require.

But it is not pedantic to rejoin that *E* may not require that
essential activity be performed in a satisfactory fashion. One
might, then, silence the objector by saying that people
produce because circumstances give them no other choice, but
that in producing they exercise their essential powers, yet not,
because of situational constraint, in a satisfactory way.[41]
(Note that in such a view the theory of history and the
anthropology remain substantially independent of each other,
along the lines laid out in the last paragraph of section 10
above.)

Consider now principle *F*. On its different construal of
essence, the objection fails, although it would follow that if
Arcadians are humans, then they are not flourishing ones.
Marx strongly implies, of course, that, whatever they are, they
are contented; but he did not regard contentment as a
sufficient condition of flourishing.[42]

12

I have been distinguishing production which flows from
human nature from production which reflects adverse human
circumstance, and I would like to end by quoting a politically
potent commentary by Jon Elster, which relates to that

---

[41] The view just sketched bears comparison with the following difficult
passage: 'We see how the history of *industry* and the established *objective*
existence of industry are the *open* book of *man's essential powers*, the
perceptibly existing human *psychology*. Hitherto this was not conceived in its
connection with man's essential being, but only in an external relation of
utility . . . We have before us the *objectified essential powers* of man in the form
of *sensuous, alien, useful* objects, in the form of estrangement, displayed in
ordinary material industry . . . all human activity hitherto has been labour—
that is, industry—activity estranged from itself' (*Economic and Philosophic
Manuscripts of 1844*, pp. 302–3).

[42] See the personal views he expressed in a 'Confession' reprinted in
D. McLellan, *Karl Marx* (London: Macmillan, 1973), pp. 456–7.

distinction. In a liberating inversion of conventional wisdom about 'the problem of incentives', he claims that they are needed not in order to get people to produce, but to get them to produce in circumstances of scarcity which prevent their natural creativity from expressing itself. Having quoted Marx's statement that in the future society 'the free, unobstructed, progressive and universal development of the forces of production is itself the presupposition of society and hence of its reproduction',[43] he goes on:

According to the view of human nature worked out in the *Economic and Philosophic Manuscripts*, innovative and creative activity is natural for man. Contrary to the usual approach in political economy, the problem is not one of creating incentives to innovation, but of removing the obstacles to the natural creative urge of the individual 'in whom his own realization exists as an inner necessity'.[44] Special incentives are needed only under conditions of scarcity and poverty, in which the needs of the individual are twisted and his capacities developed only in a one-sided way. In the early stages of capitalism there was indeed a great deal of scarcity and poverty . . .

so that incentives to innovation, such as the patent system, and extravagant rewards to entrepreneurship, were required. But

given the technology developed by capitalism itself, it is materially feasible to install a regime in which the level of want satisfaction is so high that innovation as a spontaneous activity comes into its own— as part of the general self-actualization of individuals. The result will be a rate of innovation far in excess of anything seen before.[45]

The main contentions of this chapter are as follows:

1. Marxist philosophical anthropology is one-sided. Its conception of human nature and human good overlooks the need for self identity than which nothing is more essentially human. (See sections 6 and 7.)

2. Marx and his followers have underestimated the importance of phenomena, such as religion and nationalism, which satisfy the need for self identity. (Section 8.)

---

[43] *Grundrisse*, p. 540.
[44] *Economic and Philosophic Manuscripts of 1844*, p. 304.
[45] J. Elster, *Making Sense of Marx* (Cambridge, 1985), pp. 261–2.

3. It is unclear whether or not phenomena of that kind impinge in a damaging way on historical materialism. (Section 9.)

4. Historical materialism and Marxist philosophical anthropology are independent of, though also consistent with, each other. (Sections 10 and 11.)

5. If historical materialism is, as (3) allows it may be, false, then, in virtue of (4), it is not false because it relies on a false anthropology, but it and the anthropology are false for parallel reasons.

Is historical materialism false? Some distinctions which are relevant to the task of answering that question are provided in chapter 9 of my *History, Labour, and Freedom*.

6

MARX AND ARISTOTLE:
A KIND OF CONSEQUENTIALISM

RICHARD W. MILLER

In English-speaking universities, political philosophy has long been dominated by two moral outlooks, the judgement of institutions by the utility they create and the judgement of institutions by conformity to rights held to be binding apart from their consequences. In the history of philosophy, Marx and Aristotle are the most striking and attractive contrasts to both alternatives. As against rights-based morality, both judge institutions by the kinds of lives they promote and judge proposed rights by assessing the consequences, of embodying them in institutions. At the same time, their general conceptions of the kinds of lives worth promoting are highly similar, and emphatically opposed to utilitarianism. In short, as political philosophers they are non-utilitarian consequentialists.

In arguing for this conception of Marx and Aristotle, I hope to shed light on some obscure texts and to correct some misinterpretations. But my main intention is to help the case for consequentialism of Marx's sort. In the Philosopher's Heaven that is an occasional fantasy even of atheist philosophy teachers, Marx and Aristotle are a good team. Aristotle often develops in subtle and useful detail distinctions and arguments to which Marx alludes in passing. Because of his insight into history and the social sources of ideas, and his acquaintance with a wider range of political philosophies, Marx can answer certain questions of which Aristotle is, at best, vaguely aware.

First published in Canadian Journal of Philosophy, Supp. Vol. VIII (1981), pp. 323–52. Used with permission.

HAPPINESS AND COMMUNISM

In the concrete social arrangements they ultimately recommend, Marx and Aristotle are enormously different, as different as slavery on the one hand, and, on the other, 'an association in which the free development of each is the condition for the free development of all' (*CM*, 353).[1] If their general, fundamental ethical ideas were nearly as different, it would be misleading, at best, to discuss them as representatives of a single approach to the judgement of institutions, using the arguments of each to justify the outlook common to both. I will begin, therefore, with a sketch of the general principles of each thinker, so far as the two agree.

Aristotle repeatedly insists that the goal of society is to promote good lives on the part of its members. 'Politics takes very great care about making citizens have a certain character; that is, good people who will be able to do fine actions' (*EN* 1099^{b}30 f., p. 297; see also ibid. 1102^{a}5–25, 1103^{b}3–6).[2] Though it owed its origin to the bare necessities

[1] In referring to Marx's writings, I shall use the following abbreviations. *CM* for *Communist Manifesto*, *CGP* for 'Critique of the Gotha Programme', *IA* for 'Inaugural Address of the International Workingman's Association', *CWF* for *The Civil War in France*, *WL* for *Wage-Labour and Capital*, all with page references to Robert C. Tucker, ed., *The Marx-Engels Reader* (New York, 1972); *C* for *Capital* (vol. i unless otherwise indicated) (Moscow, n.d.); *EP* for *Economic and Philosophic Manuscripts*, and *OJ* for 'On the Jewish Question', both in T. B. Bottomore, tr. and ed., *Karl Marx: Early Writings* (New York, 1964); *SC* for Marx and Engels, *Selected Correspondence* (Moscow, n.d.); *GI* for *The German Ideology*, C. J. Arthur, ed. (New York, 1970); *G* for the *Grundrisse*, M. Nicolaus, tr. (New York, 1972); *I* for Marx and Engels, *Ireland and the Irish Question* (Moscow, n.d.); *WPP* for *Wages, Price and Profit*, in Marx and Engels, *Selected Works in Three Volumes* (Moscow, n.d.), ii.

[2] When I present a translation from Aristotle in direct quotes, I shall either note that it is my own, or give a page number referring to the translation I have adopted. For the *Politics*, I have relied on John Warrington, *Aristotle's Politics and the Athenian Constitution* (New York, 1959). For the *Nicomachean Ethics*, I sometimes rely on the translation by Wardman and Creed in *The Philosophy of Aristotle*, R. Bambrough, ed. (New York, 1963), sometimes that of Ross in *The Basic Works of Aristotle*, R. McKeon, ed. (New York, 1941). Wardman and Creed translations are cited using unadorned page numbers, Ross translations using page numbers prefaced by 'R'.

of life, it [the state] continues to exist for the sake of a good life'
(*Pol.* 1252^{b}30 f., p. 7). The good life and its essence, happiness
('well-being' and 'flourishing' are alternative translations),
are activity of human life in accordance with virtue (or
'excellence', *EN* 1098^{a}16 f.). Aristotle has much to say, filling
in the outlines of this broad definition. Indeed, the whole of
the *Nicomachean Ethics* is devoted to this task. Here are some of
the main points (all references are to the *Nicomachean Ethics*,
except as noted):

1. Since happiness is an activity, it requires a minimum of
material goods and physical energy as the prerequisites for the
appropriate actions (1099^{a}31–^{b}8, 1122^{b}26–9, 1153^{b}16–8).

2. The good life must give priority to the exercise of the best
human capacities, the ones which remove a person the
farthest from an animal existence (1097^{b}23–4).

3. Intelligence, above all, separates men from animals. The
exercise of intelligence is an especially important aspect of the
good life (1097^{b}23–1098^{a}5).

4. The moulding of one's life through deliberation and
choice is an important, characteristically human ability. It
expresses one's human capacity to act in accordance with
reason. Hence, so far as one's life is determined by forces
beyond one's control, it is not a good life (1105^{a}30–^{b}4,
1112^{a}19–29).

5. Action in accordance with virtue must express one's
good character. One must choose such an action for its own
sake (1105^{a}33). Moreover, what is done for its own sake is
better than what is done for the sake of something else
(1097^{b}1–6, 9). Again, it follows that the best life consists of
activities engaged in for their own sakes (1176^{b}4 f.).

6. To be happy, people need friendship (*philia*, a broad
term encompassing relations between parents and children,
lovers, and fellow-citizens, as well as non-erotic intimates)
(1155^{a}5 f.). Friendship, as Aristotle explains it, is mutual
caring among those with common goals, conscious of their
association and engaging in discussion of their common
interests (1156^{a}3–5, 1170^{b}10–14, 1172^{a}2–9). Friendship is or
implies virtue and is essential to a good life (1155^{a}4,
1170^{b}18 f.). In genuine friendship, each cares for the other for
his own sake, not for the sake of the goods that can be

extracted from him (1156^a3-^b10). Friendship holds a good society together (115^a23-8).

7. Pleasure, although not the sole good, is a good (1172^b27 f., 1175^a10-22). It is the unimpeded exercise of a human faculty (1153^a12-6, 1153^b10 f.).

8. The pursuit of money for its own sake is unnatural and undesirable. It leads to the neglect and atrophy of the many human faculties which have non-monetary and non-acquisitive goals. Money should only be acquired in order to provide the means for the exercise of these capacities (*Pol.* $1257^b1-1258^a18$).

When one turns to Marx's writings, an amazing similarity emerges, uniting the great opponent of exploitation with the most celebrated defender of slavery. Briefly put, Marx's theory of alienated labour is, in its more abstract features, largely a description of deprivations which, in *Aristotle's* view, would deny people a good life. The best way to establish this point at somewhat greater length is through a sketch of most of Marx's theory, paralleling the previous one point-by-point.

Marx, like Aristotle, judges societies by the kinds of human lives they create. Sometimes, he directly describes the life mankind should ultimately promote, life in communist society. Usually, though, he describes the best life indirectly, by presenting the main features of its opposite, a life of alienated labour, in which the worker's labour power is put under the control of another. In his discussion of alienated labour, Marx emphasizes the following points:

1. Capitalism degrades workers by depriving them of the material means and the physical energies to exercise most of their capacities (*EP* 70 f., 73, 124 f., *G* 294, *C.*, chapter 10 passim). (Here, as elsewhere in this list, 'capitalism' means 'capitalism, so far as workers do not organize to resist the tendencies of capitalist market-forces and the bourgeois state'. Marx refers to this phenomenon as 'the tendency of *things*' under capitalism, in *WPP*, 75.)

2. Worse yet, workers are forced to spend most of their waking lives providing for the physical needs they share with animals, and most of the rest recovering through mere relaxation (*EP* 72, 123, 125, *WL* 170 f.).

3. Capitalism, while organizing production in accordance

with the most advanced science, forces workers to engage in monotonous, repetitive activity, of unparalleled stupidity (*C* 340 f., 604, *EP* 124, *CGP* 388).

4. Under capitalism, the worker's life is largely determined by forces beyond his control. He is 'a plaything of alien powers' (*OJ* 13. See also *EP* 178, *G* 306 f.).

5. Under capitalism the worker sells his labour-power as a mere means to obtain necessities. 'He works in order to live. He does not even reckon his labour as part of his life. It is rather a sacrifice of his life' (*WL* 170). No one would take part in his activity except to avoid the consequences of unemployment. By contrast, in communist society, 'labour has become not only a means of life, but life's prime want' (*CGP* 368). Only on this basis can work be a means of self-expression for the worker. (See also *EP* 69, 122, 125, *WL* 1704.)

6. Because everything, including labour-power, is a commodity competing in the market, everyone 'treats other men as means' (*OJ* 13), 'is separated from the community, withdrawn into himself, wholly preoccupied with his private interest and acting in accordance with his private caprice' (*OJ* 26). 'Social connectedness becomes a mere means to private purposes, an external necessity' (*G* 84. Later, on page 226, Marx repeats this point and contrasts this estrangement with the appreciation of social connectedness—in effect, *philia*—characteristic of antiquity.). By contrast, communist society is 'an association to which the free development of each is the condition for the free development of all' (*CM* 353). It is held together by mutual caring expressed in the rule 'from each according to his abilities, to each according to his need' (*CGP* 388).

7. Part, though not all, of the damage done by capitalism is the infliction of pain on workers and the impairment of their ability to function (*EP* 73, *G* 294).

8. Capitalism encourages people to pursue money for its own sake. If the only significance, for the agent, of an activity is how much money it yields, the differences between various skills and activities lose their subjective meaning. Hence, the experience of life loses diversity and individuality (*EP* 77, 139, 191, 199, *CM* 347). By contrast, in communist society the

desire to possess is replaced by the desire to enjoy diverse and complex activities (*EP* 159–61, *GI* 53, *CGP* 388).

AGAINST UTILITARIANISM

The resemblance between Marx and Aristotle is most useful philosophically when we consider their writings as a collective criticism of the moral outlooks that dominate political philosophy today. One of these is utilitarianism, the view that institutions are ultimately justifiable solely on the grounds that they maximize the total welfare of the population, this welfare being regarded as a sum of mental phenomena, to be measured in a scientific and non-evaluative manner. The other outlook I shall call 'rights-based'. (Marx and Engels call it 'juridical', reflecting the origins of many of its concepts in the legal philosophy of the bourgeois revolutions.) By a right, I mean a rule requiring that in certain circumstances (described in general terms) an individual receive or be protected in the possession of goods or opportunities, even when, on occasion, interference would promote happiness or other values in society as a whole. In Dworkin's phrase, rights are trumps against appeals to the general welfare. By a rights-based theory, I mean a political philosophy holding that certain rights should be sanctioned by all societies, regardless of the consequences of respect for those rights. Thus, a rule-utilitarianism which claims that certain rights are valid because their observance promotes the general welfare is not rights-*based*.

Marx and Aristotle are not utilitarians. Though each gives weight to pleasure, the central element in classical utilitarian notions of welfare, neither regards it as a sole basis for justifying institutions, in the final analysis. Nor do they give this role to any other psychological aggregate, measurable without first evaluating different ways of life as more or less desirable. But neither of their political philosophies is rights-based. Each regards every right with an impact on institutions as subject to evaluation and possible rejection by an assessment of the consequences of respecting that right.

In considering utilitarianism, it is helpful to begin with the version associated with Bentham and, before him, with French materialists such as Helvetius. In this version, institutions are judged by their tendency to maximize net pleasure, different pleasures and pains being distinguished solely by intensity.

Marx's most striking reference to Benthamite utilitarianism is an impolite footnote:

Bentham is a pure English phenomenon. Not even excepting our philosopher Christian Wolff, in no time and in no country has the most homespun commonplace ever strutted about in so self-satisifed a way. The principle of utility was no discovery of Bentham. He simply reproduced in his dull way what Helvetius and other Frenchmen said with *esprit* in the 18th century. To know what is useful for a dog, one must study dog-nature. This nature itself is not to be deduced from the principle of utility. Applying this to men, he that would criticise all human acts, movements, relations, etc., by the principle of utility, must first deal with human nature in general, and then with human nature as modified in each historical epoch. Bentham makes short work of it. With the driest naivete he takes the modern shopkeeper, especially the English shopkeeper, as the normal man. Whatever is useful to this queer normal man, and to his world, is absolutely useful . . . Had I the courage of my friend, Heinrich Heine, I should call Mr Jeremy a genius in the way of bourgeois stupidity. (*C* 571)

The German Ideology contains a significant addition to this indictment. In this passage (pp. 109 f.) Marx accuses utiliarianism of 'the . . . stupidity of merging all the manifold relations of people in the *one* relation of usefulness' (p. 109).

The passages to which I have alluded are suggestive, but extremely sketchy, so much so that the question of whether Marx was a closet utilitarian, appalled by incidental characteristics of Bentham's writings, is still a topic of lively debate. Here, Aristotle elaborates, supplements, and strengthens Marx's writings. Aristotle's discussions of pleasure include compelling arguments against Benthamite utilitarianism which are also the most plausible interpretations of the cited passages in Marx.

The beginning of the last book of the *Nicomachean Ethics* (x. 1–5) is largely an attack on a doctrine which is crucial to Benthamite utilitarianism: someone's well-being in the course of his life is the net amount of pleasure he experiences. Three arguments in particular expand and strengthen Marx's anti-utilitarian claims.

1. Pleasure can consist of the enjoyment of any of a great diversity of activities. But some activities are more desirable than others, apart from the amount and intensity of the pleasure produced ($1173^b25-1174^a12$). 'No one would choose to live with a child's mentality throughout the whole of his life, even though he took the greatest possible pleasure in the things that children are pleased by' (173^a1-4, p. 363). Hence, the extent of someone's well-being is not identical with the magnitude of his pleasure. Surely this idea that the different activities of which someone is capable must be distinguished, examined, and assessed before his well-being can be determined is part of Marx's indictment of Bentham for failing to discriminate among the different versions of 'human nature'.

2. Pleasure cannot be the sole good people aim at, for people prefer pleasure combined with other things to the same amount of pleasure by itself (1172^b27-34). 'The pleasant life is even more sought after when it is combined with wisdom than apart' (1172^b30f., p. 360). In *The German Ideology*, when Marx charges utilitarianism with falsely reducing the diversity of human relations to a single phenomenon, this is part of what he has in mind. Like Aristotle, he regards pleasure as a good. But it is not the sole good, in the final analysis.

3. 'Friendship, since the friend differs from the flatterer, seems to make it plain that pleasure is not the good, or else that there are different classes of pleasure. The friend associates with us with a view to the good, but the flatterer with a view to pleasure. The flatterer is reproved, but people praise the friend because he associates with us for a different purpose' (1173^b32-^a1, pp. 362 f.).

Here, Aristotle relies on the discussion of friendship which he has just completed, in books viii and ix. There, he describes real friendship as mutual caring, in which each friend cares for the other's good. A flatterer, on the other hand, says gratifying things solely with an eye to extracting advantages.

A relation of mutual flattery can provide as much pleasure as a true friendship, involving mutual caring. Most obviously, the former relation can yield intense pleasures of gratified vanity. But still, friendship would be more desirable than the debased relationship, in which each cares to preserve the association only as a means to further, self-centred ends. Aristotle is condemning pleasure-theorists for failing to take such differences into account.

In *The German Ideology*, Marx probably has the same limitation in mind when he condemns utilitarianism for reducing all human relations to that of usefulness. Marx is most plausibly taken to mean that utilitarianism, having taken one restricted good, pleasure, as the measure of all, cannot adequately discriminate between relations of convenience, in which people use one another as means, and relations characterized by mutual caring.

So far I have concentrated on the version of utilitarianism associated with Bentham. Mill, however, is often thought to have saved utilitarianism from Bentham's crudeness, through a more discriminating conception of well-being. Human welfare, in Mill's view, has both a quantitative and a qualitative dimension. To assess the morally relevant consequences of an act or institution, different kinds of pleasure must first be weighed by determining shared preferences of those who have experienced all the respective kinds of pleasures. Only when they have been thus weighted can pleasure be added up (taking intensity and extent into account), to evaluate the act or institution producing them.

If Mill believed that the use of his procedure for weighing different kinds of pleasure required an independent moral commitment, over and above the commitment to maximize total pleasure, he would not be a utilitarian in the sense I previously defined. In that sense, a utilitarian is concerned to maximize a sum of psychological phenomena which can be measured without further commitment to moral evaluations. In fact, Mill is true to the utilitarianism I have defined. He regards his procedure as one which any reasonable person, whatever his moral commitments, would, on sufficient reflection, accept as part of an accurate way of measuring welfare.

Here, Marx is a necessary supplement to Aristotle, who knew of no sophisticated pleasure-theorist who stood to Mill as Eudoxus stood to Bentham. The crucial passage in Marx's writings occurs in a discussion of 'the philosophy of enjoyment' late in *The German Ideology*:

The connection of the enjoyment of the individuals at any particular time with the class relations in which they live, and the conditions of production and intercourse which give rise to these relations, the narrowness of the hitherto existing forms of enjoyment which were outside the actual content of the life of people and in contradiction to it, the connection of every philosophy of enjoyment with the enjoyment actually present and the hypocrisy of such a philosophy when applied to all individuals without distinction—all this, of course, could only be discovered when it became possible to criticize the conditions of production and intercourse in the hitherto existing world, i.e., when the contradiction between the bourgeoisie and proletariat had given rise to communist and socialist outlooks. That shattered the basis of all morality, whether the morality of asceticism or of enjoyment. (*GI* 115)

Once one reflects on how people's social situation determines what they enjoy, Mill's weighing procedure soon appears to be either class-biased or ineffective, depending on how it is interpreted. In a class-divided society, say, a capitalist society, the experience of a wide range of kinds of pleasures is largely confined to a few, well-off social strata. Letting their consensus determine the relative worth of pleasures would be as arbitrary, especially from a worker's point of view, as Bentham's alleged choice of the English shopkeeper as the desideratum.

Suppose, however, that the consensus Mill seeks is hypothetical: that ranking should be used which reflects the preferences everyone or almost everyone *would* share if everyone experienced all kinds of pleasures. Now, the procedure is not arbitrary, but it is probably useless. For it is doubtful that industrial proletarians, farmers, professors, waitresses, bankers, coupon-clippers, housewives, executives and accountants would have a common answer to such questions as, 'How much do you like luxury goods, as compared to security?', 'How much do you like control over others, as compared to friendship?', 'How much do you like material comforts, as compared to cultural activities?'. Yet these are not trivial comparisons, for purposes of social policy. Choice among alternative ways of life is needed and Mill has not shown that reason alone yields the right decision, without further moral discriminations.

The arguments against utilitarianism that I have derived from Marx and Aristotle are explicitly concerned with pleasure as an ultimate standard. But they suggest important difficulties for any utilitarian. Any utilitarian, hedonistic or not, must provide some value-neutral way of comparing the different total effects of alternative choices on his favoured range of mental phenomena. In assigning magnitudes (or ordinal indices) to the totals, he must adopt a procedure of one of two kinds. On the one hand, he might, in Bentham's manner, only consider the intensity of the mental phenomena in question, together with the number of people who experience them. I that case, he will neglect differences in kind which, Marx and Aristotle show, make alternatives more or less desirable in their effects on human life. On the other hand, he may seek to give different weights to different kinds of phenomena, apart from differences in intensity. But he cannot give greater weight to certain kinds of phenomena on the grounds that they are more desirable, in themselves. Otherwise, he ceases to be a utilitarian. Moreover, history and social structure create so many differences in what people enjoy that he cannot weight all the phenomena relevant to social choice by appealing to a consensus which all would share, if they experienced all those phenomena. In important cases, there will be no such consensus. Some much stricter qualification for the board of judges might make a joint verdict possible. But such a qualification would probably need to be justified by moral considerations which the utilitarian must exclude as unnecessary in the final analysis. In any case, this is true of every such qualification proposed so far. No further basis for weighing different kinds of phenomena seems to be available for the construction of a plausible standard of social choice.

To say that Marx was not a utilitarian is not to deny that utilitarian considerations involving avoidable suffering and possible pleasure would, in his view, justify the changes he supports. Utilitarianism, however, is an attempt to describe the *only* kind of reason which, in the final analysis, justifies preference for an alternative. Marx, I have argued, believed on good grounds that other reasons play an independent role. Given Marx's objectives as an activist, this logical point has additional, practical importance. As Marx's writings on the Paris Commune make clear, he regarded the development of new, anti-elitist political institutions as a central task of the workers' movement (*CM* 332, *CWF* 551–9). He praises the Commune for increasing the decision-making powers and political influence of the average worker through such measures as election of all officials, including police, subject to recall, the replacement of a standing army by a people's militia, and paying officials at the same level as workers' wages. The initial efforts to increase popular control of the state take place in the midst of revolutions, and are risky experiments. They call for correspondingly powerful justifications. While anti-elitist political innovations such as the Communards' may have utilitarian justifications, they are more directly and obviously justifiable as means to self-expression and mutuality, seen as goods of great intrinsic importance. Indeed, Marx introduces his description of the Commune's innovations by quoting a Commune decree proclaiming 'The proletarians of Paris . . . have understood that it is their imperious duty and their absolute right to render themselves masters of their own destinies by seizing upon the governmental power' (*CWF* 553). In general, valid justifications which are beyond the scope of utilitarianism can play a crucial role in motivating changes that Marx sought to encourage.

CONSEQUENTIALISM

Despite their opposition to utilitarianism, neither Marx's nor Aristotle's ethics is rights-based. Admittedly, both believe that the best social arrangements may involve the enforcement of rights. But, according to both philosophers, the appopriate rights are to be chosen by assessing their consequences for the lives of people governed by them. And that assessment is not made by determining whether those effects conform to some further, more general right.

My interpretation of Aristotle is controversial. Book v of the *Nicomachean Ethics*, Aristotle's discussion of justice, looks rights-based to many readers. In fact, as I shall now argue, it is a defence of a consequentialist theory of justice, analysing a diverse catalogue of rights in a consequentialist way.

Aristotle begins book v by distinguishing, and putting to one side, justice in an extremely broad sense, viz., the behaviour of a virtuous person in his relations with others. He then discusses justice in a narrower sense in which the just person is one who does not selfishly take more than his share. Initially, he says there are two kinds of justice in this sense, distributive justice and rectificatory justice. Then, almost as an afterthought, he discusses a third form, reciprocal justice, governing exchange.

Distributive justice, says Aristotle, regulates 'the division of honour, wealth, and other divisible things of common concern in the society (*koinonousi tes politeias*)' (my translation of 1130^b31 f.). Distributive justice requires that all be treated equally in the division of social goods. But, he immediately adds, this equality is not the assignment to each of a numerically equal share, but the assignment of equal shares to the extent to which people are equal in relevant respects. And there is great disagreement as to which features of people are relevant here. 'All men agree that what is just in distribution must be according to merit in some sense, though they do not all specify the same sort of merit, but democrats identify it with the status of freeman, supporters of oligarchy with wealth (or with noble birth), and supporters of aristocracy with excellence' (1131^a25-29, R p. 1006).

Aristotle's discussion has begun like a rights-based theory, laying down a requirement that people be treated as equals. But he continues by noting disagreements concerning what is the relevant kind of equality. How are these disagreements to be resolved? This question is answered in the *Politics*, which Aristotle, in the *Ethics*, explicitly describes as the concrete application of his ethical views. There, he decides between democratic, oligarchic, and aristocratic notions of equality by considering how institutions can most effectively promote lives of virtue. '[W]hat is right is to be interpreted as what is equally right; and what is equally right is that which benefits the whole state and advances the common good of its citizens' (1283^b, p. 89. See also 132^a. Later, I will describe how Aristotle supports aristocratic equality in this consequentialist way).

Rectificatory justice deals with situations in which one person has taken what belongs to another. It readjusts the status of the parties, restoring the original state of affairs. If, contrary to Aristotle's instructions (*EN* 1180^{b}28–1181^{b}25), the *Ethics* is read in isolation from the *Politics*, the discussion of rectification seems like a rights-based part of Aristotle's philosophy. The disagreements between democrats, oligarchs, and aristocrats concerning distributive equality are irrelevant here. For, as Aristotle reminds us, rectification is still required if a good man has taken what belongs to a bad man.

When we turn to the *Politics*, however, a new complication emerges. Aristotle is acutely aware of the existence of rival rules prescribing what properly belongs to people. He discusses Phaleas' proposal that the city-state constantly equalize land-holdings, Plato's proposal that property be controlled in common by a military elite, and his own favoured alternative of private ownership combined with compulsory contributions to common meals, informally sanctioned sharing of the household surplus, and the maintenance of extensive public lands to support common projects. In not one of these cases does he judge a system of property by applying some more general standard of rights. In every case, he considers when the rules concerning property effectively and enduringly promote individual excellence in the lives of citizens.

The final form of justice that Aristotle considers is 'reciprocal justice'. This discussion is usually treated either as a rights-based theory of just price or as a primitive attempt at economic theorizing, stymied by Aristotle's failure to develop either a labour theory of value or a theory of marginal utility. These standard interpretations are thoroughly anachronistic, and obscure one of Aristotle's more resourceful exercises in non-utilitarian consequentialism.

Aristotle initially defines reciprocal justice in terms of its function. 'In exchanges involving goods of common interest (*en tais koinoniais tais allaktikais*) this kind of justice holds things together, viz., reciprocal justice based on proportion, not on numerically equal shares' (1132^b31-4, my translation). He continues, 'For it is by proportionate requital that the city holds together. Men seek to return either evil for evil—and if they cannot do so, think their position mere slavery—or good for good and if they cannot do so there is no exchange, but it is by exchange that they hold together' (1132^b35–1133^a3, R p. 1010). In the same introductory paragraph, Aristotle also insists that the justice in exchange which serves this binding function is neither distributive nor rectificatory. While his explicit arguments are sketchy, his general point is clear enough, especially in light of the examples that follow. By 'exchanges' he means interactions in which each party gains something he needs and could not otherwise (at least, not as readily) provide for himself. In such exchanges, no one requires that the gains be proportional to the individual merit of the participants, so that the more virtuous farmer, say, receives a higher price for his grain than the less virtuous one. Gain should be in proportion to contributions, but not in the way that distributive justice requires. On the other hand, rectificatory justice is not in question. While exchange changes the pattern of possession, it does not do so, Aristotle points out, as punishment for overstepping limits (1132^b 28–30).

Now Aristotle begins the discussion (1133^a5–$^b29$) that is traditionally taken to be a rights-based theory of just price, an economic theory of price-formation, or a confused attempt to create both at once. In their exchanges, different kinds of producers, say, builders and shoemakers, exchange qualitatively different objects, say, houses and shoes. Justice demands an equal bargain. But how can such different things be equated? 'Money' is part of the answer. A quantity of shoes, an amount of food, and a house can be equal in that they have the same price. But unless this equal price reflects equal worth, we do not have the equality required for justice in the exchange. This, at any rate, is the clear implication of the introductory paragraph (1132^b21–1133^a4) and the best interpretation of the extremely obscure remark, 'The number of shoes exchanged for a house must therefore correspond to the ratio of the builder to shoemaker' (1133^a21 f., R p. 1011).

Aristotle's further answer to the demand for equality centres on the concept of mutual need as holding people together. 'That it is need (*khreia*) which holds it [the exchange] together, by serving as a single standard, is shown by the fact that when there is no need for transaction on the part of both parties, or in any case one of them, no exchange takes place. . . . Money, then, serves as a measure which makes this commensurable and equates them. . . . Of course, it is not really possible that things so different [e.g., houses and shoes] should become commensurable. But they become so to a sufficient extent with respect to need' (1133^b7–10, 16, 18–20; my translation, generally following Rackham's Loeb translation, except for his anachronistic use of 'demand' for *khreia*).

As a theory of price-formation or an ethics of just price, this would be totally naive. Price-formation is governed not by the needs of the two parties to a given transaction, but by the pattern of effective demand, i.e., needs (more properly, preferences) backed up by purchasing power, as it is distributed throughout the relevant population. If purchasing power is sufficiently maldistributed, exchanges reflecting the state of effective demand may result in antagonisms which tear a society apart, rather than holding it together. As an account of price formation, then, Aristotle's remarks would miss a variety of vital points—points which Aristotle acknowledges, at least implicitly and in general terms, when he discusses the politically disruptive effects of economic inequality in the *Politics* and the *Constitution of Athens*. On the other hand, Aristotle's remarks would yield an even more unrealistic doctrine of just price. No conceivable market mechanism can guarantee that all or most individual pairs of buyers and sellers will be equally benefitted by their transaction in any sense corresponding to the intuition that good should be returned for good, evil for evil (cf. 1132^b35). Unequal distributions of purchasing power and shifting patterns of taste in the market as a whole preclude this.

To remove the appearance of naivete, we must take seriously Aristotle's introducing the notion of reciprocal justice in terms of its political function. Reciprocal justice, he says, is justice concerning exchanges which holds the city together. How does it do so? By promoting exchanges in which people rely on each other to satisfy one another's needs. Money is important as enormously expanding the scope of such exchanges. For in a money, as against a barter system, it makes sense to sell to customers who cannot offer non-monetary goods that one needs at present. ('And for the future exchange—that if we do not need a thing now we shall have it if we ever do need it—money is as it were our surety; for it must be possible for us to get what we want by bringing the money' 1133^b11-3, R p. 1011). Reciprocal justice is satisfied when exchanges are governed by whatever institutions and practices best serve the *political* goal of exchange: holding the city-state together on the basis of mutual need.

From this point of view, it is easy to see why Aristotle lays down no substantive, general rules for the determination of just price. Those practices and institutions governing exchange that are best suited to promoting a stable society within which virtue will flourish vary from social setting to social setting. Restrictions on the sale of land, government control of import and export transactions, maximum prices for necessities, and, conversely, unrestricted market trans-actions—all of these were accepted practice in Aristotle's Greece and all are accepted as valid, in appropriate settings, in the *Politics* and the *Constitution of Athens*. In economic justice, politics is primary. Reciprocal justice has a specific subject-matter, exchange, and is helped by a specific social phenomenon, money. But its goal is the same as that of the other forms of justice, the creation of a stable social framework for the exercise of virtue. Reciprocal justice consists of whatever rules governing exchange best promote that goal.

Turning to Marx, we discover the same consequentialist outlook we have encountered in Aristotle. As in Aristotle, rights-based theories are undermined by showing that a proposed basic right has a plausible rival, and that the rivalry is most reasonably adjudicated by assessing the effects of institutionalizing the rivals, using non-rights-based considera-tions as one's standard. Moreover, apart from analyses of particular rights, Marx has a general argument to offer against rights-based morality.

Again, my consequentialist interpretation is controversial. Many commentators have claimed that Marx is making a rights-based criticism of capitalism when he argues that capitalism depends on the exploitation of workers.

Marx certainly does argue that a capitalist economy cannot survive without the pervasive existence of exploitation in the following sense of the word. The time a typical worker spends on the job must be greater than the time required to produce the goods he acquires with his wage. Moreover, Marx regards this surplus as serving to maintain kinds of capitalist production indifferent to workers' needs, and other kinds which are used against workers. There is an appearance, then, that Marx is condemning capitalists for violating a fundamental, universal right to receive what one contributes to an exchange.

Precisely because of this appearance, Marx, in *Capital* and in popular writings, is at pains to deny that the typical capitalist wage-bargain is an unfair violation of a right to equal exchange. 'To the purchaser of a commodity belongs its use, and the seller of labour-power, by giving his labour, does no more in reality than part with the use-value he has sold' (*C* 180). The renter of a horse's powers for a day does not, Marx reminds us, violate the horse-owner's rights because he gives a rent worth less than what the horse adds to the harvest. The purchaser of grapes and yeast does not cheat when those materials create a product worth more than they cost. No more does the capitalist violate a worker's rights when his payment for a day's labour-power is worth less than the products added by the use of that labour-power (see also *C* 172, *WL* 169 f., *WPP* 56 f.). Production using wage-labour should be overthrown because of its consequences, not because it violates rights.

Like Aristotle in book v, Marx is very far from opposing the institutionalization of rights, as such. He devoted his life to the fight for an initial stage of socialism in which the economy is governed by a right to income in proportion to one's labour-time (assuming equality of skills). But Marx believes rights are to be justified by their effects. Like Aristotle, he undermines claims that rights have independent, fundamental status by investigating the clash between systems of rights and their rivals.

Consider, for example, the contrast between the rights

characteristic of capitalism and those characteristic of the first stage of socialism. Socialism includes rights absent from capitalism, such as the right to a job. But there are capitalist rights absent from socialism. Under socialism—as Marx describes it—no one has a right to use his savings to purchase factories or land, on which he then employs wage-labourers to make a profit. Socialism, in Nozick's phrase, 'prohibits capitalist acts between consenting adults'. These acts are not prohibited because profit based on wages is a violation of another, stronger right. As we have seen, Marx denies that there is anything intrinsically unfair about a profitable wage-bargain. Rather, the right to capitalist investment is denied because of the consequences of respecting it. The presence of capitalist activity in a largely socialist economy may sufficiently encourage competitiveness and contempt for manual work to tip the scales in favour of counter-revolution, when added to a heritage of hundreds of years of bourgeois ideology and the special organizational skills of deposed capitalists and bourgeois politicians. A successful counter-revolution would restore a system producing much suffering and degradation. On these grounds, which are not grounds of rights, a new social system should be maintained from which old rights are missing.

The arguments that I have associated with Marx so far are directed against the alleged primacy of a few specific rights, the right to receive the equivalent of what one contributes to an exchange, the right to the results of one's honest toil and exchange, the right to income in proportion to one's labour-time. If Marx is a consequentialist, he needs a discussion of rights-based morality that is much more general than these. This discussion occurs in the 'Critique of the Gotha Programme', when he comments on the following passage from a draft programme for the German Social Democratic party: 'The emancipation of labour demands the promotion of the instruments of labour to the common property of society and the cooperative regulation of the total labour with a fair distribution of the proceeds of labour' (p. 385). In discussing this passage, he also refers to a previous claim in the draft, that 'the proceeds of labour belong . . . with equal right to all members of society' (p. 382).

These passages from the Gotha Programme present socialism as something fairness demands, without commitment to any rigid principle of fairness. Yet Marx argues at length that this talk of 'equal right' and 'fair distribution' is 'a crime', an 'attempt . . . to force on our party again, as dogmas, . . . obsolete verbal rubbish . . . ideological nonsense about rights and other trash' (p. 388). This certainly sounds like a denial that any standard of rights is the ultimate standard by which institutions should be judged. Even more important, Marx backs up this broad and vehement rejection of rights-based morality with a powerful, general argument.

The argument begins with a discussion of the socialist right, 'To each according to the length of time he or she works'. Marx points out a limitation in the sort of equality it enjoins. One worker may have less stamina than another and find an hour's work more exhausting. One may have more children to support. All are paid the same for an hour's work of equal skill. On these grounds, Marx says, of the initial socialist income-right:

It is therefore, a right of inequality, in its content, like every right. Right by its nature can consist only in the application of an equal standard. But unequal individuals (and they would not be different individuals if they were not unequal) are measurable by an equal standard only in so far as they are brought under an equal point of view, are taken from a definite side only, for instance, in the present cases are regarded only as workers, everything else being ignored. . . . To avoid all these defects, right, instead of being equal, would have to be unequal. (p. 387)

Marx then concludes with a description of a more advanced form of society which, as has become traditional, I will call 'communism', as distinct from the previous, inferior state, which I will call 'socialism'.

In a higher place of a communist society, after the enslaving subordination of the individual to the division of labour, and there-with also the antithesis between mental and physical labour, has vanished; after labour has become not only a means of life but life's prime want; after the productive forces have also increased with the all-round development of the individual, and all the springs of cooperative wealth flow more abundantly—only then can the narrow horizon of bourgeois right be crossed in its entirety and society inscribe on its banner: From each according to his ability, to each according to his needs!

This paragraph is immediately followed by the dismissal of the rights-talk of the Gotha Programme as obsolete verbal rubbish.

Appropriately expanded, the implicit argument against rights-based morality has two parts. On the one hand, the attempt to create rights-respecting institutions is doomed to failure. From the standpoint of rights-based morality, rights (equality, fairness, I follow Marx in using the terms interchangeably, here) are inevitably violated, even if everybody lives up to the rules of right embodied in their institutions. This claim is explicit in the quoted passage. However, more needs to be said, since rights-theorists might so far simply conclude that perfect fairness is unattainable. They might propose that the constant improvement of fairness is, instead, the ultimate standard of social progress. Here, further considerations are available to Marx showing that this ultimate standard is incoherent in much the same way as the standard of perfect fairness. Valid rankings of societies are only derivable from a standard of improved fairness if degrees of fairness are assessed through non-rights-based evaluations of the consequences of embodying principles of fairness of institutions. Thus, it is only reasonable to accept a fairness standard if it is not ultimate. The ultimate goal of social change is, not fairness, but the promotion of a variety of goods such as those to which Marx refers in his sketch of communism.

First, here is the argument about the self-defeating nature of the pursuit of perfect fairness suggested by Marx's criticism of socialist distribution. A proposal that society or a major part of it, say, the economy, be governed by fairness or rights cannot be taken seriously unless fairly specific principles of fairness are described, which are supposed to regulate institutions. Like Aristotle in the *Nicomachean Ethics*, Marx notes in the 'Critique of the Gotha Programme' (p. 385) that different people have utterly different notions of what is fair. A stable society cannot simply be regulated by the vague moral principle 'Be fair to one another'. However, while stability requires specificity, the differences between people in their different situations which are relevant to judgements of fairness are extremely diverse. A principle of fairness specific enough to co-ordinate stable social processes will produce violations of some other specific principle of fairness, which also has some intrinsic worth from the standpoint of rights-based morality. In any case, this is true of all that have been proposed so far. 'To each according to the length of time he works' sometimes violates 'To each according to his needs'. Both violate 'To each the results of his honest toil and exchanges'. And so on. So long as we refuse to rest the validity of principles of fairness (right, equality) on their consequences, too many principles demand recognition, at the level of specificity we require.

A rights-theorist might respond by admitting that perfect fairness is unattainable, but setting greater fairness as the goal. But there seems to be no rational rights-based understanding of 'greater fairness' which produces appropriate rankings of societies.

It might seem that the fairer society simply violates rights less frequently. But numbers need not be so important. Because of difficulties in assessing needs, communist society may frequently produce violations of its own favoured (non-bourgeois) right, while neglecting socialist and capitalist ones entirely. If it has the other consequences Marx describes, it is preferable, none the less. Even apart from problems of implementation, numbers need not count. Though such differences no doubt tend to be exaggerated, some people do make a greater contribution to society than others. In paying no attention to these differences communism often violates a distributive right which seems to have intrinsic worth if any right does, 'The one who contributes more to a common enterprise has a right to more.' When these violations are counted, there are no grounds for supposing that communism violates rights less frequently than inferior forms of society.

A more plausible proposal is to rate a society as fairer if the rights-violations it permits are less serious than those it prohibits, or otherwise discourages. But considered apart from consequences, a violation of the right to get more if one needs more does not seem more serious than a violation of the right to get more if one contributes more. Indeed, various stories in Nozick's *Anarchy, State and Utopia* suggest that neither violation is intrinsically more serious than a violation of the capitalist right to dispose of accumulated resources as one sees fit. Of course, one might evaluate seriousness by assessing the consequences of shifting from a society dominated by one right to a society dominated by another, but to do so is to lapse into Marx's consequentialism.

Finally, the rights-theorist might, in Rawls' phrase, take the basic structure of society as his subject. He might ask what basic institutions would be chosen according to considerations which are fair to all. In such a choice, principles of fairness that are otherwise pressing may be inappropriate. For example, it would not be appropriate to give greater weight to the interests of those who have actually contributed more to society. For social circumstances determine what capacities are productive and valuable, and the choice of social circumstances themselves, perhaps radically different ones favouring different capacities, is the issue at hand.

However, the social arrangement that it would be fair to choose might enforce unfair discriminations in particular cases. Suppose socialism would be the result of a fair decision. Still, someone solely concerned with fairness should, it seems, acknowledge that it is unfair to deny a worker who has saved up his earnings the right to employ another worker, who hasn't. The right to the results of honest toil and exchange surely has intrinsic merit if any right does. This right does not disappear if socialism would be the result of fair deliberations over what system to choose. The deliberations are purely hypothetical. The would-be capitalist worker has not actually consented to any such choice.

In principle, the particular instances of unfairness enforced by the society that would be the result of fair deliberations might make the institution of that society morally wrong. Suppose, for example, that the typical worker in a socialist economy tries every day to become a petty capitalist, only to be discouraged by the restriction of income to actual labour-time. Such pervasive unfairness in particular cases could surely counterbalance the fairness of the choice of the basic structure. The situational fairness produced by the fairly chosen hypothetical contract needs to be balanced against the fairness of individual acts in particular situations. There is no apparent way to do this except by assessing the consequences of switching from the arrangements that would be fairly chosen to others which would remove the individual violations of rights in particular cases. To do so is, once again, to lapse into consequentialism.

The remarks in the 'Critique of the Gotha Programme' are criticisms of the rights-based evaluation of economic institutions. But similar problems undermine the rights-based view of politics. From the standpoint of rights-based morality, two very different kinds of political rights have intrinsic merit, rights to participation and rights to non-interference. Since we all live under government and are affected by it, to a more or less equal and enormous extent, we all have a right to equal influence over the government. At the same time, even the most democratic government should not have total power. There should be a right to freedom from interference with non-coercive acts. These two rights conflict. The growth of the realm of sacrosanct private power means the growth of inequalities that make it inevitable that influence over government will not be equal. Again, in the face of conflicts between rights it is tempting simply to change the goal of rights-based morality, from the achievement of perfect political fairness to the achievement of advances in fairness. But appropriate rankings depend on the evaluation of rights by their consequences.

I have been speaking of Marx's evaluations of proposed rights by their consequences without specifying the forms which those evaluations would take. In light of the controversy over Allen Wood's article, 'The Marxian Critique of Justice',[3] the relevant kinds of evaluations need to be specified with care. For, if Wood is right, Marx regarded capitalist trans-actions as just, and rights-respecting, despite the appalling consequences of a system dominated by such transactions.

When Marx positively evaluates a proposed right (for example, in the 'Critique of the Gotha Programme') he approves of its institution, in a given historical context and along with other appropriate measures, as something to fight for. He wants the struggle to institute or to defend the right to

---

[3] In Marshall Cohen, *et al.*, eds., *Marx, Justice and History* (Princeton, 1980 (originally: *Philosophy and Public Affairs*, 1 (1971–2)).

succeed, and regards such struggle as rational, for himself and those for whose interests he is concerned, even if considerable self-sacrifice is involved. Because rational self-sacrifice can be involved, indeed actually was, especially in 1848–9 and in the Paris Commune, we may speak of such approval as 'moral preference'. That is all I have intended by such phrases.

It may be that Marx was also concerned to evaluate social proposals and institutions in other ways which might be called 'moral'. I am not sure, the issues are complex, and the comparison with Aristotle would probable be illuminating. But if Marx evaluated in these other ways, he did so as a consequentialist.

Because 'evaluation' might be understood in the way I have sketched, the claim that Marx was a consequentialist is compatible with Wood's view of Marx. According to Wood, Marx believed that 'the justice of the transactions in capitalist production rests on the fact that they arise out of capitalist production relations, that they are adequate to, and correspond to, the capitalist mode of production as a whole.'[4] In other words, what is just and what rights there are (Wood makes clear that both questions are at issue) is a non-evaluative, sociological fact concerning what regulating practices and institutions would effectively maintain the existing mode of production. Marx can certainly say all this, and also adopt a rational commitment to help create a new kind of justice and new rights in the course of helping to create a new mode of production. Needless to say, Marx could also be a consequentialist if Wood is wrong. He could, for example, condemn capitalism as unjust on the grounds that it violates the principles of right that it would now be best to institute, on consequentialist grounds.

The arguments for consequentialism have so far been negative ones, to the effect that rights are too conflicting, partial and one-sided to be the foundation for the judgement of institutions. However, the kinds of ultimate goods that are acknowledged by Marx and Aristotle make possible positive arguments, as well. Reflecting on the goods to be promoted, in particular, self-control, mutuality, and rationality, they argue

[1] Ibid., p. 24.

that appeals to rights, in political argument, are valid so far as those rights are means to those goods.

Since around the seventeenth century, the most urgent appeals to rights have been motivated by concern that people will be denied control over their lives. A central concern of Marx's consequentialism, perhaps the most important one, is the promotion of self-control (i.e., control over one's life) and allied goods of dignity, self-expression and mutual respect. Socialism, he argues, is the only means by which these goods can be promoted, given that our material needs have so developed that only large-scale specialized production, co-ordinated over vast territories, can satisfy them. Without collective control over the means of production, competition among producers will ultimately lead to the concentration of means of production in a few hands, and the reduction of self-control for the vast majority. (See, e.g., *EP* 120, *CM* 342, 355, *G* 249, *C* 586–8.) Concern with the goods of self-control, which people seek to promote through appeals to rights, is characteristic of Marx throughout his life, from the early 1840s to his last major work, the 'Critique of The Gotha Programme' (see, for example, *EP* 17, 31, 213, *CM* 352, 357, *C* iii, 810, *CGP* 394, 396).

In emphasizing these libertarian aspects of Marx, I do not mean, in Lenin's pungent phrase, to 'render Marx more profound and turn him into an ordinary liberal'. As a social theorist, Marx believes that self-control and self-expression for the vast majority would mean the suppression of self-control or self-expression for a minority. As a consequentialist, Marx is committed to rejecting or restricting rights which would protect the minority from such interference. The abolition of the right to acquire private property in the means of production is one clear case of such a denial to some of control over their lives and of the means to express their desires and personalities. In principle, rights to speech, voting, or political organizing might also be restricted, to promote self-control and self-expression, in society as a whole. After a socialist revolution, such restrictions might reflect the advantages, in organizing skills and nation-wide connections, of former businessmen and politicians, the remnants of centuries of bourgeois ideology, or the existence of powerful capitalist states elsewhere in the world. Because the promotion of self-control, on balance, may require the suppression of one class by another, Marx calls for a 'revolutionary dictatorship of the proletariat' (*CGP* 395) in which the realm of rights is tailored to the promotion of self-control, not the other way around. Some will take this to show that Marx's consequentialism gives rights too little weight. Others, though, even if they do not accept Marx's factual claims about class conflict, will agree that rights should not be preserved at the cost of self-control and related goods. For them, Marx's consequentialism will be a compelling account of the force and limits of appeals to rights.

Similarly, Aristotle tries to show that his theory of the good life as the proper goal of politics accounts for deeply-held convictions of his times concerning political justice. Aristotle is especially concerned to provide justifications for the conviction that justice requires proportionate return, so that in a just relationship (political or otherwise) people who are equal in relevant ways are equally benefited, while someone who is relevantly superior receives proportionately more. One extremely general argument for this rule concerns the dictates of rationality in human relations. A virtuous person is guided by his reason, the best part of him. His feelings and attitudes toward someone else will, accordingly, be based on an accurate appreciation of what is of value in the other person. In the case of friendship, for example, he will appreciate the friend for his pleasantness, his usefulness, or (most valuable, fundamental, and enduring) his good character. Moreover, because he is fully rational, his feelings and attitudes will be of kinds and degrees appropriate to the worth he sees in the other. For example, it would be unreasonable to feel affection for another or to wish him well out of proportion to the worth that motivates the affection and well-wishing. (See *EN* 1157^{b}11–37, 1163^{b}30–1164^{a}22.) Aristotle applies such considerations far and wide among human relations, in cases as disparate as the stupidity of the ugly lover of a beautiful person who expects equal return of erotic feelings (1159^{b}15–20), the rationality of virtuous friends keeping their relations on an equal footing (1157^{b}34–7), and the hard-won rationality of a citizenry who voluntarily give kingship to a preeminently virtuous person (*Pol.* 1284^{b}28–34).

Aristotle is so concerned to do justice to demands for equality and proportion that he develops additional arguments, sometimes quite elaborate ones, in connection with particular relationships, above all the supremely important one of friendship. The specific arguments concerning proportionate return in friendship implicitly rely on the notion that a friend is a kind of second self (*EN* 1166^{a}31, 1168^{a}35–^{b}11). In effect, Aristotle accepts this truism as reflecting at least three different aspects of friendship. The caring and understanding involved in friendship require a capacity and a desire to identify empathetically with one's friend (1166^{a}6–9, 1170^{a}26–^{b}19). A virtuous person uses the lives of his virtuous friends as a kind of mirror in which he learns about himself (1169^{b}28–1170^{a}4). One wants to help a friend for his own sake, and this means experiencing his happiness as part of one's own happiness (1168^{a}35–^{b}11, 1166^{a}1–5).

These aspects of friendship provide reasons why the virtuous will be guided, in their friendships, by the principle of proportionate return. A rational person cannot regard another as a kind of second self, if he regards the other as of significantly different worth. Hence, virtuous friends, wanting to keep their friendship going, will act so as to preserve their equality as flourishing people leading good lives (1158^{b}29–^{a}12). Moreover, a certain amount of inequality between people can be adjusted through proportionate return, so that mutual identification is possible. The inferior gives more in affection and other goods. As a result, in this particular relation, he is an equal, on balance. For such voluntary giving is an important expression of virtue (1159^{a}13–^{b}2, 1168^a–18). This giving of more to the superior also makes it possible to reconcile the mutual concern and respect of the friendship with the rational principle that greater worth should receive more honor. If, however, the inequality is too great, no feasible effort by the inferior can maintain the empathy on which friendship depends, or reconcile the mutuality of friendship with the demands of reason. The virtuous cannot be friends with the wicked or masters friends with their slaves (at least when they are perceiving them as slaves). (See 1158^{b}29–1159^{a}13, 1161^{b}2–10.)

These arguments about equality and proportion have

immense consequences in the political realm. For Aristotle, human capacities and resources are normally such that a minority in a population will lead lives of virtue. Their virtue will normally be roughly equal. Or, in any case, effective general laws and stable institutions could not discriminate among them on grounds of virtue (*Pol.* 1284ᵃ11–4, 1332ᵇ13–25). As rational people, then, they will want the activities of ruling to be parcelled out equally among them, by rotation or lot, while these activities are denied their inferiors (1324ᵃ24 f., 1332ᵇ11–42). Moreover, this equal citizenship of the virtuous will be dictated by friendship among them as fellow-citizens, a form of friendship that is desirable in itself, and essential to the survival of the city-state (1295ᵇ21–9). Indeed, Aristotle goes so far as to say that the creation of civic friendship is the first concern of lawgivers (*EN* 1155ᵃ23–8). In this way, the equalities, and the inequalities, of Aristotle's ideal state result from his identification of the good life as the proper goal of the state. The consequentialism which might seem to threaten the demand that equals be treated as equals turns out to justify and clarify it.

The other deeply-held political conviction that Aristotle seeks to justify in his consequentialist-style is the condemnation of tyranny. Here he refuses to take the easy way out, by supposing that tyranny will inevitably deprive people of goods outside the political realm. The tyrant may benefit the subject, as a benevolent master benefits his slave and the rational mind benefits the body (*EN* 1161ᵃ35–ᵇ1). However, the tyrant, as Aristotle defines him, rules out of certain motives, whatever the effects of his rule. Taking politics as a kind of business proposition, he rules with his private advantage in mind, not the common interest (*Pol.* 1295ᵃ19–22, *EN* 1150ᵇ1–2). Thus, the intrinsic goods of friendship and concord, which are based on mutual concern, do not exist as political ties, binding members of tyrannical states together. 'In a tyranny there is little or no friendship' (*EN* 1160ᵇ30–1, R p. 1071). Also, the tyrant is no more virtuous than the virtuous minority among his citizens. (If he were, he would not rule in the selfish way.) The principle of proportionate return is, therefore, violated, and political life is thoroughly irrational. The virtuous must give the tyrant honour and power out of proportion to his worth. He gives the virtuous less honour and power than they are worth. Finally, in tyranny, people are deprived of the self-control that the good life requires (*Pol.* 1195^{a}19–23, 1181^{a}20–4).

In the arguments we have considered, Aristotle is sometimes appealing to the *egalitarian* implications of friendship. To this extent, he suggests an important addition to Marx's consequentialist arguments for liberty. Equality, after all, is another watchword of the mass movements that Marx supported. Yet in Marx's writings, he is concerned to show that demands for equality are confused. Many readers have felt that this emphasis is one-sided. The classless society which Marx supports seems to be a description of what many workers have in mind when they call for equality. Moreover, when people discuss whether a society is socialist, say, in connection with Russia or China, both sides find it natural to count the distribution of income as a high relevant fact.

Aristotle's reasoning about friendship helps us to see why Marx has a certain bias toward equal distribution, even though his ultimate standards are not distributive at all. Socialism and communism can only reconcile the goods of self-control with a highly interdependent system of production because people are developing increased mutual concern and respect. Also, such mutuality is an intrinsic good. When he explores the implications of the truism, 'A friend is a second self', Aristotle gives us reasons to suppose that friendship, indeed, any enduring and substantial mutual well-wishing, will require at least rough equality. This is an important reason for the implicit bias toward equality that readers have perceived in Marx. In addition, large inequalities of income, in Marx's view, tend to produce differences in power, both economic and political, with consequent threats to people's autonomy. These considerations, not a tendency of marginal utility to decline with increased goods, are the main support for Marx's somewhat egalitarian bias. Equality gets what importance it has from liberty and fraternity. While this consequentialist reasoning is not commonplace, many, I suspect, will recognize their own inclinations in the outcome: Equal distribution is not intrinsically desirable, but large inequalities are a sure sign that something is wrong with a society.

BEYOND ARISTOTLE: HIERARCHY AND HISTORY

Marx's and Aristotle's consequentialism is especially attractive because of the diversity of the goods it recognizes. But this diversity creates a problem. Situations may arise in which the promotion of one good reduces the availability of another. How should we rank alternatives, when such trade-offs must be judged? At the abstract level at which I have compared them, Marx and Aristotle differ most dramatically in their contributions to this question.

Whether he is judging individuals ways of life or whole societies, Aristotle employs fixed, hierarchical rankings of human capacities in which what is less than best should, so far as possible, contribute to the activity of the best. In the best life, he argues, a man subordinates everything else to the best activity, the contemplation of eternal truths, concerning things that do not change, engaged in without consideration of practical human concerns (*EN* vi. 3, x. 7). Very few, he concedes, can approach this ideal. A more feasible way of life is one in which non-intellectual activities, in particular perceptual activies and the fulfilment of appetites, serve as means for the greatest exercise of intelligence in a broad sense, i.e., the capacity for rational and insightful thinking (*EN* 1098^{a}1–17). In the *Politics*, when Aristotle turns from individual ways of life to whole city-states, he follows a similar pattern. He unhesitatingly ranks political arrangements according to the quality of the best lives they promote, quite apart from costs to the majority. For example, his ideal society is an aristocracy in which leisured philosophers, political leaders, and military men are provided for by the farming of their slaves and the handiwork of artisans and tradesmen who are excluded from politics (*Pol.* xii. 9). The non-slave non-citizens are consigned to inferior lives, in part through their political exclusion, even though they are not innately incapable of leading good lives (*Pol.* 1260^{b}1 f.). By contrast, Aristotle ranks as merely the best version of a bad arrangement a democracy of small farmers, all of whom can exercise significant moral virtues even though they lack sufficient leisure for the best sorts of lives (*Pol.* 1318^{b}6–1319^{a}19).

Because of his hostility toward attempts to reduce all goods to a single good or measure, Marx is sensitive to the problems of trade-off that Aristotle's hierarchies would neatly solve. In effect, his remarks on these conflicts are a highly non-Aristotelian argument for the central role of historical change and social context in the assessment of consequences.

Marx's alternative is clearest where the assessment of whole societies is concerned. Of course, he differs from Aristotle in his concern for the suffering of the many which may serve as the basis for the good lives of the few. However, because he recognizes important incommensurable goods, Marx does not think a final judgement of such trade-offs can always be reached by summing up individual happiness and unhappiness.

Marx believes that in many societies in the past, including Aristotle's, valuable activities, above all, the production of cultural goods, could only be sustained through a social division of labour that oppresses the vast majority, and cuts them off from the enjoyment of those activities. In the 'Critique of the Gotha Programme' he calls this situation a 'social curse' which can only be lifted when the development of capitalism first makes a socialist revolution feasible (p. 384). In *Capital*, he characterizes the ancient Greek social ideal as one in which the full development of some was purchased at the cost of the slavery of others (p. 385).

Marx never says whether these societies were desirable or undesirable on balance. He never tells us whether Athenian slavery was worth it. A definite attitude toward the evaluation of institutions seems to lie behind this silence.

In Marx's consequentialism, the question 'Which basic social arrangement is desirable?' has a rational answer, at a given time, only if there is a single basic arrangement that best promotes all the important ultimate goods, among the feasible alternatives. Marx believed, on empirical grounds, that socialism, in his time, had become such a feasible alternative. On the other hand, in past societies, important ultimate goods have depended on human misery. Marx does not rate these societies as desirable or undesirable, because, here, no valid, rational answer exists. The availability of a rational and effective guide to political action, in accord with relevant facts, depends on historical change.

Even if this approach to the judgement of basic social arrangements is correct, the assessment of the relative importance of ultimate goods could play a role in many political discussions. Even if socialism is the best basic arrangement along all dimensions of choice, still, under socialism, policy choices will have to be made which require a real sacrifice of some goods for others. These trade-offs might be faced, for example, when leisure is balanced against consumption, in fixing the length of the working day, or when sharing is balanced against privacy in choosing institutions and practices to govern neighbourhood life. For Marx, it is a distinctive advantage of socialism that it can resolve such questions through rational deliberation, rather than leaving them to be settled through uncontrolled social processes based on the necessities of capitalist competition. But a rational choice, here, may sometimes require a preference among different goods of intrinsic worth. At this point, people need to compare different ultimate goods, the task that Aristotle pursues in ranking human capacities.

Nothing could be further from Aristotle's hierarchy of activities than Marx's view, asserted throughout his writings, that the most desirable life is many-sided, expressing a diversity of intellectual, perceptual, and manual activities, and overcoming the distinction between mind-work and handwork (see, e.g., *EP* 159 f., *GI* 53, *CGP* 388). Not only does he reject Aristotle's hierarchical conception, he offers, in effect, penetrating criticisms of Aristotle's rationale for it.

Aristotle's main arguments appeal to the alleged superiority of self-sufficiency, intrinsic desirability, and humanity. One of his arguments for the supremacy of contemplation is that it alone is 'admired for its own sake . . . whereas, in matters of action we hope for something more or less apart from the action' (*EN* 1177^{b}1–4, p. 370). There seems to be a confusion, here, which Marx carefully avoids in his discussion of alienated labour. Consider Phidias, sculpting a statue. Of course, if the marble were constantly to disintegrate, Phidias would not enjoy what he is doing and we would not admire it. But, given the effectiveness of his sculpting, Phidias would not be willing to leave off sculpting if his life were otherwise left unchanged, in honour, income, and so forth, even if beautiful statues were supplied as part of the bargain. He enjoys his activity for its own sake, and we may admire it, in the same spirit. Marx respects this distinction in his portrayal of alienated labour. What is degraded about such work is not that its enjoyment is only rational if objects are produced, but that the kinds and destinies of objects produced are determined by social processes that make production an unpleasant necessity, not a means of self-expression.

Aristotle's other main argument for the contemplative life (the others are question-begging) concerns the importance of self-sufficiency. 'The just man needs people with and towards whom he may perform just acts, and the same applies to the temperate man, the brave man, and so forth. But the wise man is able to contemplate, even when he is on his own' ($1177^a29–^b1$, p. 370). Very likely, the same attitude toward dependence supports the ranking of production as inferior to contemplation, since producers depend on nature and other people for their materials. But this wholly negative assessment of dependence is one-sided, as Marx clearly sees and as Aristotle should have seen, in light of his discussion of friendship. Friendship, like any important relation of mutual caring, involves dependency and vulnerability in at least two ways. It is sustained by cooperation in which each depends on the other. And it carries at least some risk of frustration or betrayal by the other. That hardly means that friendship is nothing more than an unfortunate necessity. Marx states the point in a touching paradox: 'Not only the wealth but also the poverty of man acquires, in a socialist perspective, a human and thus a social meaning. Poverty is the passive bond which leads man to experience the need for the greatest wealth, the other person' (*EP* 165).

The remaining argument for Aristotle's hierarchy of capacities is meant to support the thesis that all perceptual and appetitive activities should serve to promote activities of intelligent thinking. Aristotle bases this supremacy of the intellect on the claim that intelligence, not perception or the satisfaction of bodily appetite is what separates humans from animals (*EN* $1097^b23–1098^a18$). Marx reveals a way in which this reasoning depends on a one-sided conception of what is distinctively human, based on a neglect of history. The quality of a capacity changes as history modifies the human environment and man's interactions with it. Activities which, abstractly defined, are shared by humans and animals, for example, listening and eating, may become humanized, as a result, so that their exercise expresses someone's humaneness, his or her non-brutishness.

Man's musical ear is only awakened by music. . . . The cultivation of the five senses is the work of all previous history. . . . For a starving man, a human form of food does not exist, but only its abstract character as food. It could just as well exist in the most crude form, and it is impossible to say in what way this feeding-activity would differ from that of animals. . . . Thus, the objectification of the human essence, both theoretically and practically [at this point, a jargon-phrase for the creation of communist society] is necessary in order to humanize man's senses. (*EP* 161 f.; see also ibid. 125, 159, and *G* 92)

Of course, these criticisms of Aristotle, even if sound, do not constitute an alternative procedure for resolving the competing demands of different human activities. In Marx's writings, so far as I can see, there is, not an outline, but only fragments of an outline of an alternative. The fragments, as I see them (sometimes dimly), are these. Socialism is now rationally preferable as the one basic arrangement best promoting all ultimate goods. Under socialism, specific policies are best if they best serve the needs of participants in the working class which now runs society (a class which may contain many former professionals, perhaps some former managers), and if they best serve the needs of the working class world-wide. If these needs are too diverse and conflicting to be best served by one alternative, the appropriate choice is simply the result of whatever forms of deliberation should be adopted under socialism to promote mutuality and self-control.

Two gaps in this outline are especially big. It is unclear to what extent a common order of needs exists among most people, which creates a determinate answer to questions of social policy. Some possibilities for such ranking are suggested by Marx's notion that a secure sense of possessing a real self, acceptance of one's own individuality, and a capacity to enjoy the contents of one's present experience can only flourish when social relations are characterized by mutual caring (*EP passim*, *G* 156–65). If this empirical, controversial claim is true, then the need for such relations has a surprisingly high rank among human needs. In recent research in the development of personality and personality disorders, this conception of how the self depends on relations to others has been elaborated and supported in great detail.[5] This research and philosophical reflection on it, may establish an important priority among needs and suggest what kinds of empirical considerations could justify further rankings.

The other great gap in the fragmentary outline concerns the relations between the needs of a proletarian ruling class and the needs of others. Do the needs of opponents of socialism have any weight? What is and what should be the relation between the needs of workers in the socialist country and those of workers world-wide? As theorist and political activist, Marx placed great weight on international solidarity (see, for example, *CM* 346, *I* 292–5, *IA* 380f., *CGP* 390f.). But twentieth-century developments have called for a more specific account of working-class internationalism.[6]

Non-utilitarian consequentialism is a two-thousand-year-old project which is as yet incomplete. I hope to have shown that it is worth pursuing. In part, I have tried to do so by a legitimate appeal to authority. Consequentialism without utilitarianism may appear to be a ploy, a way of being essentially utilitarian while avoiding hard consequences of utilitarianism through vagueness and muddle. But no one regards Aristotle as muddle-headed. No one calls Marx or Aristotle a timid thinker, whatever else is said. Here, at least, their path is worth exploring and extending.

[5] See, in particular, Harry Guntrip, *Schizoid Phenomena, Object-Relations and the Self* (New York, 1969); D. W. Winnicott, *The Maturational Processes and the Facilitating Environment* (New York, 1974); Margaret Mahler *et al.*, *The Psychological Birth of the Human Infant* (New York, 1978).

[6] The role of internationalism in Marx's thought and the implications of his basic ideas for contemporary international issues are discussed in Alan Gilbert, 'Marx on Internationalism and War', *Philosophy and Public Affairs*, 7 (1977–8), 347–70.

7

THE CONTROVERSY ABOUT
MARX AND JUSTICE

NORMAN GERAS

In this essay I review a fast-growing sector of the current literature on Marx and the controversy that has fuelled its growth. During the last decade or so, the keen interest within moral and political philosophy in the concept of justice has left its mark on the philosophical discussion of his work. It has left it in the shape of the question: did Marx himself condemn capitalism as unjust? There are those who have argued energetically that he did not; and as many who are equally insistent that he did—a straightforward enough division, despite some differences of approach on either side of it. To prevent misunderstanding, it is worth underlining at the outset that the question being addressed is not that of whether Marx did indeed *condemn* capitalism, as opposed just to analysing, describing, explaining its nature and tendencies. All parties to this dispute agree that he did, agree in other words that there is some such normative dimension to his thought, and frankly, I do not think the denial of it worth taking seriously any longer. The question is the more specific one: does Marx condemn capitalism in the light of any principle of justice?

I shall survey the case for thinking he does not and the case for thinking that he does; the textual evidence adduced and supporting argument put forth on behalf of each. Given the extent of the literature being surveyed—some three dozen items (all but one of which have appeared since 1970; and incidentally, of largely, indeed overwhelmingly, North American provenance, twenty-one of the twenty-four authors

From *New Left Review*, 150 (1985), pp. 47–85. Used with permission.

cited here either writing or hailing from that continent)—each case as I present it is a kind of composite. No one of its proponents necessarily makes use of all the texts and arguments I shall enumerate and they sometimes emphasize or formulate differently those that they do use in common. Still, I give what I hope is an accurate overall map of this dispute, before going on to venture my own judgement on it. The main body of the essay falls, therefore, into three parts. First, I review the texts and arguments put forward by those who deny that Marx condemned capitalism as unjust. Second, I review the texts and arguments put forward by those who claim he did so condemn it. I try in these two sections to present each case broadly as made, with a minimum of critical comment. Third, I then offer some conclusions, and argument in support of them.[1]

[1] For convenience of reference, bibliographical details of the literature under review are assembled here. In subsequent citation I then give just the author's name (followed, where there is more than one publication by the same author, by an identifying numeral in parenthesis as designated below in this note) and page number(s). Several of the articles are cited from the following collections: M. Cohen, T. Nagel and T. Scanlon (eds.), *Marx, Justice, and History* (Princeton, 1980); K. Nielsen and S. C. Patten (eds.), *Marx and Morality* (*Canadian Journal of Philosophy*, suppl. vol. 1981); J. R. Pennock and J. W. Chapman (eds.), *Marxism* (*Nomos XXVI*, New York and London, 1983). Contributors to the debate may be grouped as follows:
1. Those according to whom Marx did not criticize capitalism as unjust: D. P. H. Allen, (1) 'Is Marxism a Philosophy?', *Journal of Philosophy*, 71 (1974), 601–12, (2) 'Marx and Engels on the Distributive Justice of Capitalism', in Nielsen and Patten, pp. 221–50; G. G. Brenkert, (1) 'Freedom and Private Property in Marx', in M. Cohen *et al.*, pp. 80–105 (reprinted from *Philosophy and Public Affairs*, 8, 2 (winter, 1979), 122–47), (2) *Marx's Ethics of Freedom* (London, 1983), ch. 5; A. Buchanan, (1) 'Exploitation, Alienation and Injustice', *Canadian Journal of Philosophy*, 9. 1 (1979), 121–39, (2) *Marx and Justice* (London, 1982), ch. 4 (a revised version of 'The Marxian Critique of Justice and Rights', in Nielsen and Patten, pp. 269–306); L. Crocker, 'Marx's Concept of Exploitation', *Social Theory and Practice* (autumn, 1972), 201–15; S. Lukes, (1) 'Marxism, Morality and Justice', in G. H. R. Parkinson (ed.), *Marx and Marxisms* (Cambridge, 1982), pp. 177–205, (2) 'Morals', in T. Bottomore (ed.), *A Dictionary of Marxist Thought* (Oxford, 1983), pp. 341–2, (3) *Marxism and Morality* (Oxford, 1985), chs. 3–5; R. W. Miller, (1) 'Marx and Aristotle: A Kind of Consequentialism', in Nielsen and Patten, pp. 323–52, (2) *Analyzing Marx* (Princeton, 1984), chs. 1 and 2; R. C. Tucker, *The Marxian Revolutionary Idea* (London, 1970), ch. 2 (which is reprinted from C. J. Friedrich and J. W. Chapman (eds.),

Before getting under way, however, there is one indispensable preliminary and that is to sketch briefly a part of the theoretical background to this debate, the general lines of Marx's account of capitalist exploitation. One may speak for this purpose of the 'two faces' of it distinguishable in the wage relation. The first and more benign of them is seen in the sphere of circulation, where there is according to Marx an exchange of equivalent values, wages on the one side for labour-power on the other. The workers sell their

Justice (*Nomos VI*, New York, 1963), pp. 306–25); A. W. Wood, (1) 'The Marxian Critique of Justice', in M. Cohen *et al.*, pp. 3–41 (reprinted from *Philosophy and Public Affairs*, 1. 3 (spring, 1972), 244–82), (2) 'Marx on Right and Justice: A Reply to Husami', in M. Cohen *et al.*, pp. 106–34 (reprinted from *Philosophy and Public Affairs*, 8. 3 (spring, 1979), 267–95), (3) *Karl Marx* (London, 1981), pt. 3, (4) 'Marx and Equality', in J. Mepham and D. H. Ruben (eds.), *Issues in Marxist Philosophy*, iv (Brighton, 1981), pp. 195–221, (5) 'Justice and Class Interests', in *Philosophica* (Ghent) 1984.

2. Those according to whom Marx did criticize capitalism as unjust: R. J. Arneson, 'What's Wrong with Exploitation?', *Ethics*, 91 (1981), 202–27; G. A. Cohen, (1) 'Freedom, Justice and Capitalism', *New Left Review*, 126 (1981), 3–16, (2) review of *Karl Marx* by Allen W. Wood, *Mind*, 92. 367 (1983), 440–5; J. Elster, (1) 'Exploitation, Freedom, and Justice', in Pennock and Chapman, pp. 277–304, (2) *Making Sense of Marx* (Cambridge 1985), ch. 4; M. Green, 'Marx, Utility, and Right', *Political Theory*, 11. 3 (1983), 433–46; R. Hancock, 'Marx's Theory of Justice', *Social Theory and Practice*, 1 (1971), 65–71; Z. I. Husami, 'Marx on Distributive Justice', in M. Cohen *et al.*, pp. 42–79 (reprinted from *Philosophy and Public Affairs*, 8. 1 (autumn, 1978), 27–64); P. Riley, 'Marx and Morality: A Reply to Richard Miller', in Pennock and Chapman, pp. 33–53; C. C. Ryan, 'Socialist Justice and the Right to the Labour Product', *Political Theory*, 8. 4 (1980), 503–24; H. van der Linden, 'Marx and Morality: An Impossible Synthesis?', *Theory and Society*, 13. 1 (1984), 119–35; D. van de Veer, 'Marx's View of Justice', *Philosophy and Phenomenological Research*, 33 (1973), 366–86; G. Young, (1) 'Justice and Capitalist Production: Marx and Bourgeois Ideology', *Canadian Journal of Philosophy*, 8. 3 (1978), 421–55, (2) 'Doing Marx Justice', in Nielsen and Patten, pp. 251–68.

2*. A group not altogether distinct from (2) but rather more tentative, expressing reservations of one sort or another about the interpretation of (1) without directly challenging it: N. Holmstrom, 'Exploitation', *Canadian Journal of Philosophy*, 7. 2 (1977), 353–69; W. L. McBride, 'The Concept of Justice in Marx, Engels, and Others', *Ethics*, 85 (1975), 204–18; J. H. Reiman, 'The Possibility of a Marxian Theory of Justice', in Nielsen and Patten, pp. 307–22; W. H. Shaw, 'Marxism and Moral Objectivity', in Nielsen and Patten, pp. 19–44; R. J. van der Veen, 'Property, Exploitation, Justice', *Acta Politica* (Amsterdam), 13 (1978), 433–65.

commodity—the capacity to work—and from the capitalist they receive in exchange, in the form of wages, the value of the commodity they sell, which is to say the value of what goes into producing it, of the things workers consume by way of their historically defined subsistence. What they receive from the capitalist, Marx goes out of his way to insist, is the full equivalent in value of what they sell and so involves no cheating. The second and uglier face of the relationship now shows itself, however, in the sphere of production. Here the workers, whose labour is itself the source of the value that commodities contain, will have to work longer than the time which is necessary to reproduce the value of their own labour-power, longer than is necessary to replace the value of the wage they have received. They will perform, that is to say, surplus labour, and the surplus-value they create thereby will be appropriated by the capitalist as profit. Labour-power in operation creates a value greater than the value labour-power itself embodies and is sold for. The two faces by turns reveal their contrasting features across the pages of *Capital*, complementary aspects of the wage relation: in the sphere of circulation, an equal exchange freely contracted; in the sphere of production, the compulsion to labour some hours without reward.

This, then, is the character of capitalist exploitation. Does Marx think it unjust?

I. MARX AGAINST JUSTICE

i. A first and, on the face of it, compelling piece of evidence against supposing so is that he actually says it is not. Once the purchase of labour-power has been effected, according to Marx, this commodity belongs to the capitalist as of right, and so therefore does its use and so do the products of its use.[2] Or, expressed from the worker's point of view, 'As soon as his labour actually begins, it has already ceased to belong to him'.[3] The capitalist, Marx says in the passage most often

---

[2] Karl Marx, *Capital*, i (Penguin edn., Harmondsworth, 1976), pp. 292, 303, and *Theories of Surplus Value* (Moscow, 1968–72), i. 315.
[3] *Capital*, i. 677.

referred to in this connection, has paid for the value of labour-power, and the fact that the use of the latter now creates a greater value, this 'is a piece of good luck for the buyer, but by no means an injustice towards the seller'.[4] Similarly: 'The fact that this particular commodity, labour-power, possesses the peculiar use-value of supplying labour, and therefore of creating value, cannot affect the general law of commodity production. If, therefore, the amount of value advanced in wages is not merely found again in the product, but augmented by a surplus-value, this is not because the seller has been defrauded, for he has really received the value of his commodity; it is due solely to the fact that this commodity has been used up by the buyer.'[5]

ii. Consistently with this denial that the wage relation is unjust, Marx also rails against socialists who want for their part to appeal to considerations of justice. The best-known occasion is his polemic, in 'Critique of the Gotha Programme', against the notion of a fair distribution of the proceeds of labour. 'What is "a fair distribution"?' he asks pointedly. 'Do not the bourgeois assert that the present-day distribution is "fair"? And is it not, in fact, the only "fair" distribution on the basis of the present-day mode of production? Are economic relations regulated by legal conceptions or do not, on the contrary, legal relations arise from economic ones? Have not also the socialist sectarians the most varied notions about "fair" distribution?' Shortly afterwards, he refers to such notions as 'obsolete verbal rubbish' and 'ideological nonsense about right and other trash so common among the democrats and French Socialists'—the gist of all of which seems clear enough.[6] Again, in a letter of 1877, he writes contemptuously of 'a whole gang of half-mature students and super-wise diplomaed doctors who want to give socialism a "higher, idealistic" orientation, that is to say, to replace its materialistic basis (which demands serious objective study from anyone who tries to use it) by modern mythology with its goddesses of

[4] Ibid. 301.
[5] Ibid. 731. See also the 'Notes on Adolph Wagner' in Karl Marx, *Texts on Method*, T. Carver, ed. (Oxford, 1975), at p. 216.
[6] Karl Marx and Frederick Engels, *Selected Works* (Moscow, 1969–70), iii. 16, 19.

Justice, Liberty, Equality, and Fraternity'.[7] On the one
occasion when Marx himself makes use of some phrases
about rights and justice—in his Inaugural Address to, and
Preamble to the Rules of, the First International—he explains
carefully in a letter to Engels: 'I was obliged to insert two
phrases about "duty" and "right" into the Preamble to the
Rules, ditto about "truth, morality and justice", but these are
placed in such a way that they can do no harm.'[8]

iii. What motivates the above polemics, as well as Marx's
denial of any injustice in the wage relation, is perhaps already
evident. It is what is suggested to many, including those
whose interpretation we are presently rehearsing, by another
formulation from 'Critique of the Gotha Programme'; namely,
that 'Right can never be higher than the economic structure of
society and its cultural development conditioned thereby'.[9]
Standards of justice, this may be taken to mean, are relative or
internal to specific historical modes of production. It is not
merely that they are generated by these—that juridical
relations and the 'forms of social consciousness' corresponding
to them 'originate in the material conditions of life'[10]—but
that, in addition, they are only applicable to and valid for
them. The only principles of justice which are appropriate to
judging a particular mode of production are those that in fact
'correspond' to it, that are functional to sustaining and
legitimating it. In the words of another much-quoted passage:
'It is nonsense for Gilbart to speak of natural justice in this
connection [interest payment on loans—N.G.]. The justice of
transactions between agents of production consists in the fact
that these transactions arise from the relations of production
as their natural consequence. The legal forms in which these
economic transactions appear as voluntary actions of the
participants, as the expressions of their common will and as
contracts that can be enforced on the parties concerned by the

[7] Karl Marx and Frederick Engels, *Selected Correspondence* (Moscow,
n.d.), pp. 375–6; see also *Capital*, i. 178–9 n. 2.
[8] *Selected Correspondence*, p. 182; and see *Selected Works*, ii. 18–20, for the
phrases in question.
[9] *Selected Works*, iii. 19.
[10] Karl Marx, *A Contribution to the Critique of Political Economy* (London,
1971), p. 20.

power of the state, are mere forms that cannot themselves determine this content. They simply express it. The content is just so long as it corresponds to the mode of production and is adequate to it. It is unjust as soon as it contradicts it. Slavery, on the basis of the capitalist mode of production, is unjust; so is cheating on the quality of commodities.'[11] Now, if by relativism in this regard we understand a conception in which what is just is simply a matter of subjective viewpoint, then Marx's conception may be said not to be a relativist one. It has, on the contrary, a firmly objective basis, since it construes the standards of justice appropriate to any society as being so by virtue of the real social function they perform.[12] It remains relativist, however, in the different sense of tying every principle of justice to a specific mode of production in the way described, and thus rendering each such principle unfit to provide a basis for trans-historical judgement. On this account of things, there cannot be an independent standard of justice, external to capitalism, yet appropriate to assessing it. There can be no principle transcending historical epochs and in the light of which Marx would have been able to condemn capitalism as unjust.

iv. We can put the same point in another way. Moral norms and notions come within the compass of Marx's theory of ideology. Not only, therefore, do ideas about justice, but so does morality more generally, belong to the superstructure of any social formation. As *The German Ideology* has it, 'Morality, religion, metaphysics, and all the rest of ideology as well as the forms of consciousness corresponding to these, thus no longer retain the semblance of independence'.[13] It is not consistent with his views on ideology that Marx should have found capitalist society to be unjust by reference to historically quite general norms of justice.[14]

Reformism

v. Justice being an essentially distributive value, it is argued

[11] *Capital*, iii (Penguin edn., Harmondsworth, 1981), pp. 460–1; see also ibid. i. 178.
[12] Wood (1), pp. 18–19, (3), pp. 131–2.
[13] Karl Marx and Frederick Engels, *Collected Works* (London, 1975–) v. 36–7.   [14] Brenkert (1), p. 90, (2), pp. 150, 154–5.

furthermore, to attribute to Marx a concern with it is to inflect his critique of capitalism in a direction he explicitly repudiated and leads to a reformist conclusion he did not accept. For it focuses attention too narrowly on the distribution of income and the differentials within it: on the share of the social product received by the workers, the inadequate level of their remuneration. And it suggests that their exploitation might be eliminated by alteration and regulation of this sphere, in other words, merely by reforms in the distribution of income. As we know, however, for Marx exploitation is in the very nature of capitalism, integral to its relations of production on which the distribution of income largely depends. His preoccupation is with this more fundamental issue of the production relations and the need for a thoroughgoing revolution in them. As important as they are, reforms in the matter of wage levels simply cannot lead to the abolition of exploitation.[15] So, Marx chides the authors of the Gotha Programme with having made a fuss about 'so-called *distribution*'. The distribution of 'the means of consumption' cannot be treated independently of the mode of production.[16] So too, in *Wages, Price and Profit*, he speaks of 'that false and superficial radicalism that accepts premisses and tries to evade conclusions', and he goes on: 'To clamour for *equal or even equitable retribution* on the basis of the wages system is the same as to clamour for *freedom* on the basis of the slavery system. What you think just or equitable is out of the question. The question is: What is necessary and unavoidable with a given system of production?' Later in the same work Marx proclaims, 'Instead of the *conservative* motto, "A fair day's wage for a fair day's work!" they [the workers—N.G.] ought to inscribe on their banner the *revolutionary* watchword, "*Abolition of the wages system!*" '[17]

vi. The focus on distributive justice, some say, is also reformist in another way. It leads back from Marx's materialist enterprise of seeking the real revolutionary tendencies which will overturn the capitalist order to projects of moral enlightenment and legal reform. As one commentator puts

[15] See Tucker, pp. 50–1; Wood (1), p. 27; Buchanan (1), p. 134, (2), pp. 56–7.
[16] *Selected Works*, iii. 19–20.   [17] *Selected Works*, ii. 56–7, 75.

this, it 'directs attention toward confused abstract ideals of justice and away from concrete revolutionary goals'.[18] The line of thought here is that for Marx it is a form of idealism to believe historical progress occurs through a change for the better in people's moral or juridical ideas. Such a change is secondary, derivative of the transformations in society's production relations. What counts, therefore, is to identify the actual historical tendencies that make for this sort of transformation and the social forces and movements at work that are capable of consummating it. Relative to this materialist task, a critique of capitalism in the name of justice represents a retreat—just equipping the would-be revolutionary, determined and passionate as may be, 'to deliver the keynote address at the next Democratic Convention'.[19]

vii. Principles of justice are, in any case, precisely *juridical* principles. As such, they have their place within that whole institutional apparatus of state, law, sanctions and so on, by which obligatory modes of conduct are imposed upon the members of a social order. According to Marx, however, a communist society will not have this sort of apparatus. The state here withers away. Communism as envisaged by him cannot then be seen as realizing a juridical principle like one of distributive justice, as conforming to and institutionalizing this where capitalism is to be criticized for violating it.[20]

Beyond Scarcity

viii. A communist society as Marx envisages it, indeed, is a society beyond justice. That is the claim of the commentators whose case we are presenting and the main textual authority for it is the same section from 'Critique of the Gotha Programme' we have already cited, in which Marx speaks his mind about 'fair distribution' and about 'right'. For, in that context, he also anticipates two sorts of distributional criterion for the different phases of a post-capitalist society and discusses them in a way these commentators take to prove

[18] Buchanan (1), p. 134.
[19] Wood (1), p. 30—and see also (2), p. 133, (3), p. 143.
[20] Wood (1), pp. 26–7, 30; Lukes (1), p. 198.

their point. For convenience, I refer hereafter to the two principles involved as, respectively, the *contribution principle* and the *needs principle*. The former will apply, Marx thinks, during an earlier period of emergent communism, 'still stamped with the birth marks of the old society'. After some necessary deductions from the total social product have been made—for infrastructural and similar social purposes and the provision of public goods—each individual will receive from it, by way of means of personal consumption, an amount in proportion to his or her labour contribution. Each will be rewarded, therefore, according to an equal standard, constitutive of a situation of 'equal right'. But this is an equal right, Marx says, 'still constantly stigmatized by a bourgeois limitation'. Though it no longer permits class differences or privileges, nevertheless by measuring people solely according to their labour contribution, it allows those relatively well endowed, whether with physical or with intellectual ability, to benefit from the greater contribution they can thereby make, and it entails, conversely, for those with relatively large needs or responsibilities, greater burdens and disadvantages than others will have to bear: '*It is, therefore, a right of inequality, in its content, like every right.* Right by its very nature can consist only in the application of an equal standard; but unequal individuals (and they would not be different individuals if they were not unequal) are measurable only by an equal standard in so far as they are brought under an equal point of view, are taken from one *definite* side only, for instance, in the present case, are regarded *only as workers* and nothing more is seen in them, everything else being ignored.' Such a one-sided approach, so to speak levelling the complex individuality of persons, is unavoidable, Marx holds, in the initial stage of communism. Only in a later period will it be possible to implement the needs principle, better able, this, to match each person's individuality: 'In a higher phase of communist society, after the enslaving subordination of the individual to the division of labour, and therewith also the antithesis between mental and physical labour, has vanished; after labour has become not only a means of life but life's prime want; after the productive forces have also increased with the all-round development of the individual, and all the springs of co-operative wealth flow more abundantly—only then can the narrow horizon of bourgeois right be crossed in its entirety and society inscribe on its banners: From each according to his ability, to each according to his needs!'[21]

Now, it is argued in the light of these passages that the needs principle—which I shall render henceforth: 'From each according to their ability, to each according to their needs!'— is not a principle of distributive justice; and that in the higher phase of communism Marx speaks of, the very circumstances, of scarcity and conflict, that make such principles necessary will no longer exist. The formula is not intended by him as a principle of justice, so the argument goes, since it is clear here that he regards principles of justice, and concepts of rights associated with them, as inadequate by their nature, unable in their generality and formalism, indeed unable owing to their egalitarianism, to take account of the specific individuality of each person. The needs principle is not such a general or formal rule, because it does not subsume people under any equal standard or point of view but takes them in their specificity and variety. It is not, some even suggest, a prescriptive principle at all but simply a description of how things will eventually be. When Marx talks, therefore, of 'the narrow horizon of bourgeois right' being crossed, we must take him to mean that it is considerations of rights and justice as such that are transcended and left behind: 'to mean, not merely that there will be no more *bourgeois* right, but that there will be no more *Recht*, no more legal and moral rules'.[22] This possibility is based upon the hypothesis of a progressive disappearance of those conditions which create the need for codes of rights and norms of distributive justice. It is predicated, that is, on the elimination of scarcity and of other sources of human conflict, or at least on their diminution to a point of insignificance. With increasing material productivity yielding an abundance of resources; with less selfish, more sympathetic and generous interpersonal attitudes and qualities; with more harmonious and co-operative relationships all round—what from Hume to Rawls have been perceived as 'the circumstances of justice' will be present no more. If Marx

[21] *Selected Works*, iii. 16–19.
[22] Lukes (1), p. 200.

sees this communist society as being 'higher' than all preceding social forms, then obviously, given what has gone before, this cannot mean he regards it as *more just*. No, it is higher according to some other standard of value.[23]

ix. For—finally, in our review of this side of the argument—Marx *is* committed to certain other values. As was made clear at the very beginning, no one here is denying that he condemned capitalism, and he did so in the light precisely of values other than justice: the most commonly mentioned in this connection being freedom; but also self-realization, well-being and community.[24] Unlike norms of justice, it is held, such values are not wholly relative or internal to historically specific modes of production and so are able to serve as universal criteria of judgement. There is a subordinate dispute, 'on this side of the line' as it were, as to whether they are themselves also *moral* values or are, rather, values of a different, non-moral sort, but I shall ignore that issue as of secondary significance, in view of the position I take in the last section of this essay on the principal issue of disagreement.

2. MARX FOR JUSTICE

i. If Marx sees no injustice or fraud in the wage paid by the capitalist to the labourer, then that is because these two, as he insists, exchange fully equivalent values. However, it is only in the narrow and preliminary perspective of the circulation process (so says our second group of interpreters in reply) that he does treat the wage relation as an exchange of equivalents. Only within the sphere of exchange itself, where commodities are bought and sold, and only in accordance with the criteria internal to it, with the law of value which governs the purchase and sale of commodities, does Marx depict the

[23] For this paragraph see Tucker, p. 48; Brenkert (1), p. 91, (2), pp. 153, 162; Buchanan (1), p. 139, (2), pp. 57–9; Lukes (1), pp. 198–203, (3), chs. 3 and 4; Wood (2), p. 131, (3), pp. 138–9, (4), pp. 203–11; Miller (1), pp. 338–9; Allen (1), p. 609.

[24] See Tucker, p. 50; Wood (1), pp. 34–41, (2), pp. 119–28, (3), pp. 125–30, 138; Brenkert (1), pp. 81–6, 93–105, (2), ch. 4 and pp. 155–7; Allen (1), pp. 609–11; Lukes (1), p. 201, (2), p. 342, (3), chs. 3 and 5; Miller (2), chs. 1 and 2.

relation in that way. Once he moves forward, the wage contract behind him, to deal with the surplus labour that must be rendered by the worker to the capitalist within the production process, and once he sets this individual relationship in its broader class context, with the capitalist class facing the workers and exploiting them repeatedly and continuously, he goes on to represent the wage relation as *not* in fact an exchange of equivalents, not a genuine exchange at all. That the capitalist advances anything in exchange for labour-power, let alone something of an equivalent value, this, Marx now says, is 'only illusory' and a 'mere semblance' or 'form'.[25] It is an 'appearance', a 'mere pretence'.[26] There is no true equivalence in the exchange, for the worker must perform more labour than that which is necessary to replace the value of the wage; and thus Marx speaks of the surplus labour involved as done 'gratis' for the capitalist and as 'uncompensated', or often calls it simply 'unpaid labour'.[27] And the exchange is only an apparent one anyway since the capitalist just contributes to it what has been appropriated— gratis!—from the product of the labour of other workers. As Marx puts it in *Capital*: 'The exchange of equivalents, the original operation with which we started, is now turned round in such a way that there is only an apparent exchange, since, firstly, the capital which is exchanged for labour-power is itself merely a portion of the product of the labour of others which has been appropriated without an equivalent; and, secondly, this capital must not only be replaced by its producer, the worker, but replaced together with an added surplus. The relation of exchange between capitalist and worker becomes a mere semblance belonging only to the process of circulation, it becomes a mere form, which is alien to the content of the transaction itself, and merely mystifies it. The constant sale and purchase of labour-power is the form; the content is the constant appropriation by the capitalist, without equivalent, of a portion of the labour of others which

[25] Karl Marx, *Grundrisse* (Harmondsworth, 1973), pp. 458, 509, 551, 674.
[26] *Theories of Surplus Value*, iii. 92–3, i. 316.
[27] *Capital*, i. 346, 680, and pp. 672, 689, 691, 693, 714, 715, 728, 729, 732, 733, 757, 769, 771; ibid. iii. 509; *Theories of Surplus Value*, ii. 29; *Grundrisse*, pp. 570–1.

has already been objectified, and his repeated exchange of this labour for a greater quantity of the living labour of others.'[28]

There is a parallel to be noted here between Marx's treatment of the apparent equivalence in the wage contract and his treatment of the freedom the worker enjoys in choosing to enter that contract. For the worker may appear to do this quite voluntarily and the sphere of circulation to be, therefore, 'a very Eden of the innate rights of man . . . the exclusive realm of Freedom, Equality, Property and Bentham'.[29] But the reality is different and, again, not so benign: 'the "free" worker', Marx writes, 'makes a voluntary agreement, i.e. is compelled by social conditions to sell the whole of his active life, his very capacity for labour'; and 'the period of time for which he is free to sell his labour-power is the period of time for which he is forced to sell it'.[30] As, in the one case, unilateral appropriation of the labour of others is the reality behind an appearance of equal exchange, so in the other, compulsion is the real content of the appearance of voluntary contract: 'capital . . . pumps out a certain specific quantum of surplus labour from the direct producers or workers, surplus labour that it receives without an equivalent and which by its very nature always remains forced labour, however much it might appear as the result of free contractual agreement.'[31] The supposed justice *of* the wage relation is comparable, then, to the worker's freedom *in* it. It is an appearance whose real content or essence is a radically different one. It is asserted by Marx provisionally and in the context only of the circulation process where capitalist and worker treat with one another exclusively as individuals, but is then revealed in due course as mere appearance, within the overall perspective of the relations of, and in, production, a perspective this, by contrast, of the relationship of class to class.[32]

---

[28] *Capital*, i. 729–30.
[29] Ibid. 280.
[30] Ibid. 382, 415.
[31] Ibid. iii. 957–8; see also *Grundrisse*, pp. 247–9, 464.
[32] This is the argument of Holmstrom, pp. 366–8; Husami, pp. 66–7; Young (1), pp. 441–50; Ryan, pp. 512–13; Arneson, pp. 218–19—and of my own 'Essence and Appearance: Aspects of Fetishism in Marx's *Capital*', *New Left Review*, 65 (1971), at pp. 80–1, 84.

Exploitation as Theft

ii. But if Marx, so to speak, takes back his assertion of an equivalence in this matter, does he also clearly take back his denial that there is any injustice involved? Does he say, in fact, and in defiance of his own strictures of other socialists, that the real and exploitative content of the wage relation is *unjust* or is in violation of anyone's *rights*? In so many words he does not, but in effect—this case continues—he does. For he often talks of the capitalist's appropriation of surplus-value in terms of 'robbery', 'theft' and the like, which is tantamount to saying that the capitalist has no right to appropriate it and that his doing so is, therefore, indeed wrongful or unjust. Thus, referring in one place to the surplus product as 'the tribute annually exacted from the working class by the capitalist class', Marx goes on: 'Even if the latter uses a portion of that tribute to purchase the additional labour-power at its full price, so that equivalent is exchanged for equivalent, the whole thing still remains the age-old activity of the conqueror, who buys commodities from the conquered with the money he has stolen from them.'[33] That is not a maverick usage on Marx's part. On the contrary. He also speaks of the annual surplus product 'embezzled from the English workers without any equivalent being given in return', and he says that 'all progress in capitalist agriculture is a progress in the art, not only of robbing the worker, but of robbing the soil'.[34] He refers to 'the booty pumped out of the workers' and 'the total surplus-value extorted . . . the common booty' and 'the loot of other people's labour'.[35] The prospective abolition of capitalist property he describes as 'the expropriation of a few usurpers'.[36] And the wealth produced under capitalism, he says, is based on the 'theft of alien labour time'.[37] Now it is perfectly possible, of course, to use the language of robbery without intending, for one's own part, any charge of injustice and wrong. One may mean by it simply to invoke, and not to

---

[33] *Capital*, i. 728.   [34] Ibid. 761, 638.
[35] Ibid. i. 743; ibid. iii. 312–13; *Theories of Surplus Value*, ii. 29.
[36] *Capital*, i. 930.
[37] *Grundrisse*, p. 705. For a more ambiguous, and disputed, passage, see *Texts on Method*, p. 186—and Wood (2), pp. 115–16; Young (2), pp. 259–60.

endorse, some prevailing or conventional standard of rightful ownership. Thus, Robin Hood stole from the rich to help the poor, and so forth. But the whole point here is that according to Marx, as should be clear enough by now, exploitation is not robbery by prevailing and conventional standards, wrong by the norms of capitalist society. This point has been well put by Jerry Cohen: 'since . . . Marx did not think that by capitalist criteria the capitalist steals, and since he did think he steals, he must have meant that he steals in some appropriately non-relativist sense. And since to steal is, in general, wrongly to take what rightly belongs to another, to steal is to commit an injustice, and a system which is "based on theft" is based on injustice.'[38]

Some see it as significant, moreover, that in his discussion of primitive capitalist accumulation in the concluding part of the first volume of *Capital*, Marx should have emphasized, amongst other violent and bloody methods, the robbery that marked this process too—robbery of 'all their own means of production' from the direct producers, theft of the common lands from the people.[39] Not right and labour, as in the idyll of political economy, but 'in actual history . . . conquest, enslavement, robbery, murder, in short force, play the greatest part'.[40] This actual history may not be decisive from a purely theoretical point of view, since one could envisage a capitalism with clean origins or at least with cleaner origins than these, and it is capitalism in general, and by its very nature, that falls foul of Marx's charge of wrong, irrespective of how salubrious or otherwise its origins. Nevertheless, if he highlighted the robbery that actually occurred, he did so in order to draw attention to capitalism's unjust historical foundation. And since the context of this condemnation is precisely a transition period between modes of production, it shows surely, against what is argued on the other side, that not every standard of justice was, for him, internal to a particular mode of production.[41]

[38] Cohen (2), p. 443; and see Husami, pp. 45, 63; Young (1), pp. 431–3; Ryan, p. 513; Elster (1), pp. 291–3, (2), ch. 4; van der Linden, pp. 128–9.
[39] *Capital*, i. 875, 885, 889, 895.   [40] Ibid. 874.
[41] See Arneson, p. 204; Cohen (1), p. 15; and—especially on this last point—Young (2), pp. 262–3.

iii. From what Marx says about capitalist robbery, therefore, we can infer a commitment to independent and tran-
scendent standards of justice, and further evidence of the
same thing is provided by his way of characterizing the two
principles of distribution that he anticipates for post-capitalist
society. I shall come presently—at 2. viii—to the interpretation of the second of them, the needs principle, that responds
to what we have seen the other group of commentators aver
about it. Of import here is that, and how, Marx ranks these
principles relative both to what precedes them historically
and to one another. The contribution principle, by which
distribution of consumption goods is based exclusively on the
labour one has done, he explicitly calls an 'advance'. This
principle—where 'no one can give anything except his labour,
and . . . nothing can pass to the ownership of individuals
except individual means of consumption'—is a superior one,
then, to the norms of capitalist distribution. But on the other
hand, because as was earlier explained, it takes no account
either of differential individual endowment or of differential
needs, Marx says also that it possesses 'defects' relative to the
needs principle which will eventually replace it, so that we
must take the needs principle as being a yet superior one.
He proposes, in other words, a hierarchy of distributive
principles; and as they are not ranked by him according to any
extrinsic standard of value, it is a reasonable supposition that
he simply sees some principles as fairer or more just than
others intrinsically, on a trans-historical standard of justice.[42]

Moral Realism

iv. Marx's seemingly relativist statements in this area are not,
in fact, what many have taken them to be. They are
statements not of moral relativism but rather, as we may call
this, of moral realism. That standards of right are, for him,
sociologically grounded or determined means that the norms
people believe in and live by will be powerfully influenced by
the nature of their society, their class position in it, and so on.

---

[42] See *Selected Works*, iii. 18–19; and Hancock, p. 66; van de Veer, p. 373;
Husami, p. 58; Arneson, pp. 214–15; Riley, pp. 39–42; Elster (1), pp. 290–
1, 296, (2), ch. 4.

It means, more particularly, that what standards of right can actually be implemented effectively and secured—this is constrained by the economic structure and resources of the given society. It does not mean that the standards to be used in evaluating or assessing a society must necessarily also be constrained by the same economic configuration; that the only valid criteria of assessment are those actually prevalent, those harmonious with the mode of production.[43] Marx's assertion that right cannot be 'higher than the economic structure' is a case in point. Its context makes clear that it is a realist, not a relativist, one. He first speaks of the contribution principle as an advance over capitalism, then explains why it is defective none the less, and says that the defects are inevitable, however, during the first phase of communism. Then he makes the statement in question and says, immediately afterwards, that the different conditions of a higher phase of communism will permit the implementation of the needs principle. Implanted in this context, Marx's statement is plausibly one concerning the real prerequisites of achieving progressively higher or more advanced standards of right. It is obviously not a statement that there can be no higher or lower in this matter on account of each such standard being relative to its appropriate economic structure.[44]

v. There is nothing at all either reformist or contrary to the cast of Marx's thought, it is argued in addition, about a preoccupation with distribution as such. He does object to any over-restricted focus upon the social *division of income*, but that is because he sees the latter as more or less a consequence of the relations of production, and it is both politically misguided and theoretically senseless to condemn the necessary effects of a cause which is itself left uncriticized. On any broader view of distribution, however, Marx is clearly concerned with it: with the distribution of free time, of opportunities for fulfilling activity, of unpleasant or rebarbative work; with the distribution of welfare more generally, of social and economic benefits and burdens. And he is concerned, in particular and above all, with the distribution of productive resources, on which

[43] Van de Veer, pp. 371–3; Holmstrom, p. 368; Husami, pp. 49–51; Arneson, p. 216; Shaw, p. 28; Hancock, pp. 66–7.

[44] *Selected Works*, iii. 18–19.

according to him this wider distribution depends. That is clear even in the passage of 'Critique of the Gotha Programme' from which his putative anti-distributive orientation is usually derived. For, insisting that the distribution of means of consumption cannot be viewed as independent of the mode of production, Marx speaks of the mode of production as itself a kind of—more basic—distribution: 'the distribution of the conditions of production'.[45] His belittling of the 'fuss' about distribution, therefore, is aimed at distribution too narrowly construed and not in general. His own attention to the production relations is precisely a preoccupation with distribution, with for him the most fundamental one of all, namely that of the means of production; and as such this preoccupation is revolutionary *par excellence*.[46]

vi. Equally, there is nothing inherently reformist or idealist, from Marx's point of view, in criticism of capitalism by appeal to ethical norms or ideals, like justice. True, if such is the sole and self-sufficient, or even the principal, burden of a critical discussion of capitalism, then he does find it so wanting, but while clearly inadequate for him as an impulse to, or instrumentality of, revolutionary change, moral criticism and argument are in no way incompatible with the sort of materialist analysis—of the real historical tendencies towards revolution—that he sees as indispensable. In conjunction with that analysis, and with the actual movement and the struggles of the workers against capitalism, and with the social and economic transformations which these struggles and other developments bring about, a normative critique is perfectly in place and the denial of this just a form of what is called economism. Moral censure and justification are certainly the accompaniment of, and arguably they are a relatively independent contribution to, processes constituting the human agency of revolutionary change, the formation of a desire and a consciousness for socialism.[47]

vii. So, whatever else may be the force of categorizing principles of justice and right as juridical ones, the categorization is

[45] Ibid.
[46] Van de Veer, p. 376; Husami, p. 75; Cohen (1), pp. 13–14; Arneson, pp. 222–5; van der Veen, p. 455.
[47] Holmstrom, p. 368; Husami, pp. 53–4; Ryan, p. 516; Elster (2), ch. 4.

unacceptably narrow if it is meant to bind them indissolubly
to the existence of law, in a strict and positivist sense. They
are, of course, as Marx knew well, standardly embodied in
legal codes, backed up by the apparatus of enforcement that is
a part of the state. However, such principles can be too, in the
first instance, simply ethical ones concerning what is and what
is not a morally defensible distribution of goods and bads;
and it is possible to conceive their realization without the
paraphernalia of state coercion. If these points do not make a
juridical conception, then Marx had, or he *also* had, a non-
juridical conception of justice.[48]

The Needs Principle

viii. That is what the principle, 'From each according to their
ability, to each according to their needs!', amounts to. It is
in substance a principle of distributive justice even if its
attainment is envisaged together with the death of the state.
There are some differences worth noting in the way this is
argued, amongst the writers whose interpretation is being
outlined, but the common ground is that, whether knowingly
or not, Marx retains a notion of rights even for the higher
phase of communism. Severe as his 'Critique of the Gotha
Programme' may be about a certain sort of formalism
exemplified by the contribution principle, the strictures there
do not finish by disposing of all types of right, or of general
rules as such. They simply reveal, in effect, what rights and
rules Marx finds morally inadequate. As one commentator
has written, 'it is only the horizon of bourgeois right, not that
of rights *überhaupt*, that is superseded in the transition to the
higher stage'.[49] The general rule, indeed, marked down for
this higher stage is the fulfilment of individual needs, and the
right that it generalizes a right, amongst other things, to the
means of personal development or self-realization. Its comple-
ment (expressed in the first half of the famous slogan) is that
each person makes an effort commensurate with her or his
abilities, in taking on a share of the common tasks. If

[48] Husami, pp. 78–9; Shaw, pp. 41–2; Riley, pp. 49–50 n. 40.
[49] Arneson, p. 216; see also van de Veer, p. 372, and compare the text to
n. 22 above.

they succeed, these standards, in making good the defects of the principle they supplant—which, sensitive only to the magnitude of labour contribution, gives out larger rewards to greater capabilities and talents—this is not because they are free of either the generality or the prescriptive force characteristic of rights. It is only because Marx obviously regards need and effort as morally more appropriate, in a word *fairer*, criteria of distribution than individual endowment. Why else should he say of the contribution principle that 'it tacitly recognizes unequal individual endowment and thus productive capacity as natural privileges',[50] whilst looking forward to the implementation of the needs principle, quite happy therefore to countenance its recognition of unequal need, forgoing with respect to this any such talk of privilege? The element of plain good fortune in the possession of great or exceptional abilities he clearly does not see as meriting any larger reward than is inherent in the very exercise and enjoyment of them. That Marx himself thinks of the needs principle as less formalistic, or more concrete, than the one it supplants, more exactly attuned, morally speaking, to the specific individuality of each person, does not for all that undo its generality as a normative principle.

Now, it is just because of the idea of its greater responsiveness to the specificity of every individual that some of the writers who view the needs principle, along the above lines, as a standard of right and justice, agree nevertheless, with those who reject that view, that it is not a principle of equality: under it, different individuals are accepted as being, by definition, unequal individuals.[51] Others—a majority—of these writers, however, do not agree. Marx must be understood, they think, as proposing, in place of a false equality, a truer or a better one. For, the sole charge laid by him, by way of its aforesaid 'defects', against the contribution principle, is in essence that it yields unjustifiable inequalities, unequal rewards based on differences in individual ability that are for him of no moral relevance. What Marx foresees in its stead is equality not in the sense of a right to equivalent rewards for equivalent amounts of labour, nor yet in the sense of the right

[50] *Selected Works*, iii. 18.
[51] Riley, pp. 39–43; Husami, p. 61.

of each person to exactly the same things or to an identical
share of social wealth; it is, rather, an equality of self-
realization—everyone's right, equally, to the means of his or
her own.[52] As for the prospect of an eventual abundance of
resources, this is either not discussed at all here or else,
acknowledged as the precondition of giving effect to the needs
principle, obviously not thought incompatible with construing
the latter as a principle of distributive justice. Only one writer
explicitly—though another perhaps implicitly—treats the
assumption of unconditional abundance as a problematic
one.[53]

ix. The claim, finally, that Marx's condemnation of capitalism rests on values such as freedom and self-actualization,
though not on any conception of justice, involves an inconsistent
usage of his texts. Whether these other values are said
themselves to constitute an ethic ('of freedom') or morality
('of emancipation'), or are regarded, on the contrary, as being
non-moral goods,[54] it makes no difference in this matter; the
claim sets up a distinction in his thought between two sorts
of values: on the one hand, those—to do with rights and
justice—necessarily dependent on and relative to historically
particular social formations and hence unsuitable for the
revolutionary criticism of them; on the other hand, those—
like freedom and self-realization—not so dependent or relative
and apt consequently for critical use. The distinction is
unfounded. To the extent that Marx does postulate an
ideological limitation or relativity of values, his theory of
ideology is perfectly general in its reach, encompassing every
sort of normative concept and not only ideas about justice.
Sociology of normative belief in attempting to explain the
historical bases of different values, it is consistent, however,
with his also making evaluative judgements of universal range
on his own behalf. Marx does, of course, condemn capitalism
for its unfreedom, oppression, coercion, but so does he in
substance condemn it for its injustice. And just as, conversely,

[52] Hancock, pp. 69–70; Arneson, pp. 214–16; Reiman, pp. 316–17,
321–2; Elster (1), p. 296, (2), ch. 4; Green, pp. 438–42.
[53] Respectively Elster and—with the appearance of some inconsistency—
Reiman.
[54] Respectively, here, Brenkert, Lukes and Wood.

he does indeed identify principles of justice that are internal to and functional for the capitalist mode of production, so also does he identify conceptions of freedom and of self-development historically relative in exactly the same way.[55] To take account only of texts in which he does the first is in the circumstances exegetically arbitrary.[56]

3. MARX AGAINST MARX

In the face of two so opposed construals of a single author's meaning, each apparently supported by a plethora of both direct citation of, and inferential reasoning from, his works, it is probably as well to begin by posing, point-blank, the question of whether a definitive resolution of this issue is possible by reference only to the letter of Marx's texts. I think there are reasons for doubting that it is. I shall mention two such, at any rate, one a consideration of a general kind, the other a more specific doctrinal point.

The first is that Marx was not a moral philosopher and there is more than likely to be some incoherence in what he gives out on these matters. To say he was no moral philosopher actually understates the relevant point. For, it is not just that he was primarily something else, scientific historian, critic of political economy, theoretician of proletarian revolution, or what have you; but in any case mere non-practitioner of moral philosophy and neutrally disposed towards it. It is that Marx, as is well known, was quite impatient and dismissive of overt theoretical reflection about normative questions, condescending only rarely to engage in it himself. He was hostile, not neutral, towards the explicit elaboration of socialist ethical theory, disdained in this area the kind of rigorous examination of problems and concepts he so insisted upon elsewhere. At the same time, and despite this, like just about everyone else he was given to the use of moral judgement. Normative viewpoints lie upon, or just beneath the surface of, his writings, and they lie there abundantly, albeit in an unsystematic form. This being so, some, perhaps even

<hr>

[55] See *Collected Works*, vi. 464, 499–500, and *Grundrisse*, pp. 487–8, 651–2.
[56] Young (2), pp. 266–8; Arneson, pp. 219–20; Husami, p. 52–3.

major, inconsistency here on his part is not to be excluded. The details of our two antithetical interpretations do at least suggest the possibility of it.

The second reason needs more extended exposition. It concerns what I should like to call the 'dialectical play' indulged in by Marx as to whether or not the wage relation constitutes an exchange of equivalents. Does it? The answer is: yes and no. Viewed as an exchange of commodities in the market, it does. The capitalist pays for the value of labour-power; the worker gives this commodity and receives, in exchange, a wage of equal value. But, viewed as a relation in production, the wage relation is not an exchange of equivalents. For, here the worker has still to give something: not in the sense of selling it, since the sale has already been concluded, but in the sense of personal effort; and this personal effort is the substance of a value that is larger than the value of the wage. The same thing can be expressed in other terms. Does the accumulation of value and capital which takes place result from labour that is the capitalist's? Yes and no. The labour which is its source belongs to the capitalist, for it has been bought and paid for; but it is not the labour of his (more rarely, her) own body, not the sweat of his (or her) brow. It is, if you like, labour that the capitalist owns but not the capitalist's own labour. Now, there is nothing mysterious about all this (leave alone whether the theory of value that it depends on is defensible)—it is spelled out plainly by Marx himself and careful readers of *Capital* have no trouble grasping it. Considered from one point of view, the wage relation is an exchange of equivalents and the accumulation of capital due only to the use of what is the capitalist's. Considered from another point of view, the wage relation is not an exchange of equivalents and the accumulation of capital is due to the labour of the worker. The two points of view are simply that, two different angles of vision on a single phenomenon. They depend on two different senses of what counts as an exchange of equivalents. They are in no way contradictory, but mutually consistent parts of the doctrine that labour is the source and substance of all value: that labour-power, sold for what it is worth as a commodity, in operation creates something that is worth more.

An Equivocal Dialectic

Which of them, however, is the appropriate point of view in
the present context, the controversy about Marx and justice?
Those according to whom he sees no injustice in the wage
relation privilege the first, that there is an exchange of
equivalents. Many (not all) of those according to whom he
does regard the wage relation as unjust privilege the second,
that there is not. Each side says, in effect, '*This* point of view is
the only one relevant to the question of whether or not
capitalism is for him unjust.'[57] But what of Marx himself?
Well, Marx has it both ways, and that is at least one root of
the difficulty. Note, here, that the problem is *not* that he
affirms both points of view. As has just been said, they are
mutually consistent parts of one doctrine. The problem is that
he equivocates as to which of them is the one relevant to the
moral question, so that it is legitimate in a way for each side to
claim, about the two different perspectives: Marx *really* means
us to adopt this one. For, he does say that, so far as justice is at
issue, all that matters is that equal values are exchanged, in
accordance with the laws of commodity production, and he
thereby legitimates the view of one side in this dispute. But
then, by a piece of dialectical wizardry in Chapter 24 of the
first volume of *Capital*, he has these same laws turning
into their very opposite. In his own words, 'the laws of
appropriation or of private property, laws based on the
production and circulation of commodities, become changed
into their direct opposite through their own internal and
inexorable dialectic.' He speaks here, similarly, of the
occurrence of a 'dialectical inversion'. The exchange of
equivalents has now become, accordingly, only apparent, not
an exchange of equivalents—in fact theft. A passage from the
Grundrisse tells us, in the same vein, that 'the right of property
undergoes a dialectical inversion, so that on the side of capital
it becomes the right to an alien product.'[58] If the laws of
commodity production and exchange have actually turned
into their opposite, then that legitimates the view of the other

---

[57] See, for example, Allen (2), pp. 234–7, and Young (2), pp. 263–6.
[58] *Capital*, i. 725–34 (the quoted material appears at pp. 729, 730 n. 6,
734); *Grundrisse*, p. 458.

side in this dispute as well, that, when all is said and done, there is no genuine equivalence or reciprocity here.

But this turning into opposites is just a logical trick, or more generously perhaps—though that point stands—the enjoyment of intellectual paradox and surprise. It is a game with the two different senses of equivalence. Nothing, in fact, changes into its opposite in this matter. Everything persists. In so far as the laws of commodity production require that equal values be exchanged in the market, they are, and this remains so when labour-power is sold as a commodity. And in so far as these laws allow that labour-power may indeed be sold as a commodity, being itself alienable, they allow *ab initio* a relation other than, but consistent with, equal exchange in the market, a relation in which the capitalist uses the worker to reap a profit over the wage, while the worker for her or his part simply works, just giving the portion of value that the other just takes. The right of property involved is always a right of persons to use what they own, thus what they have paid the value of in exchange; and it is, consistently with that, always a right to profit from the labour of others. Both the equivalence or reciprocity and the lack of it are there from beginning to end. Marx knows all this—it is, after all, his own theory—and he says as much even in expounding the 'dialectical inversion'. But, as is so often the way with it, the dialectic here only muddies the water. A thing cannot be its opposite. If the wage relation is an exchange of equivalents and just, then that, finally, is what it is, and this can be maintained, even to the point of extreme stubbornness,[59] in the face of Marx clearly speaking otherwise. But if it does indeed turn into its direct opposite, then it is not, finally, an exchange of equivalents or just, and therefore Marx cannot really mean what he says when he says that it is. The confusion amongst his commentators is a fruit, then, of his own: of his prevarication over which perspective, equivalence or non-equivalence, really counts for this purpose; of the consequent willingness and ability to assert, to all appearances in his own voice, both that the wage relation is not unjust and that it is theft. There are other and perhaps more important

[59] See, for instance, Wood (3), p. 256 n. 21, and the apt comment on it by Cohen (2), p. 443.

causes of Marx's confusion, causes I shall come to shortly. But the path is certainly smoothed for it by his use in this context of the language of the dialectic.

In view of these considerations, any attempt to resolve the central issue in dispute must bring with it some measure of reconstruction beyond mere exegesis, and I will contend for my own part that the most cogent such reconstruction broadly vindicates those who say Marx did think capitalism unjust. It gives them the better of this argument. The enterprise requires that one be as faithful as possible to the spirit of all the pertinent texts, both those already adduced on each side and others to be cited in what follows. One should not deny the elements of confusion and inconsistency in them, a common though not a universal temptation in this debate. Rather, acknowledging their presence there, one should seek to make the best sense that can be made of them. A reconstruction along these lines, however, broadly vindicates the view that Marx thought capitalism unjust, because it is better able to explain the apparent evidence to the contrary than are those who gainsay that he did able to explain what speaks against them. The issue turns, in my opinion, on two questions. Each of them is sorely embarrassing to the case I shall henceforth here oppose, and neither has elicited a satisfactory response from its proponents. On the principle that a good test of any intellectual position is the answers it has to the strongest questions that can be put against it, the view that Marx did not condemn capitalism as unjust must be judged to be uncompelling, for all the passages from his work seemingly in its favour. I shall, in any case, now take the two crucial questions in turn, interposing between them, though, what I think needs to be conceded on account of those passages. First, I endorse the claim, against inadequate attempts to explain such talk of his away, that in characterizing exploitation as robbery, Marx was impugning the justice of it. Second, I qualify this claim in the light of his own disavowal of a critique of capitalism in the name of justice. Third, I argue that the counter-claim, that his real critique was, instead, one on behalf of freedom and self-actualization, bears within it a fatal logical flaw: probed, this reveals, at the heart of his very critique on behalf of these other values, a concern for distributive justice.

'Explanations'

Why then, firstly, does Marx use 'robbery' and cognate terms in describing the realities of capitalism, unless it is because he thinks them unjust? The force of this question is not lost on those who deny that he thinks so and, in general, they do not flinch from responding to it.[60] Nor are they short of suggested answers. On the contrary, they offer, between them, a surprisingly large number. I shall set down their suggestions here. (*1*) In some of the usages in question, Marx has in mind the theft, not of surplus-value, but of the worker's health or time. (*2*) As regards the robbery involved in particular in the primitive accumulation of capital, this has the 'straightforward' sense that some people took what did not belong to them: wrong, therefore, according to prevailing standards of rightful ownership, it does not necessarily entail a charge of injustice on Marx's own part. (*3*) Similarly, but with regard now to capitalist exploitation in general, this is robbery only on bourgeois society's own conceptions of justice, and not by any standard that he himself entertains. At any rate, 'it appears that' the passages under discussion can be accounted for in this way. (*4*) Marx's model here might be a relationship of more or less regular plunder, as of a conquering from a conquered people, and in that case 'it is not so clear that' the robbery is unjust, since, being regular, such plunder must be based on existing material possibilities, hence correspond to the given mode of production, and if it corresponds to the mode of production, then it is, we know, just, on Marx's conception of justice. (*5*) His talk of theft and the like is aimed in fact at the disguised coercion, or merely at the coercion, whether disguised or open, rather than at the injustice of capitalist exploitation. (*6*) Or it is 'rhetoric pure and simple', 'Marx . . . speaking figuratively', or 'speaking falsely', misrepresenting his own view of things. (*7*) In any event, it simply cannot be taken as levelling a charge of injustice on the basis of a principle that transcends capitalism, for

[60] But see Tucker, p. 46; having perhaps overlooked the relevant material, he says that Marx and Engels 'do not admit that profit derived from wage labour under the capitalist system is "theft" '.

Marx's views on ideology prohibit him from doing that.[61]

The secret of these attempted explanations is discovered in the last of them. It might be thought that the plurality of their number testifies to the soundness and security of the interpretation of Marx they are deployed to defend, able to throw so much against a potentially damaging criticism. But it only testifies, in fact, to the feebleness of each one. If the texts themselves pointed to some strong and obvious explanation, then the authors of the above suggestions might have been expected to converge on it. In the absence of this, they do the best they can, each in his own particular way. The first three suggestions merit some detailed individual comment. Briefer and more generalized treatment then disposes of the rest of them.

As to (*1*), Marx does sometimes say that capital robs the workers of their time and health, or that it 'usurps' these things.[62] But, with respect to the passages in dispute in this debate, that accounts only partially for one or two of them, as open-minded readers may satisfy themselves. The main point of these passages is the theft of surplus labour and surplus-value. More importantly, even where it is time and health that is the point, does not this, as one commentator has observed, 'show *at least* that on Marx's view capitalist production essentially involves the theft of the worker's time and health, and is for *that* reason unjust?'[63] As for (*2*), the argument has some logical force but is for all that wanting. That is, it is possible that, in speaking of the robbery that marked the dawn of capitalist society, Marx meant only to register the violation of pre-existing property rights and not himself to condemn it; to record a wrong by the then prevailing standards rather than injustice by his own. Abstractly considered, therefore, the circumstance that he was dealing with a transition between modes of production does not in itself conclusively prove that he subscribed to some trans-

---

[61] See, for (*1*): Allen (2), p. 248; for (*2*): Brenkert (2), p. 148; for (*3*): Buchanan (2), pp. 187–8 n. 31; for (*4*): Wood (2), pp. 117–18 (3), pp. 137–8; for (*5*): Wood (2), p. 119 (3), p. 138, and Brenkert (2), pp. 147–8; for (*6*): Allen (2), pp. 246–9; for (*7*): Brenkert (2), pp. 149–50.

[62] *Capital*, i. 375–6, 553, 591, 599.

[63] See the references at nn. 33–7 above, and Young (2), pp. 256–8.

historical principle of justice. He might simply have been speaking relative to positive property rights.[64] But what tells us that this abstract possibility is a fact—that Marx in reality did mean what he possibly might have meant? Nothing does, absolutely nothing in the relevant texts. On the contrary, the passion of his treatment of primitive accumulation indicates the opposite, that his description of this process is also a denunciation of the brutal methods it involved. We are offered no reason here for thinking that his talk of robbery was not intended in his own name—unless inconsistency with the view that he did not consider capitalism to be unjust can itself be counted as such a reason. The argument, in other words, is merely an explanation of convenience. It responds to a need that must be met if that view is to be sustained, and has no independent textual foundation.

The same goes for the argument—(3)—that, in calling capitalist exploitation 'robbery', Marx implicitly invokes standards of justice internal to capitalism and records an injustice relative only to these. Since he never says explicitly that exploitation is unjust, whether by standards internal to capitalism or by standards external to it, how do we know that such is the burden of the robbery passages? We do not. It just 'appears that' they can be accounted for in that way. What appears, however, to others is Marx himself simply saying that the capitalist robs the worker, and as the passages themselves give not so much as a hint of any appeal to someone else's norms of justice, saying it in his own right. It is again, not the texts, but the needs of the interpretation that are the real foundation of the argument. I shall digress briefly to point out that the latter is part of a subordinate difference amongst those who concur that Marx does not himself view capitalism as unjust. Some of them claim that he does, at least, see it as unjust by its own criteria.[65] It is true that he seeks to expose an ideology of bourgeois society according to which the worker receives full recompense for all the value his or her labour-power creates. The worker, Marx holds, receives the equivalent only of some of that value, of a part of

[64] See text to n. 41 above.

[65] See Allen (1), pp. 603–7 (2), pp. 240–1; Buchanan (1), p. 138 (2), pp. 54–5.

it equal to the value of labour-power itself. However, this is all that the capitalist is required to pay according to the laws of commodity production and exchange, and it is these which Marx plainly takes as the real standard of bourgeois right in this matter. If, therefore, the ideology is a deception or hypocrisy, the relation between capitalist and worker still satisfies what are for him the sole effective juridical norms of capitalist exchange.[66] So the claim is unconvincing. But, convincing or not, it makes no difference: it cannot establish that when he terms exploitation, repeatedly—without qualification—'robbery', 'theft', 'embezzlement', and surplus-value 'loot' or 'booty', and capitalists 'usurpers', this does not imply that, right or wrong by bourgeois society's standards, exploitation is an injustice by Marx's own lights. It cannot establish it save via the pure presumption that exploitation cannot be that, on account of other things he says, which is the presumption generating speculation as to what else these usages might mean.

Double-counting

And this is the crux of it all. What we have here are precisely *ad hoc* and speculative attempts to explain away material that embarrasses the interpretation of Marx these writers favour. They are speculative attempts because there is nothing in the robbery passages themselves, or in their context, to confirm that they in fact have the character attributed to them in the explanations suggested. Detailed consideration of the remainder of these would involve unwarranted repetition. (7) just *asserts* that the talk of robbery cannot carry a charge of injustice, on the basis of this presumption of consistency. Doubtless on the same basis, (6) equally, and very conveniently, just discounts such talk as rhetoric and self-misrepresentation. (5) is a quite arbitrary displacement; 'robbery' has a meaning distinct from 'coercion' and we are given no reason to believe either that Marx was ignorant of the distinction or that he chose to overlook it. And the tautological inadequacy of (4) is manifest. It tells us in essence, albeit with a tentativeness surely due to its own inadequacy, that 'it is not so clear that'

[66] Ryan, p. 510; Brenkert (2), pp. 139–40.

Marx regards this particular form of robbery as unjust, because we know that it is for him *not* unjust if it corresponds, as regular plunder necessarily would, to the prevailing mode of production. But the question remains, why then does he characterize it as robbery? This attempt at a response, like all the others, is just based on a kind of exegetical double-counting: there must be some such explanation as these, for we already *know* that Marx says capitalist exploitation is not unjust and so he cannot *really* mean robbery. One can just as well reason, as others in effect do: we *know* he thinks exploitation is robbery, so he cannot *really* mean it is not unjust. Either way the reasoning begets a forced and conjectural reading of some passages from Marx's work, a reading strained against the evidence internal to them.

The assumption of some consistency is, of course, a rational principle of textual interpretation. Where an author's work reveals the clear commitment to a certain intellectual position and we nevertheless find there also some few formulations which seem to contradict that, interpretative charity demands that we should enquire whether the inconsistency is not merely an apparent one or seek some other way of explaining the formulations in question. Elsewhere, for example, I have myself argued that Marx obviously did have a concept of 'human nature' and that the one lonely—and ambiguous— passage which has encouraged many to believe otherwise is susceptible to such treatment and must be given it. The same applies to a single phrase, concerning 'uninterrupted revolution', in Lenin's writings before 1917, a phrase often used to denature the sense of his conception of the Russian revolution up to that year.[67] However, the assumption of consistency has its limits. It cannot be absolute. Otherwise, one will simply presume complete theoretical coherence where it may be lacking. When not just one or a few formulations, but a whole body of formulations, arguments, concepts, stands in the way of one of a thinker's putative intellectual commitments, then an assumption of full consistency is no longer either rational or justified. The whole of section 2 of

[67] See *Marx and Human Nature: Refutation of a Legend* (Verso, London, 1983), and in particular the remarks at pp. 57–8; and *The Legacy of Rosa Luxemburg* (Verso/NLB, London, 1976), pp. 70–100.

this essay, and the literature there summarized, is testimony to the fact that this is the case with respect to Marx's disavowal of any critique of capitalist injustice. In such circumstances, the argument that he cannot have held one viewpoint because to have done so would have been inconsistent with another he affirmed, is not a good one.

In the absence, therefore, of any convincing answer to the question, why Marx should have called exploitation 'robbery' if not because he considered it unjust, one must accept the most natural reading of the passages where he so characterizes it, which is that he did consider it unjust. To treat exploitation as theft is to treat the appropriation of surplus-value and, with it, capitalist property rights as wrongs. That such was Marx's view of things, however, is a claim that has to be qualified— and this brings me to the second part of my argument. For one can no more wish away the material that is troubling to this claim than one can Marx's talk of robbery. He does explicitly deny that there is injustice in the relationship between capitalist and worker, eschews and derides any appeal on behalf of socialism to the language of rights or justice, and appears more generally to underwrite a conception wherein standards of justice are merely relative to each mode of production. Some commentators have been tempted to propose that it is in fact this sort of material which is not to be taken at face value: that his denial of any injustice in the wage relation is made 'tongue-in-cheek' or with satirical, 'ironic' intent; that he means by it to say simply—this is what is called or what is taken to be just, or this is what is just by capitalist criteria, or this is a mere appearance of justice inasmuch as the exchange to which it relates is itself a mere appearance; and that, correspondingly, the object of his impatience with socialist appeals to notions of what is just or fair is only the rhetoric of justice and not its substance.[68] In other words Marx, on these proposals, is either not speaking literally and seriously here or not speaking in his own voice. As I have already intimated, I think the temptation to have recourse to this kind of explanation is mistaken. It gives us a mirror-image of the procedure of those who would explain

[68] Holmstrom, p. 368; Husami, pp. 45, 67; Arneson, pp. 217–18; Young (1), pp. 441, 446 (2), p. 252; van de Veer, pp. 369–70.

away Marx's assertions of robbery, just switching from one side of the intellectual profile to the other the values of what he means literally and what he does not; conveniently discounting, exactly as do writers of the opposite viewpoint, what cannot readily be accommodated within the interpretation proffered: in the present case, not the charge of theft but rather the relativizing discourse about justice.

An Unacknowledged Thought

But the procedure is equally unconvincing with respect to this. On internal textual evidence Marx speaks in these matters both seriously and for himself. It is true, to be sure, that it is on criteria internal to capitalism that his judgement of the equity of the wage relation is based. But then, according to the *only* direct and explicit statements Marx makes concerning justice, it is precisely and solely such internal and, thus, relative criteria that are relevant to deciding what is just and what is not. If the relation is just by capitalist standards, it is also just on the only explicit conception of justice that Marx himself puts forward. There is at any rate no conscious irony involved—if one does not, in the manner I have criticized, simply presume that there *must* be, given other things we know. So far as his own intentions are concerned, Marx has to be taken as meaning both that the wage contract is not unjust according to the appropriate, internal, bourgeois standards and—therefore!—that it is not unjust according to him, that is, according to the relativist definition of justice to which he expressly commits himself. From this it should be clear that in my view one cannot plausibly dispose of all of what I have termed his relativizing discourse by representing it as only apparently that and really something else. It may be true of some of his statements standardly read as relativist ones that they are not. The argument, in particular, that the proposition, 'Right can never be higher than the economic structure of society', signifies rather a sober moral realism, seems to me from the details of the proposition's context to be a cogent one, in any case no less plausible than the common relativist interpretation of these words. More generally, such a sense of or care for moral realism is unquestionably an important dimension of Marx's thought, thereby also of the problem under discussion, and it is one to which I shall later advert. All the same, I think it idle to hope to liquidate, by appeal either to this or to other considerations, what is at the very least a strong tendency on his part, one that pervades his mature writings, whatever else he may *also* do or say inconsistently with it; a tendency to relativize the status of norms and values, and whose most incontrovertible manifestation is the treatment of these as ideological, hence superstructural and merely derivative, without independent validity or trans-historical reach.

Is there, then, no way of resolving the conflict between Marx's explicit statements that are the product and reflection of this tendency and his implicit charge that capitalism is unjust, borne by, amongst other things, his usage of the terminology of robbery? I believe there is, although what I propose has itself an air of paradox about it. Not only is it perfectly coherent, however; it is the virtually mandatory conclusion in the light of all the relevant textual evidence. The proposal is: Marx did think capitalism was unjust but he did not think he thought so.[69] This is because in so far as he indeed thought directly about and formulated any opinion concerning justice, which he did only intermittently, he expressed himself as subscribing to an extremely narrow conception of it. The conception was narrow in two respects: associating justice, firstly, in more or less legal positivist fashion, with prevailing or conventional juridical norms, the standards internal to each social order; and associating it, secondly, with the distribution of consumption goods or, as this relates to capitalism, the distribution of income, and hence with a too partial focus upon the process of exchange in

[69] Two other writers make this point: see Cohen (2), pp. 443–4—also (1), p. 12—and Elster (1), pp. 289–90, 303 n. 44 (2), ch. 4. Oddly, so does a third, Steven Lukes, from the other side of the debate: his essay on the subject, however, minimizes the force of the point, consigning to a footnote Marx's belief that capitalism was unjust and simply declaring it an 'unofficial' view; and while his forthcoming book appears to concede a larger place in Marx's thinking to this unofficial view, the appearance is basically deceptive since Lukes does not in fact concede what really matters here, that the belief in question shows Marx's attachment to some *non-relativist* standards of justice. See Lukes (1), p. 197 n. 83 (3), ch. 4.

the market. This double association is manifest in the material cited at section 1, paras. i–v above and it is obvious why on the basis of it Marx should have treated the wage contract as not unjust and justice as not a revolutionary notion. But it is these two conceptual associations that are, along with the 'dialectical inversion' discussed earlier, the source of his confusion.[70]

For neither of them is obligatory in estimating the justice of a society, which is to say that there are alternative and broader conceptions of distributive justice than they define. One may consider what is proper in virtue of a supposed set of *moral*, rather than legal or conventional, rights or entitlements—the rational content of notions of natural right—and one may also take account, in doing so, of the distribution of advantages and disadvantages quite generally, including here consequently the distribution of control over productive resources. And that is exactly what Marx does and does frequently, even if the concept, 'justice', is not expressly present to his mind and under his pen when he does it. Not compelled by the aforementioned conceptual associations, we can legitimately say, therefore, that inasmuch as he obviously finds the distribution of benefits and burdens under capitalism morally objectionable, impugning the capitalist's right to the best of it, he does think capitalism is unjust. Implicit in his work is a broader conception of justice than the one he actually formulates, notwithstanding the fact that he never himself identifies it as being such. This is not a question of simply imputing to Marx something alien to his own ways of thought. On the contrary, it is *he* who clearly, albeit *malgré lui*, challenges the moral propriety of the distributive patterns typical of capitalism—distribution in this context, mark you, taken in its widest sense—and that he does not realize what he is doing in challenging it, precisely criticizing capitalism as unjust, is merely a confusion on his part about the potential scope of the concept of justice and thus neither here nor there so far as the substance of the issue is concerned. The challenge, by its nature, cannot be anything else than a critique of injustice. We have seen this with respect to the

[70] See also, in connection with this paragraph and the next, Hancock, p. 66; Shaw, pp. 41–2; Ryan, pp. 516–17; van der Veen, pp. 434, 448, 455.

matter of robbery: to say that this is what capitalists are engaged in just *is*, so long as one has no well-founded alternative explanation of its meaning, to question their right to what they appropriate and so the justice of that appropriation. We may now go on to adduce further confirmation of the resolution of this controversy I have here proposed, by examining how things stand with the third matter for discussion previously signalled: Marx's commitment to the values of freedom and self-development.

The Distribution of Freedom

It is this commitment, remember, that is urged upon us, by those who deny his attachment to considerations of justice, as being the real basis of his condemnation of capitalism. But such a delineation of putative alternatives is a false one, as immediately becomes clear if we proceed to put the second of the two questions I have said are embarrassing to the case these writers make. Whose freedom and self-development or self-realization are at issue? The answer to this question, Marx's answer, is—tendentially everybody's. Tendentially, because of course for Marx universal freedom can only come through class struggle, the dictatorship of the proletariat, a transitional economic formation and so on, in the course of which there should be, certainly, a progressive enlargement of freedom and of opportunities for individual self-realization, but only over time and in the face of social and also material obstacles. Everybody's, however, because it is after all a universal freedom and self-development that he both envisages and looks forward to at the end of the line. And this is to say that it is the distribution and not just the extent of these, not just the aggregate quantity so to speak, that matters to him. Communist society is a better society in Marx's eyes and capitalism condemned by him at least partly because of the way in which the former makes such 'goods' available to all where the latter allots them unevenly and grossly so. His concern with distribution in the broad sense, in other words, takes in the very values said to distance him from any preoccupation with justice, so that these do not in truth supply the foundation of a separate and alternative critique of capitalism. His critique in the light of freedom and self-actualization, on the contrary, is *itself* in part a critique in the light of a conception of distributive justice, and though it is so in part only, since there is also an aggregative aspect involved, Marx clearly believing that communism will provide greater freedoms overall than has any preceding social form,[71] the identity is none the less real or important for all that.

Considering, indeed, this point's logical centrality to the whole controversy, it is surprising how little discussion there has been of it in the literature here being reviewed. For it vitiates a claim quite fundamental to the 'anti-justice' interpretation. That Marx does care about distribution broadly construed has, as I have made clear, been effectively argued by opponents of this. But the theoretical hole, the incoherence, in the interpretation that is revealed once the goods themselves of freedom and self-development are seen to fall within the scope of this distributive concern of his is something noted by few commentators and then only fleetingly, in passing.[72] In any event, the distributive dimension of Marx's treatment of these values may now be documented. I cite material relevant both to the distribution of advantages and disadvantages in general and to the distribution of freedom and self-development in particular.

In *The German Ideology*, Marx refers to the proletariat as 'a class . . . which has to bear all the burdens of society without enjoying its advantages'. One sort of advantage he has in mind is evident from the following, in the same work: 'All emancipation carried through hitherto has been based . . . on restricted productive forces. The production which these productive forces could provide was insufficient for the whole of society and made development possible only if some persons satisfied their needs at the expense of others, and therefore some—the minority—obtained the monopoly of development, while others—the majority—owing to the constant struggle to satisfy their most essential needs, were for the time being (i.e., until the creation of new revolutionary productive forces) excluded from any development.'[73] This

---

[71] Here I disagree with Arneson, pp. 220–1.

[72] See Arneson, pp. 220–1; Riley, p. 50 n. 40—and cf. Hancock, pp. 68–9.   [73] *Collected Works*, v. 52, 431–2.

disparity is also registered in the later, economic writings. Marx speaks on one occasion, for example, of 'the contradiction between those who have to work too much and those who are idlers' and of its projected disappearance with the end of capitalism.[74] Amplifying the point in *Capital* itself, he writes: 'The intensity and productivity of labour being given, the part of the social working day necessarily taken up with material production is shorter and, as a consequence, the time at society's disposal for the free intellectual and social activity of the individual is greater, in proportion as work is more and more evenly divided among all the able-bodied members of society, and a particular social stratum is more and more deprived of the ability to shift the burden of labour (which is a necessity imposed by nature) from its own shoulders to those of another social stratum. The absolute minimum limit to the shortening of the working day is, from this point of view, the universality of labour. In capitalist society, free time is produced for one class by the conversion of the whole lifetime of the masses into labour-time.'[75]

Some readers will think they detect, in Marx's way of putting things here, the signs of a definite evaluative attitude to the distributive imbalance he describes, and they will be right to think so. Lest it be said, however, that this thought is just prompted by their, and my, own intellectual predilections, not by anything Marx himself says, we can point to other passages of the same general type, in which a charge of moral wrong is not merely signalled obliquely but is there black on white. Thus, speaking, in a famous summary paragraph, of the cumulative processes of capitalist development, Marx says *inter alia*: 'Along with the constant decrease in the number of capitalist magnates, who usurp and monopolize all the advantages of this process of transformation, the mass of misery, oppression, slavery, degradation and exploitation grows.'[76] Note: the capitalists not only monopolize all advantages, they also *usurp* them, which is just to say that they have no right to what they monopolize. And included under this rubric of the usurpation of advantages is, once again, self-development; in the *Grundrisse* Marx writes: 'Since all *free time*

[74] *Theories of Surplus Value*, iii 256.
[75] *Capital*, i. 667.   [76] Ibid. 929.

is time for free development, the capitalist usurps the *free time* created by the workers for society.[77] So, the distribution of advantages, amongst them free time and free development, and also, conversely, of burdens, is morally illegitimate, and this entails a commitment to some more acceptable, some fairer, distribution of both the first and the second.

That such indeed is what Marx is committed to, another and a better standard of distributive justice than prevails under capitalism, is also brought out clearly in a passage from the third volume of *Capital*, concerning capitalism's 'civilizing' mission. He states first: 'It is one of the civilizing aspects of capital that it extorts this surplus labour in a manner and in conditions that are more advantageous to social relations and to the creation of elements for a new and higher formation than was the case under the earlier forms of slavery, serfdom, etc.' Then, proceeding to elaborate on this statement, Marx says immediately after it: 'Thus on the one hand it leads towards a stage at which compulsion and the monopolization of social development (with its material and intellectual advantages) by one section of society at the expense of another disappears.'[78] It could not be more direct. The social formation in prospect is 'higher', and it is higher in part because compulsion disappears, but *also* because so does the monopolization of social development by some at the expense of others. The positive distributive principle that is implicit in this judgement is spelled out by Marx elsewhere. He refers, in the first volume of *Capital*, to: 'those material conditions of production which alone can form the real basis of a higher form of society, a society in which the full and free development of every individual forms the ruling principle.'[79] Or, in the celebrated formula of the *Communist Manifesto*: 'In place of the old bourgeois society, with its classes and class antagonisms, we shall have an association, in which the free development of each is the condition for the free development of all.'[80]

---

[77] *Grundrisse*, p. 634.
[78] *Capital*, iii. 958.
[79] Ibid., i. 739.
[80] *Collected Works*, vi. 506.

Justice and Class Interests

So soon, therefore, as the ambit of 'distribution' is extended to cover the generality of social advantages, especially the relative availability of free time, time, that is, for autonomous individual development, itself a crucial component in Marx's conception of human freedom, it becomes evident that his critique of capitalism is motivated by distributive considerations, at least amongst others. Do those who claim that he did not think capitalism unjust have any persuasive answer to this apparent evidence against their claim? None that I have been able to discover. In fact, for the most part they do not even attempt one, either ignoring or being unaware of the problem for them here. Taking those who do have something to say about this, however, we may quickly pass over, as not worthy of serious attention in view of the texts just cited, the bare assertion of one author that 'Marxist freedom' should not be thought of as a social good to be distributed. Those texts, I submit, suffice to show the opposite. We can be nearly as quick with the argument of the same author that, since the capitalist like the worker is in a significant sense unfree so long as capitalism persists, it is not the point of Marx's critique that the former enjoys freedoms which the latter lacks.[81] It is unquestionably true, on the doctrine of alienation, that everybody is to some degree unfree under capitalism. But the passages I have quoted demonstrate, equally, that it is also part of Marx's criticism of this society that it privileges some with advantages, opportunities for free development included, which others are denied, by contrast with what he envisages as the principle of a communist society.

More space needs to be given to the only substantial attempt at a counter-argument in this matter. It is to be found in a recent paper by Allen Wood, whose earlier articles played so prominent a part in stimulating the whole debate. Wood concedes that Marx 'clearly objects to the prevailing distribution of such entities as effective control over the means of production, leisure time, and the opportunity to acquire education and skills'; but such objection, he claims, cannot be

[81] See Brenkert (2), p. 158, for both arguments.

counted a criticism of capitalism as unjust, since to be that it would have to be urged on the basis of 'disinterested or impartial considerations' and it is not consistent with what Wood calls the 'class interests thesis' that Marx should have urged it on this kind of basis. The class interests thesis, part and parcel of historical materialism, is stated thus: 'Marx believes that our actions are historically effective only in so far as they involve the pursuit of class interests, and that the historical meaning of our actions consists in their functional role in the struggle between such interests.' For a rational or self-conscious historical agent, Wood argues, practical recognition of this thesis is incompatible with taking justice, in the sense of impartially grounded distributive principles, as a primary concern.[82]

Two things may be said in response to Wood's argument. The first is that the incompatibility it alleges is open to question. It is Marx's belief, certainly, that where there are classes and class struggle, disinterested or impartial consideration of the interests of everyone is merely an ideological illusion, and he aligns himself unambiguously with one set of interests, the proletariat's, against those of its exploiters. The goal of communism, furthermore, he treats as being in the interests of the proletariat and absolutely not in the interests of the capitalist, as a capitalist, and it is a goal for him that cannot be effectively secured except on the basis of proletarian interests and of the social and political movement that pursues them. However, to limit the 'historical meaning' of action along this path to its functional role within a struggle so characterized, just one sectional interest against another, is radically to diminish, to impoverish, the sense which Marx himself—everywhere—gives it. For, as partial and as 'interested' as he unashamedly proclaims it to be, such action also has a universal aspect, in virtue of the character of its historical objective, of what the proletariat's struggle is a struggle *for*. This universality, I have already said, is tendential; it cannot be immediate. Some genuine social interests, of really existing people, first of all the interest of the beneficiaries of exploitation in its continuance, are not allowed by Marx morally to count for anything. That is the truth in Wood's argument. But if the proletariat's struggle for its own interests can still be viewed as being of ultimately universal significance, it is just and indeed because, considered from an impartial and disinterested standpoint, the goal of this struggle, 'the free development of all', is for Marx a moral advance on the sectional monopoly of social advantages that capitalism entails. Is it, after all, a feature special to his intellectual outlook that in the pursuit of just arrangements, the interests some will have in the preservation of injustices from which they benefit must be set aside? Scarcely. In returning to someone what rightfully belongs to her, you may legitimately disregard, so far as it is only justice that is at issue, any interest that, say, I may have in holding on to it. Nor, for the rest, is there anything in itself remarkable about the fact that the historical objective or ideal which Marx adumbrates he also sees as not being immediately or straightforwardly realizable, but rather as mediated by obstacles, opposed by vested interests, as something therefore that must be fought for through a long and difficult process on which 'causes' other than the ideal in view will inevitably leave their mark. This is in the nature of many political ends and it is a problem for everyone, although some give themselves the luxury of pretending that it is not.[83]

The second thing to say is that even if one does not—as I do—contest the incompatibility Wood argues there to be between the so-called class interests thesis and any too central preoccupation with disinterested principles of justice, but grants him it for the sake of exhausting exegetical possibilities, it will not suffice for his defensive purpose. For it only shows that if Marx expressed a commitment to disinterested distributive principles, he did so inconsistently with other beliefs he held. It cannot show that he did not *in fact* express such a commitment, because he in fact did, as is manifest from the textual evidence assembled above. Wood himself in some sort acknowledges the existence of this evidence. In his own words, 'Marx often describes the results of the communist revolution in terms which suggest that if one accepts the

---

[83] See my 'Bourgeois Power and Socialist Democracy: On the Relation of Ends and Means', *The Legacy of Rosa Luxemburg*, ch. 4.

description, then one has reasons for considering these results as impartially or disinterestedly good. For example, Marx claims that the revolution will put an end to alienation, that it will enable *every member of society* to develop his or her capacities, that it will promote community and solidarity between people, and that it will facilitate the expansion of human productive powers and the *universal* satisfaction of human needs'.[84] But then the passages in which these claims are made are promptly discounted as 'the liturgy which self-styled "Marxist humanism" never tires of chanting'. Sharp stuff, but what is its justification? What, in other words, saves Wood from giving their due weight to the passages which he himself so aptly characterizes? Well, just the class interests thesis and other passages said to be its consequence, and which he takes—wrongly, but we have decided here to let this pass—as evincing a contempt on Marx's part for humanitarianism. Exegetically, however, it is no more legitimate to set aside the first sort of passage for not squaring with the second than it would be to set aside the second sort, therefore the class interests thesis itself, for not squaring with the first. If the object is to understand Marx's own thought, as for Wood it emphatically is, then the only proper procedure would be to register a large inconsistency there. Simply to decide that the apparent evidence of a disinterested concern with the distribution of human goods—and, *Wood says it*, such is what the texts in question suggest—cannot really be what it gives every appearance of being, is to indulge in that double-counting we have already, in the matter of robbery, uncovered and dismissed.

On this issue as on that, proponents of the 'anti-justice' interpretation default. They are unable satisfactorily to answer the questions they must, unable to explain the data they must if they are to render plausible the interpretation they propose. Their account of Marx, one must conclude, is mistaken. The negative part of my critique of it is here completed, and it remains only to spell out positively what the substance of the conception of justice is that is implicit in his writings. The strands of it already run through the foregoing

[84] Wood (5), my emphasis.

discussion and it is just a matter now of trying to draw them out more clearly.

The Conditions of Production

Fundamental to that conception is that there is no moral right to the private ownership and control of productive resources.[85] Treating exploitation as theft, Marx challenges the legitimacy of some people being in a position to appropriate the surplus product of social labour, and he thereby challenges the legitimacy of the system of property rights whose consequence such appropriation is. The positive titles to property embodied in capitalist law, therefore, are condemned as unjust by reference to a generalized moral entitlement—to control over the means of production—which for him has precedence over them. Some will doubtless find it mildly shocking that I attribute to Marx what is in effect a notion of natural right, and this is understandable in view of his overt hostility to the natural rights tradition. Consider, however, how he regards the private ownership of land: 'From the standpoint of a higher socio-economic formation, the private property of particular individuals in the earth will appear just as absurd as the private property of one man in other men. Even an entire society, a nation, or all simultaneously existing societies taken together, are not the owners of the earth. They are simply its possessors, its beneficiaries, and have to bequeath it in an improved state to succeeding generations, as *boni patres familias*.'[86] What *can* he be saying? That no one owns or that no one can own land? But Marx knows all too well that individuals both can and do privately own it. Their positive legal titles to such ownership are no mystery to him. That no one, then, legal titles notwithstanding, *truly* owns it—truly *owns* it—in the sense of having a right to it which *legitimately* excludes others? Exactly. He is saying no more nor less than that people are not morally entitled to exclusive use of the productive resources of the earth; saying that private ownership of these constitutes a wrong. What else could his meaning be? There is even, according to the above passage ('They . . . have to bequeath it

[85] See Cohen (1), p. 13; Ryan, p. 521.   [86] *Capital*, iii. 911.

in an improved state' etc.), a moral obligation in this matter to later generations. The same judgements are betrayed by the tenor of other, similar texts. Thus, in connection with rent, Marx writes that 'the tremendous power [of] landed property when it is combined together with industrial capital in the same hands enables capital practically to exclude workers engaged in a struggle over wages from the very earth itself as their habitat. One section of society here demands a tribute from the other for the very right to live on the earth.' And of capitalist agriculture he says: 'Instead of a conscious and rational treatment of the land as permanent communal property, as the *inalienable* condition for the existence and reproduction of the chain of human generations, we have the exploitation and the squandering of the powers of the earth.'[87]

Taken together with the language of usurpation and robbery, passages like these put beyond doubt Marx's conviction that the 'distribution of the conditions of production' in capitalist society is unjust.[88] Now, I have said that this conviction is fundamental to his conception of justice, but it does not exhaust it. The normative principle it entails, that of collective democratic control over productive resources, is complemented by another, the needs principle, covering the distribution, broadly speaking, of individual welfare, with this second principle seen by Marx as the eventual consequence of realizing the first. And I do not agree with a suggestion which

---

[87] Capital, iii. pp. 908, 948–9—emphasis added.

[88] The bland assertion according to which (once again) 'it appears that' Marx's criticisms of capitalism are not based on any conception of 'productive-distributive' justice—and by this the assertion's author has in mind just what I have argued for in the text—is itself based, it appears, on his forbearing to give us some account of these passages. See Buchanan (2), pp. 59–60. And it is, candidly, no more than a desperate intellectual ruse to say—see Brenkert (2), p. 162—that, collective property being 'a qualitatively different institution' from private property, it has to be regarded simply as something radically new, not as a different, more just arrangement, a *redistribution*, of the means of production. This is the discourse of the pure, unconstrained 'leap' and quite foreign to Marx's own sense of the continuities of history which, despite all novelty and change, and the growth in human productive powers, make the comparative analysis of social institutions a rational enterprise. The 'distribution of the conditions of production' (see text to n. 45 above) is, unproblematically, a trans-historical category for him.

has been made on both sides of the debate that it is not the particular content of the needs principle, or of any other distributive principle which might govern access to individual welfare in a classless society, that is of moment, but just the fact that any such principle will be the result of collective democratic decision.[89] I do not agree with this because one can easily imagine distributive norms or practices which, endorsed by the most democratic procedures of a social collective, will be morally objectionable none the less. Not to put too fine a point on it: a stable majority, whatever the basis of its self-definition, arbitrarily, regularly and over an extended period votes advantages and benefits for its members and relative disadvantages for the members of some minority, whatever, in turn, the basis of its identification.[90] Of course, Marx himself plainly did *not* envisage the possibility that a classless society might so combine collective control over the conditions of production with sheer moral arbitrariness in the distribution of welfare. Whether that was simply a sign of utopian optimism on his part, as non-socialists and perhaps even some socialists may be likely to think, or rather evidence of a bold, far-sighted realism, is an issue that may be left aside, for the point here is a different one. It is that if Marx himself upholds the principle of collective control over resources with the clear expectation that its implementation will have a certain kind of further distributive consequence and will not have a certain other kind of distributive consequence for the enjoyment of basic human goods, then it is a strange caprice to make abstraction from this expectation concerning distributive consequences and impute to him an ethical conception in which it is just collective control that matters, more or less irrespective of the nature of its ulterior distributive results. Such results must surely participate in defining the value he attaches to a future communist society. It is, in any case, a fact that he expressly formulates a principle to cover them.

So I take the principle he formulates, 'From each according to their ability, to each according to their needs!', as also integral to his notion of a just society and I want now to say

[89] See Crocker, p. 207, and Ryan, pp. 521–2.

[90] A less 'extreme' example is given by Arneson, p. 226.

something additional to the arguments reported at 2. viii, in defence of construing it thus as a standard of distributive justice. There are essentially two reasons advanced against regarding it as such, and I shall consider these in turn. They are (A) that the needs principle is not a standard of equality but meant on the contrary to respond to the unique individuality of each person, to the variety of personal character and need, and is therefore a formula for treating people differentially; and (B) that by anticipating a time when 'all the springs of co-operative wealth flow more abundantly', Marx envisages an end to scarcity and so to the very circumstances requiring principles of justice.[91]

Needs and Equality

As to (A), attention should be drawn to another text that is of interest in this connection, yet neglected in the argument over Marx's meaning in 'Critique of the Gotha Programme'. For there is also a passage in *The German Ideology* which, from the standpoint of a sort of needs principle, takes issue with a version of the contribution principle, criticizing the view 'that the "possession" and "enjoyment" of each should correspond to his "labour"'. 'But one of the most vital principles of communism, a principle which distinguishes it from all reactionary socialism, is . . . that differences of *brain* and of intellectual ability do not imply any differences whatsoever in the nature of the *stomach* and of physical *needs*; therefore the false tenet, based upon existing circumstances, "to each according to his abilities", must be changed, in so far as it relates to enjoyment in its narrower sense, into the tenet, "*to each according to his need*"; in other words, a *different form* of activity, of labour, does not justify *inequality*, confers no *privileges* in respect of possession and enjoyment.'[92] What this passage rejects, it rejects precisely as justifying inequality, and therefore the needs principle which it commends by contrast cannot reasonably be regarded as anything but a standard of equality. The passage, however, was probably written by Moses Hess and not by Marx and Engels, who are thought only to have edited the chapter of *The German Ideology* from

---

[91] See I. viii above.   [92] *Collected Works*, v. 537–8.

which it comes.[93] Needs are here construed, moreover, in an explicitly narrow sense, as basic physical needs, and as I shall argue shortly, one cannot take that as having been Marx's intention in 'Critique of the Gotha Programme'. We must be circumspect, then, as to what may legitimately be made of this passage in the present context. It would plainly be wrong to jump, without more ado, to the conclusion that, because of the manifestly egalitarian import of lines penned some thirty years earlier by another hand, the kindred formulations of Marx in the later text just have to be of identical import. But if such quick certainty would be unwarranted on our part, we may fairly ask how, in the light of these lines, the diametrically opposite certainty can be warranted on the part of those insisting that the principle he puts forward is not one of equality. The need for circumspection here cuts both ways. And these commentators, it should be noted, simply ignore this passage from *The German Ideology*.

Exercising all due care and caution, we are entitled none the less to make the following observations about it. First, there is no other passage in the Marx-Engels Works that has so obvious a bearing on the famous slogan from 'Critique of the Gotha Programme' as this one does, notwithstanding the assumption concerning its probable authorship. Second, it provides a salutary reminder that the tenet, 'to each according to their needs', was already part of the tradition of socialist discourse before Marx himself employed it. Third, the passage shows that this tenet was understood by others as a principle of equality and that one of these others, an erstwhile collaborator, openly proposed it as such within a work that was intended to bear Marx's name. These three points must surely suffice to open anyone's mind to there being at least a reasonable possibility—let us say no more yet than that—that Marx in turn espoused the principle in question out of a similar, egalitarian concern. In any case, fourthly and decisively, between the earlier passage from *The German Ideology* and the text of 'Critique of the Gotha Programme' there is an undeniable internal likeness which confirms that this possibility is a fact. For just as the burden of the former is

[93] See ibid. 586 n. 7, 606 n. 143.

that 'differences of . . . intellectual ability' and thus of 'labour'
cannot justify '*inequality*' or '*privileges*', so part of the burden of
the latter is to find fault with the contribution principle
because 'it tacitly recognizes unequal individual endowment
and thus productive capacity as natural privileges' and so
amounts to '*a right of inequality*'.[94]

Consideration of the earlier passage, therefore, just serves to
highlight the fact that when Marx speaks of the 'defects' of the
contribution principle, he clearly refers to inequalities entailed
by it which are morally unacceptable in his eyes. That he does
this, and in accordance, we can now see, with a pre-existing
tradition of argument, supports the claim that the needs
principle as he presents it is a principle of equality. It is
obviously true, on the other hand, that in envisaging equal
treatment from one point of view, that principle necessarily
countenances unequal treatment from other points of view.
All people, equally, will be able to satisfy their needs. But the
means of consumption will not be divided into exactly
equivalent individual shares; even equal labour contributions
will not, or will not invariably, be matched by such shares
being of the same size; some but not all, only those who need
them, will have access to expensive drugs or medical
treatment; and so forth. There is nothing unusual in this,
however. The same applies to absolutely every substantive
conception of social justice or principle of equality. If
distribution is to be according to some standard of need, then
people who make the same labour contribution, or people for
that matter of the same height or born under the same
astrological sign, may well not receive equivalent resources.
But, likewise, if distribution is according to some standard of
achievement or merit, then those with identical needs or who
have made similar efforts may just as well find that their needs
are not equally provided for or their efforts not equally
rewarded, as the case may be. It is indeed a truism of the
philosophical analysis of both justice and equality that the
formal principle involved here—'Treat like cases alike and
different cases commensurately with their differences'—is
practically useless until one has specified *substantive* criteria

[94] *Selected Works*, iii. 18.

regarding what sort of likenesses and what sort of differences are morally relevant; what kind of equality it is, in other words, that matters. Marx for his part comes down in favour of need, and against 'individual endowment', as the decisive criterion. There is no question that, in doing so, he himself emphasizes how adoption of this criterion—responding to the specific needs of each individual—must, *in some senses*, mean unequal individual treatment. It is a mistake, however, to get carried away by this emphasis of his, as are so many of the contributors to this debate. For they cannot, simply by verbal fiat, stipulate that there is not then *any* sense in which equal consideration and treatment are involved. There is, and Marx shows himself aware of it in the way he criticizes the contribution principle. The needs of all, irrespective of individual endowment, irrespective also of such other and many differentiating characteristics as will be judged to be morally irrelevant—the needs of all equally, therefore, are to be met.

Communist Abundance

We may turn now to (B), the argument that since the prospective abundance of communist society will 'permit everyone's needs to be fully satisfied',[95] principles of distributive justice will have become redundant there. There will no longer be any necessity for authoritative norms or rules that lay down what sort of distribution is fair, and thus the needs principle as proposed by Marx cannot be taken for one. The argument does not withstand close scrutiny. Some critical reflection on the concept of 'abundance', which means also on the concept of human 'needs', will show what is wrong with it. To this end, the following passage supplies a useful background to Marx's thinking on the subject. 'Man is distinguished from all other animals by the limitless and flexible nature of his needs. But it is equally true that no animal is able to restrict his needs to the same unbelievable degree and to reduce the conditions of his life to the absolute minimum.'[96] Now, when Marx anticipates the springs of

[95] Wood (4), p. 211; and see also Lukes (1), p. 201.
[96] 'Results of the Immediate Process of Production', Appendix to *Capital*, i. 1068.

wealth flowing 'more abundantly', what is his idea of abundance? He does not say directly. Indeed, there is no evidence that he gave the question any very rigorous consideration. We are obliged, in trying to answer it, to see what can be extrapolated from any texts that may be relevant—as accords with my earlier remarks about the need to find the best reconstruction we can. But there are, in any event, only three pertinently different 'possibilities' here, the terms of the above passage providing us with a convenient framework for distinguishing what they are. (*a*) There is abundance relative to an 'absolute minimum', a bare physical subsistence, definition of needs. (*b*) There is, at the other end of the scale, abundance relative to a 'limitless and flexible' notion of needs; in the sense, that is, of everyone being able to have or do whatever they might conceivably feel themselves as needing to. (*c*) And there is abundance relative to some standard of 'reasonableness'—there could of course, be more than one such standard—intermediate between (*a*) and (*b*).

We can discount (*a*) on the grounds that there is a lot of textual evidence that it is not Marx's notion for a communist society. He thinks in terms not of a minimum standard but of the expansion of individual needs.[97] And he has in mind particularly needs of individual self-realization. This is clear from, amongst much else that could be cited, his reference in 'Critique of the Gotha Programme' itself to 'the all-round development of the individual' and from the contrast he draws in *Capital* when he refers to 'a mode of production in which the worker exists to satisfy the need of the existing values for valorization, as opposed to the inverse situation, in which objective wealth is there to satisfy the worker's own need for development.'[98] The needs principle as Marx construes it is not distinct from the other principle we have seen that he enunciates—namely, the 'free development' of each and of all[99]—but rather encompasses it and is not therefore to be understood in any minimalist sense. We can discount (*b*), on the other hand, on the grounds that it is absurd; it is not really a possibility at all. For 'flexible' needs are one thing, but

[97] *Capital*, iii. 959, 986–7, 1015–16; ibid. i. 667.
[98] See text to n. 21 above, and *Capital*, i. 772.
[99] See text to notes 79 and 80 above.

'limitless' needs quite another. If by way of means of self-development you need a violin and I need a racing bicycle, this, one may assume, will be all right. But if I need an enormously large area, say Australia, to wander around in or generally use as I see fit undisturbed by the presence of other people, then this obviously will not be all right. No conceivable abundance could satisfy needs of self-development of this magnitude, given only a modest incidence of them across some population, and it is not difficult to think of needs that are much less excessive of which the same will be true. While it will not do simply to take it as a matter of course that Marx cannot have entertained an absurdity, it is also not legitimate to impute this sort of thing to him without some textual basis for doing so, and there is no such basis. His reflections in the third volume of *Capital* on the persistence of 'the realm of necessity' betoken an altogether more sober vision of communist abundance.[100]

We are bound, consequently, to conclude in favour of (*c*), that this is abundance relative to some standard of 'reasonable' needs which, large and generous as it may be possible for it to be, still falls short of any fantasy of abundance without limits. It might be said against the reasoning by which I have reached this conclusion that the very fact that the principle under discussion is a needs principle rules out the kind of fantastic and extravagant individual requirements hypothesized in the last paragraph. Marx means precisely needs, not any old wants or fancies. But this point changes nothing at all. It is only another route to the same conclusion. So long as the relevant notion of needs covers more than 'the absolute minimum', as we have seen for Marx it does, the distinction between what may properly be counted the needs of communist women and men and what are merely wants, whims or fancies will require a standard of differentiation. It makes no difference whether this is said to distinguish reasonable from unreasonable needs, or needs *tout court* from wants and the rest. The substance is the same. There is still a determinate standard this side of unqualified abundance.

[100] *Capital*, iii. 959.

If we now ask how a standard of 'reasonableness' vis-à-vis the satisfaction of needs might be maintained without overt conflict, there are again two suggestions that we can safely reject. (i) It could be coercively imposed by a state-type body or other institution of social control. We know that this is not what Marx envisaged. (ii) The standard, if such it can be called in these circumstances, might simply be a spontaneous, unreflected one. That is to say, it might just 'so happen' that the needs of different individuals are, everywhere and always, of such a kind and such a level as to be all satisfiable in a harmonious way. I think there are good reasons for doubting that this was Marx's view of the matter. For one thing, it does not sit well with the idea of an economy subject to conscious regulation, of a *planned* use and distribution of resources. For another, the very idea of spontaneity here is open to question. These individuals will after all be 'social individuals', so that their overall needs cannot just, 'primitively', *be* thus and so. The prospect, in any case, of there never being any potentially conflicting needs of individual self-development is scarcely imaginable. So much the worse for a conception of communism that does depend on it. There is, finally, (iii) the supposition that though there can be no primitively-given co-ordination or harmony of individual needs and though these might well sometimes potentially conflict, there will be authoritative social norms, including distributive ones, which people more or less voluntarily accept. Still plenty utopian enough for many tastes, this is a more realistic supposition and it renders Marx's principle from 'Critique of the Gotha Programme' in effect one of distributive justice. It is supported by at least these aspects of his thought: that although the state, in the Marxist sense of that term, withers away, public institutions in which the community collectively deliberates and decides on its common affairs will still exist; and that though labour will have become 'life's prime want',[101] there will continue to be a 'realm of necessity', in other words some work also that is not free creation or self-realization but 'determined by necessity and external expediency', a burden Marx explicitly envisages being shared by everyone, with the obvious exception

[101] See text to n. 21 above.

of the very young, the very old, the infirm and so on[102]—even if shared only according to relative ability.

The claim, for the rest, that 'From each according to their ability, to each according to their needs!' is not meant as any kind of norm, but is merely a *description* of the future,[103] is not very plausible in the light of the fact that Marx speaks of a communist society inscribing it on its banners, no less, and with an exclamation point at that.

Conclusion

The viewpoint I have criticized in this essay may be regarded as a bogus solution to a genuine problem in Marx's thought. The problem is an inconsistency—or paradox[104]—in his attitude to normative questions. Disowning, when he is not actively ridiculing, any attachment to ideals or values, he is nevertheless quite free in making critical normative judgements, author of a discourse that is replete with the signs of an intense moral commitment. The 'anti-justice' interpretation attempts to smooth away this contradiction by representing its two sides as just applicable to different things: what Marx disowns and derides is justice, rights; the ideals of freedom, self-realization, community—these he invokes and affirms. It is a spurious resolution. The obstacle cannot be so easily levelled. Early and late, Marx's denials in this matter (efforts of repression, so to speak, of the normative dimension of his own ideas) are quite general in scope. Thus, in *The German Ideology*: 'Communism is for us not a *state of affairs* which is to be established, an *ideal* to which reality [will] have to adjust itself. We call communism the *real* movement which abolishes the present state of things.'[105] Similarly, twenty-five years on in *The Civil War in France*, the workers 'have no ideals to realize, but to set free the elements of the new society with which old collapsing bourgeois society itself is pregnant.'[106]

---

[102] *Capital*, iii. 959, 986–7, 1015–16; *Theories of Surplus Value*, iii. 256; and see also the text to n. 75 above.

[103] See i. viii.

[104] See Lukes (3), for a clear statement of the paradox as well as this solution to it.

[105] *Collected Works*, v. 49; and cf. p. 247.

[106] *Selected Works*, ii. 224.

Not, then, be it noted, the ideal of freedom or of self-actualization *as opposed to* the ideal of justice: *no* ideals to realize, just the immanent movement and that is that. The generality of this negation leaves its mark, in fact, at the most strategic conceptual point, mocking the very disjunction of which some commentators here make so much. In the *Communist Manifesto*, a hypothetical opponent is imagined as charging that communism 'abolishes eternal truths, it abolishes all religion and all morality'. The response to the charge is not a rebuttal of it, but the acknowledgement that the communist revolution 'is the most radical rupture with traditional property relations; no wonder that its development involves the most radical rupture with traditional ideas'. But what are the eternal truths actually mentioned as being, with 'all morality', candidates for abolition? I quote: 'Freedom, Justice, etc'.[107]

Marx's impatience with the language of norms and values is global in range. And yet he himself, despite it, does plainly condemn capitalism—for its oppressions and unfreedoms and also, as the argument of this essay has been, for its injustices. Denied publicly, repressed, his own ethical commitments keep returning: the values of freedom, self-development, human well-being and happiness; the ideal of a just society in which these things are decently distributed. One can perhaps go some way towards explaining this pervasive contradiction. But that does not mean either explaining it away or justifying it. It should be recognized, on the contrary, as a real and deep-seated inconsistency on Marx's part and one with not very happy effects. Some of these may have been innocent enough: the many socialists who have simply followed him in the same obfuscation, confusing both themselves and others, in one breath denying the normative standpoint clear as noonday in what they say in the next. Not so innocent, within the complex of historical causes of the crimes and tragedies which have disgraced socialism, is the moral cynicism that has sometimes dressed itself in the authority of traditional 'anti-ethical' pronouncements. Marxists should not any longer

[107] *Collected Works*, vi. 504. Allen Wood overlooks this conjunction in his use—consequently misuse—of this passage. See Wood (2), p. 128 (3), p. 129, and the comment of Arneson, p. 221.

continue to propagate the aboriginal self-contradiction and confusion in this area, but must openly take responsibility for their own ethical positions, spell them out, defend and refine them. A properly elaborated Marxist conception of justice—to take only the example that is most relevant to this debate—would not be at all premature.

A certain salutary impulse, even so, can be detected in, and partially accounts for, Marx's disavowal of all commitment to ethical principle. It is what I have referred to earlier as a sense of moral realism. Expressed negatively in a distaste for easy moral rhetoric, *mere* moralizing, unconstrained by objective knowledge of historical realities, its positive core is the convinction that ideals alone are an insufficient tool of human liberation and the consequent dedication to trying to grasp the material preconditions of this (historically unavoidable alienations, unfreedoms and injustices included) and the social agencies capable of bringing it about. Such a historical sense, all that is entailed by it in the work of Marx, is no small thing: it is Marx's strength, his greatness. The strength, I had better repeat, does not make good or excuse the deficiency. Normative analysis and judgement can be put in their proper place, a necessary if circumscribed one, without exaggerated denial or dismissive scorn. But it is relevant to remark upon the strength together with the deficiency, all the same. For there has been, and there is, no shortage of moral philosophy which, innocent of course of Marx's particular failure in this matter and generally delighted to be able to point it out, is guilty of a greater irresponsibility of its own: minute analysis of the right, the good, the just and what have you, conceptually *nice and far* from the messy throng, the scarred history of toil and comfort, power and protest, fear, hope, struggle. The contemporary discussion of precisely justice provides ample illustrative material, in the several conceptions of just social arrangements proffered in conjunction with more or less nothing, sometimes actually nothing, on how these might conceivably be achieved. The last and the largest paradox here is that Marx, despite everything, displayed a greater commitment to the creation of a just society than many more overtly interested in analysis of what justice is.

NOTES ON THE CONTRIBUTORS

ANDREW LEVINE is a Professor of Philosophy at the University of Wisconsin, Madison.

ERIK OLIN WRIGHT is a Professor of Sociology at the University of Wisconsin, Madison, and Director of the Havens Centre for the Study of Social Structure and Social Change.

JON ELSTER is a Professor of Political Science at the University of Chicago, and Research Director at the Institute for Social Research, Oslo.

G. A. COHEN is Chichele Professor of Social and Political Theory at the University of Oxford.

ALEX CALLINICOS, the editor of this volume, is a Lecturer in Politics at the University of York.

RICHARD W. MILLER is a Professor of Philosophy at Cornell University.

NORMAN GERAS is a Senior Lecturer in Government at Manchester University.

SELECT BIBLIOGRAPHY

1. INTRODUCTIONS AND COMMENTARIES

BERLIN, I., *Karl Marx*, 4th edn. (Oxford, 1978).
CALLINICOS, A., *The Revolutionary Ideas of Karl Marx* (London, 1983).
CARVER, T., *Marx's Social Theory* (Oxford, 1983).
CONWAY, D., *A Farewell to Marx* (Harmondsworth, 1987).
ELSTER, J., *Making Sense of Marx* (Cambridge, 1985).
—— *An Introduction to Karl Marx* (Cambridge, 1986).
GERAS, N., *Marx and Human Nature* (London, 1983).
HOOK, S., *Towards an Understanding of Karl Marx* (London, 1933)
MILLER, R. W., *Analysing Marx* (Princeton, NJ, 1984).
SUCHTING, W. A., *Marx: An Introduction* (Brighton, 1983).
WOOD, A. W., *Karl Marx* (London, 1981).

2. COLLECTIONS

BALL, T. and FARR, J. (eds.), *After Marx* (Cambridge, 1984).
COHEN, M. *et al.*, *Marx, Justice and History* (Princeton, NJ, 1980).
MCLELLAN, D. (ed.), *Marx: The First Hundred Years* (London, 1983).
MATTHEWS, B. (ed.), *Marx: A Hundred Years On* (London, 1983).
NEILSEN K. and PATTEN, S. C. (eds.), *Marx and Morality* (*Canadian Journal of Philosophy*, suppl. vol. vii, 1981).
New Left Review, *Western Marxism: A Critical Reader* (London, 1977).
PENNOCK, J. R. and CHAPMAN, J. W. (eds.), *Marxism* (*Nomos XXVI*, New York, 1983).
ROEMER, J. (ed.), *Analytical Marxism* (Cambridge, 1986).

3. EVOLUTION OF MARXIST THOUGHT

ANDERSON, P., *Considerations on Western Marxism* (London, 1976).
—— *In the Tracks of Historical Materialism* (London, 1983).
BENTON, T., *The Rise and Fall of Structural Marxism* (London, 1984).
CALLINICOS, A., *Marxism and Philosophy* (Oxford, 1983).
JAY, M., *The Dialectical Imagination* (London, 1973).
KOLAKOWSKI, L., *Main Currents of Marxism*, 3 vols. (Oxford, 1978).
LÖWY, M., *Georg Lukács: From Romanticism to Bolshevism* (London, 1979).
MOLYNEUX, J., *What is the Real Marxist Tradition?* (London, 1985).

4. MARXIST METHOD

ADORNO, T. W., *Negative Dialectics* (London, 1973).

ALTHUSSER, L., *For Marx* (London, 1969).

—— and BALIBAR, E., *Reading Capital* (London, 1970).

ANDERSON, P., *Arguments within English Marxism* (London, 1980).

ARTHUR, C. J., *Dialectics of Labour* (Oxford, 1986).

BINNS, P., 'What are the Tasks of Marxism in Philosophy?', *International Socialism*, 17 (1982).

CALLINICOS, A., *Is There a Future for Marxism?* (London, 1982).

—— 'Marxism and Philosophy: A Reply to Peter Binns', *International Socialism*, 19 (1983).

COHEN, G. A., 'Functional Explanation: Reply to Elster', *Political Studies*, 28. 1 (1980).

—— 'Functional Explanation, Consequence Explanation and Marxism', *Inquiry*, 25 (1982).

CUTLER, A. *et al.*, *Marx's 'Capital' and Capitalism Today*, 2 vols. (London, 1977, 1978).

ELSTER, J., *Logic and Society* (London, 1978).

—— *Ulysses and the Sirens* (Cambridge, 1979).

—— 'Cohen on Marx's Theory of History', *Political Studies*, 28. 1 (1980).

—— *Explaining Technical Change* (Cambridge, 1983).

GODELIER, M., 'Structure and Contradiction in *Capital*', in R. Blackburn (ed.), *Ideology in Social Science* (London, 1972).

HARMAN, C., 'Philosophy and Revolution', *International Socialism*, 21 (1983).

HONDERICH, T., 'Against Teleological Historical Materialism', *Inquiry*, 25 (1982).

ILIENKOV, E. V., *The Dialectic of the Abstract and the Concrete in Marx's 'Capital'* (Moscow, 1982).

LASH, S. and URRY, J., 'The New Marxism of Collective Action: A Critical Analysis', *Sociology*, 18. 1 (1984).

LEVINE, A., SOBER, E., and WRIGHT, E. O., 'Marxism and Methodological Individualism', *New Left Review*, 162 (1987).

LUKÁCS, G., *History and Class Consciousness* (London, 1971).

MEIKLE, S., *Essentialism in the Thought of Karl Marx* (London, 1985).

MEPHAM, J. and RUBEN, D.-H. (eds.), *Issues in Marxist Philosophy*, i (Brighton, 1979).

ROEMER, J., 'Methodological Individualism and Deductive Marxism', *Theory and Society*, 11 (1982).

ROSDOLSKY, R., *The Making of Marx's 'Capital'* (London, 1977).

SAYER, D., *Marx's Method* (Brighton, 1979).

THERBORN, G., *Science, Class, and Society* (London, 1976).

THOMPSON, E. P., *The Poverty of Theory and Other Essays* (London, 1978).

ZELENÝ, J. *The Logic of Marx* (Oxford, 1980).

5. HISTORICAL MATERIALISM

ANDERSON, P., *Passages from Antiquity to Feudalism* (London, 1974).
—— *Lineages of the Absolutist State* (London, 1974).
—— 'Class Struggle in the Ancient World', *History Workshop*, 16 (1983).
—— 'Those in Authority', *Times Literary Supplement*, 12 Dec. 1986.
ASTON, T. H. and PHILPIN, C. H. E. (eds.), *The Brenner Debate* (Cambridge, 1985).
BARKER, C., CALLINICOS, A., and HALLAS, D., 'Chris Harman on Base and Superstructure', *International Socialism* 2. 34 (1987).
CALLINICOS, A., *Making History* (Cambridge, 1987).
Centre for Contemporary Cultural Studies, *Making Histories* (London, 1982).
COHEN, G. A., *Karl Marx's Theory of History: A Defence* (Oxford, 1978).
—— *History, Labour, and Freedom* (Oxford, 1989).
COHEN, J., review of G. A. Cohen, *Karl Marx's Theory of History*, in *Journal of Philosophy*, 79. 5 (1982).
DOBB, M., *Studies in the Development of Capitalism* (London, 1946).
GIDDENS, A., *A Contemporary Critique of Historical Materialism* (London, 1981).
HARMAN, C., 'Base and Superstructure', *International Socialism* 2. 32 (1986).
HILTON, R. H. (ed.), *The Transition from Feudalism to Capitalism* (London, 1976).
HINDESS, B. and HIRST, P. Q., *Pre-Capitalist Modes of Production* (London, 1975).
HIRST, P. Q., *Marxism and Historical Writing* (London, 1985).
HOBSBAWM, E. J., 'Karl Marx's Contribution to Historiography', in R. Blackburn (ed.), *Ideology in Social Science* (London, 1972).
—— 'Marx and History', *New Left Review*, 143 (1984).
LEVINE, A. and SOBER, E., 'What's Historical about Historical Materialism', *Journal of Philosophy*, 82. 6 (1985).
RATTANSI, A., *Marx and the Division of Labour* (London, 1982).
STE CROIX, G. E. M. DE, *The Class Struggle in the Ancient Greek World* (London, 1981).
SAYER, D., *The Violence of Abstraction* (Oxford, 1987).
SHAW, W. H., *Marx's Theory of History* (London, 1978).
THOMPSON, E. P., *The Making of the English Working Class* (London, 1963).
—— *Whigs and Hunters* (Harmondsworth, 1977).
WOOD, E. M., 'The Separation of the Economic and Political in Capitalism', *New Left Review*, 127 (1981).
—— 'Marxism and the Course of History', *New Left Review*, 147 (1984).
WRIGHT, E. O., 'Giddens's Critique of Marxism', *New Left Review* 138 (1983).

6. MARXIST ECONOMIC THEORY

AGLIETTA, M., *A Theory of Capitalist Regulation* (London, 1979).
FARJOUN, I. and MACHOVER, M., *Laws of Chaos* (London, 1983).
FINE, B. and HARRIS, L., *Rereading Capital* (London, 1979).
HARMAN, C., *Explaining the Crisis* (London, 1984).
MANDEL, E., *Late Capitalism* (London, 1976).
—— *The Second Slump* (London, 1978).
—— and FREEMAN, A. (eds.), *Ricardo, Marx, Sraffa* (London, 1984).
ROEMER, J., *Analytical Foundations of Marxian Economic Theory* (Cambridge, 1981).
SCHWARTZ, J. (ed.), *The Subtle Anatomy of Capitalism* (Santa Monica, Cal., 1977).
STEEDMAN, I., *Marx after Sraffa* (London, 1977).
—— *et al.*, *The Value Controversy* (London, 1981).
SWEEZY, P. M., *The Theory of Capitalist Development* (New York, 1942).
WEEKS, J., *Capital and Exploitation* (London, 1981).
WOLFF, R. P., *Understanding Marx* (Oxford, 1985).

7. EXPLOITATION AND JUSTICE[1]

BUCHANAN, A. E., *Marx and Justice* (London, 1982).
CARLING, A., 'Rational Choice Marxism', *New Left Review*, 160 (1986).
COHEN, G. A., 'Freedom, Justice and Capitalism', *New Left Review*, 125 (1981).
—— review of A. W. Wood, *Karl Marx*, in *Mind*, 92 (1983).
—— 'Peter Mew on Justice and Capitalism', *Inquiry*, 29 (1986).
ELSTER, J., 'Roemer versus Roemer', *Politics and Society*, 11. 3 (1982).
LEVINE, A. E., 'Toward a Marxian Theory of Justice', *Politics and Society*, 11. 3 (1982).
—— *Arguing for Socialism* (London, 1984).
LUKES, S., *Marxism and Morality* (Oxford, 1985).
MEW, P., 'G. A. Cohen on Freedom, Justice, and Capitalism', *Inquiry*, 29 (1986).
ROEMER, J., 'Reply', *Politics and Society*, 11. 3 (1982).
—— *A General Theory of Exploitation and Class* (Cambridge, Mass., 1982).
TROTSKY, L. *et al.*, *Their Morals and Ours* (New York, 1973).
WRIGHT, E. O., 'The Status of the Political in the Concept of Class Structure', *Politics and Society*, 11. 3 (1982).

---

[1] See also the bibliography given at ch. 7 n. 1.

8. CLASSES

BRAVERMAN, H., *Labour and Monopoly Capital* (New York, 1974).
CALLINICOS, A. and HARMAN, C., *The Changing Working Class* (London, 1987).
GORZ, A., *Farewell to the Working Class* (London, 1982).
PARKIN, F., *Marxism and Class Theory* (London, 1979).
POULANTZAS, N., *Classes in Contemporary Capitalism* (London, 1975).
STE CROIX, G. E. M. DE, 'Class in Marx's Conception of History, Ancient and Modern', *New Left Review*, 146 (1984).
WALKER, P. (ed.), *Between Labour and Capital* (Hassocks, 1979).
WRIGHT, E. O., *Class, Crisis and the State* (London, 1978).
—— *Class Structure and Income Determination* (New York, 1979).
—— *Classes* (London, 1985).

9. IDEOLOGY

ABERCROMBIE, N. *et al.*, *The Dominant Ideology Thesis* (London, 1980).
—— 'Determinacy and Indeterminacy in the Theory of Ideology', *New Left Review*, 142 (1983).
ALTHUSSER, L., 'Ideology and the Ideological State Apparatuses', in id. (ed.), *Lenin and Philosophy and Other Essays* (London, 1971).
ELSTER, J., *Sour Grapes* (Cambridge, 1983).
GERAS, N., 'Essence and Appearance: Aspects of Fetishism in Marx's *Capital*', in id. *Literature of Revolution* (London, 1986).
HABERMAS, J., *Legitimation Crisis* (London, 1976).
HELD, D., 'Crisis Tendencies, Legitimation and the State', in J. B. Thompson and D. Held (eds.), *Habermas: Critical Debates* (London, 1982).
HIRST, P. Q., *On Law and Ideology* (London, 1979).
LARRAIN, J., *The Concept of Ideology* (London, 1979).
—— *Marxism and Ideology* (London, 1983).
MARCUSE, H., *One-Dimensional Man* (London, 1964).
MEPHAM, J., 'The Theory of Ideology', in J. Mepham and D.-H. Ruben (eds.), *Issues in Marxist Philosophy*, iii (Brighton, 1979).
THERBORN, G., *The Ideology of Power and the Power of Ideology* (London, 1980).
—— 'New Questions of Subjectivity', *New Left Review*, 143 (1984).

10. POLITICS AND THE STATE

BARKER, C., 'The State as Capital', *International Socialism*, 2. 1 (1978).
DRAPER, H., *Karl Marx's Theory of Revolution*, 3 vols. (New York, 1977, 1978, 1986).

GILBERT, A., *Marx's Politics* (Oxford, 1981).

HARMAN, C., *Party and Class* (Chicago, Ill., 1986).

HOLLOWAY, J. and PICCIOTTO, S. (eds.), *The State and Capital* (London, 1978).

JESSOP, B., *The Capitalist State* (Oxford, 1982).

LEVINE, A. E., *The End of the State* (London, 1987).

MILIBAND, R., *The State in Capitalist Society* (London, 1969).

—— 'Reply to Poulantzas', in R. Blackburn (ed.), *Ideology in Social Science* (London, 1972).

—— *Marxism and Politics* (Oxford, 1977).

—— *Class Power and State Power* (London, 1983).

MOLYNEUX, J., *Marxism and the Party* (London, 1978).

OFFE, C., *Contradictions of the Welfare State* (London, 1984).

POULANTZAS, N., 'The Problem of the Capitalist State', in R. Blackburn (ed.), *Ideology in Social Science* (London, 1972).

—— *Political Power and Social Class* (London, 1973).

—— *State, Power, Socialism* (London, 1978).

PRZEWORSKI, A., *Capitalism and Social Democracy* (Cambridge, 1985).

INDEX

In the following index, 'Marxism' is abbreviated to 'M.'

Index compiled by Peva Keane

DATE DUE

FEB 1 6 2015			
FEB 2 0 2017			
GAYLORD			PRINTED IN U.S.A.